IMAGES of America

WILMINGTON'S WATERFRONT

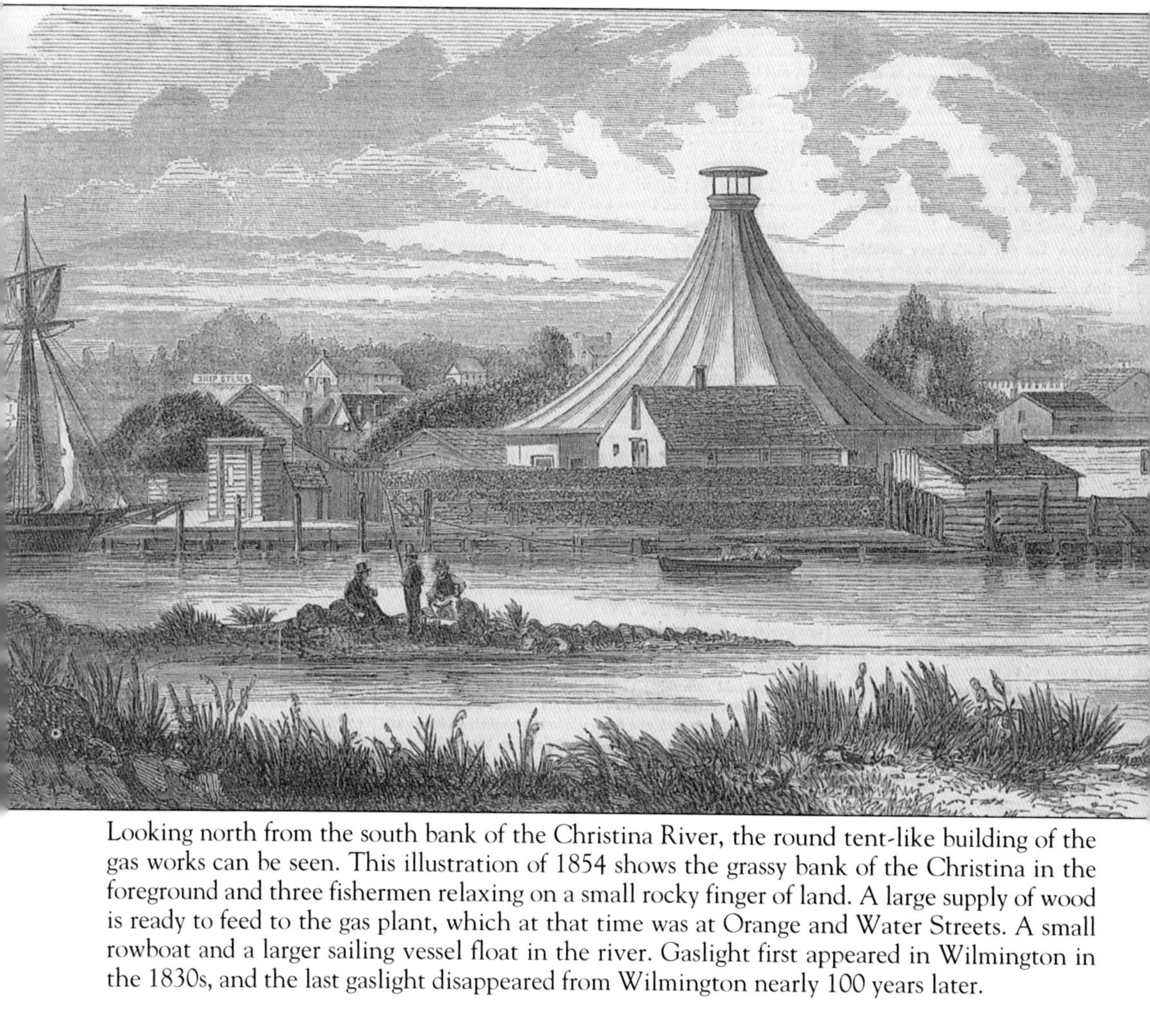

Looking north from the south bank of the Christina River, the round tent-like building of the gas works can be seen. This illustration of 1854 shows the grassy bank of the Christina in the foreground and three fishermen relaxing on a small rocky finger of land. A large supply of wood is ready to feed to the gas plant, which at that time was at Orange and Water Streets. A small rowboat and a larger sailing vessel float in the river. Gaslight first appeared in Wilmington in the 1830s, and the last gaslight disappeared from Wilmington nearly 100 years later.

IMAGES
of America

WILMINGTON'S WATERFRONT

Priscilla M. Thompson
and Sally O'Byrne

ARCADIA
PUBLISHING

ISBN 978-0-7385-0304-2

Published by Arcadia Publishing
Charleston, South Carolina

Printed in the United States of America

Library of Congress Catalog Card Number: 99-066581

For all general information contact Arcadia Publishing at:
Telephone 843-853-2070
Fax 843-853-0044
E-mail sales@arcadiapublishing.com
For customer service and orders:
Toll-Free 1-888-313-2665

Visit us on the Internet at www.arcadiapublishing.com

We dedicate this book to the thousands of people who have worked or relaxed along Wilmington's waterfront and to those who are working today to improve the city's rivers.

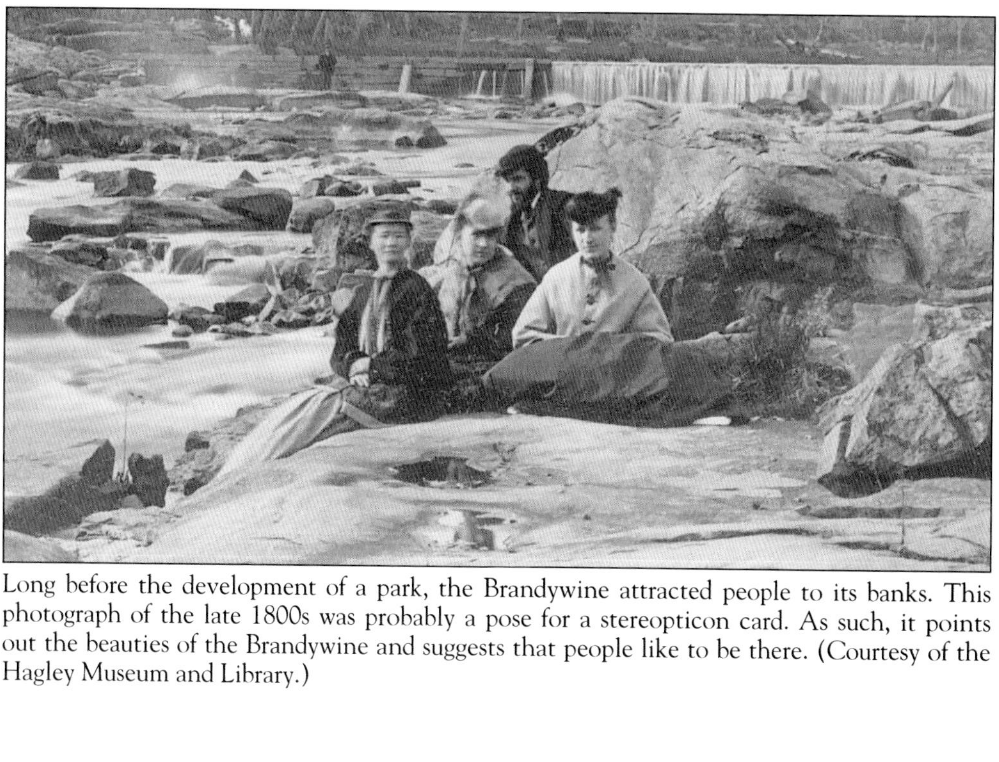

Long before the development of a park, the Brandywine attracted people to its banks. This photograph of the late 1800s was probably a pose for a stereopticon card. As such, it points out the beauties of the Brandywine and suggests that people like to be there. (Courtesy of the Hagley Museum and Library.)

Contents

Acknowledgments

Most of the pictures in this book came from collections in Delaware, and we are grateful to many people for helping us to locate photographs and for allowing us to borrow them. At the Delaware State Archives, Randy Goss led us to interesting unprocessed photographs. Dawn Mitchell, Heather Jon, Clifford Parker, and Molly Porter helped to find pictures in the archives' collection and also assisted us with ordering and other details of gathering our photos. At the Historical Society of Delaware, the director, Dr. Barbara E. Benson; L. Ellen Rendle; Constance J. Cooper; Edward W. Chichirichi; Thomas Beckman; and Richard Urban all went out of their way to help us locate photographs, secure copies, and find information. Ellen Rendle, as the curator of photographs and maps, was especially helpful. Jon M. Williams, the curator of prints and photographs, assisted at Hagley Museum and Library where Barbara Hall also helped in looking through Hagley's collection of photographs and even called us to make suggestions after we had left the library. Ken Dodunski of the Wilmington Department of Parks and Recreation gave us access to many old photographs, and his enthusiasm for our project was most helpful.

Many individuals have taken their time to talk with us and have loaned their photographs. These people include the following: Lammot Copeland; Malcolm Mackenzie; Faith Pizor; Peg Tigue of the Kalmar Nyckel Foundation; Susan Corkran; John Hanley, the city engineer of the Wilmington Department of Public Works; Margaret Owens of Riverfront Development Corporation; Irving Greenberg; Tim Bayard; Charles Lavin; Harmon Carey of the African-American Historical Society; Lisa Dyer of the Port of Wilmington; Susan Chase, who is the historian for the Friends of Wilmington Parks; Ronald Sommer of Dravo Corporation; Arden Media; Moeckel Carbonell Associates; Don Callendar; Charles Weymouth; Richard Chalfant; A. Roy Smith; Mildred Ward; Nancy Denisio; and Peter Kledaras.

We also appreciate the work of the photographers who have chosen Wilmington's rivers as their subject. Tim Bayard, John Schoonover, and Chris Queeney continue to photograph the city today, and several of their photographs appear in this book. In the past, Frank R. Zebley, Joseph Maybin, Sanborn Studios, Henry Szymanski, and David W. Allen, as well as many other anonymous photographers, engravers, and lithographers, have created a permanent pictorial record of Wilmington's rivers.

We want to acknowledge the assistance of the board members of Cityside, Inc. who secured the Maritime Preservation grant from the National Trust for Historic Preservation that first led us to study the Wilmington waterfront. We are grateful to have been able to refer to the works of the many authors who have recorded Wilmington history. They include Anna T. Lincoln, Elizabeth Montgomery, Henry Seidel Canby, and especially Carol E. Hoffecker, whose scholarly, yet lively accounts of Wilmington have set the benchmark against which all other histories of the city will be judged.

INTRODUCTION

Wilmington exists because of its rivers: the broad and navigable Christina and the rapidly flowing Brandywine. Wilmington's earliest European settlers arrived by water, her first industries used water power, and her later industries moved their products by water. By the mid-20th century, all that had changed. The miles of waterfront along Wilmington's rivers had become the home of idle industrial buildings, rusty machinery, and derelict cars and boats. Despite some productive uses of the waterfront by industry, parks, schools, and recreational interests, neglect had spawned junkyards and scrap heaps along the river banks. When the United States bicentennial approached in 1976, many Wilmington residents began to look back upon their heritage, trying to understand their past.

As a part of the Wilmington bicentennial celebration, Cityside, a local civic organization, sponsored its first "Maritime Days." Cityside was active in the Back-To-The-City Movement of the time and tried to call attention to the benefits of Wilmington's waterfront. Maritime Days included tours of the waterfront, fishing contests, a regatta, and other events. The general reaction was unenthusiastic; most people considered the riverfront, except within Brandywine Park, to be dull, dirty, and depressing.

The Cityside board members decided to take a more organized approach to studying the rivers in order to find out what really was there and what future the Wilmington waterfront might have. The organization successfully applied for a Maritime Preservation grant from the National Trust for Historic Preservation to prepare "An inventory of the historical and environmental aspects of the Christina and Brandywine Rivers in Wilmington." This became known as Project R.O.W., which stood for Reclaim Our Waterfront. Sally O'Byrne and Priscilla M. Thompson took on the task of creating the inventory, which they completed in March 1981.

The authors spent over two years visiting every lot along both sides of the Brandywine and Christina Rivers within the city of Wilmington. Using property maps provided by the city, they made notes of the uses and condition of all buildings, observed the plant life or lack of it on every lot, and looked for any remaining evidence of past uses of each piece of land. Background research included checking old land records, maps, books, and business records to compile a brief history of each lot, as well as gathering information on weather, tides, and the natural environment of the rivers and their banks.

This mountain of information resulted in a 260-page report that very few people knew about. However, it did form the basis for an exhibit by the Historical Society of Delaware, which had been cooperative with the project all along. Fortunately, by this time, the Wilmington city government had become interested in the potential for development on the waterfront, and there were glimmers of curiosity among residents. (*cont. on p. 10*)

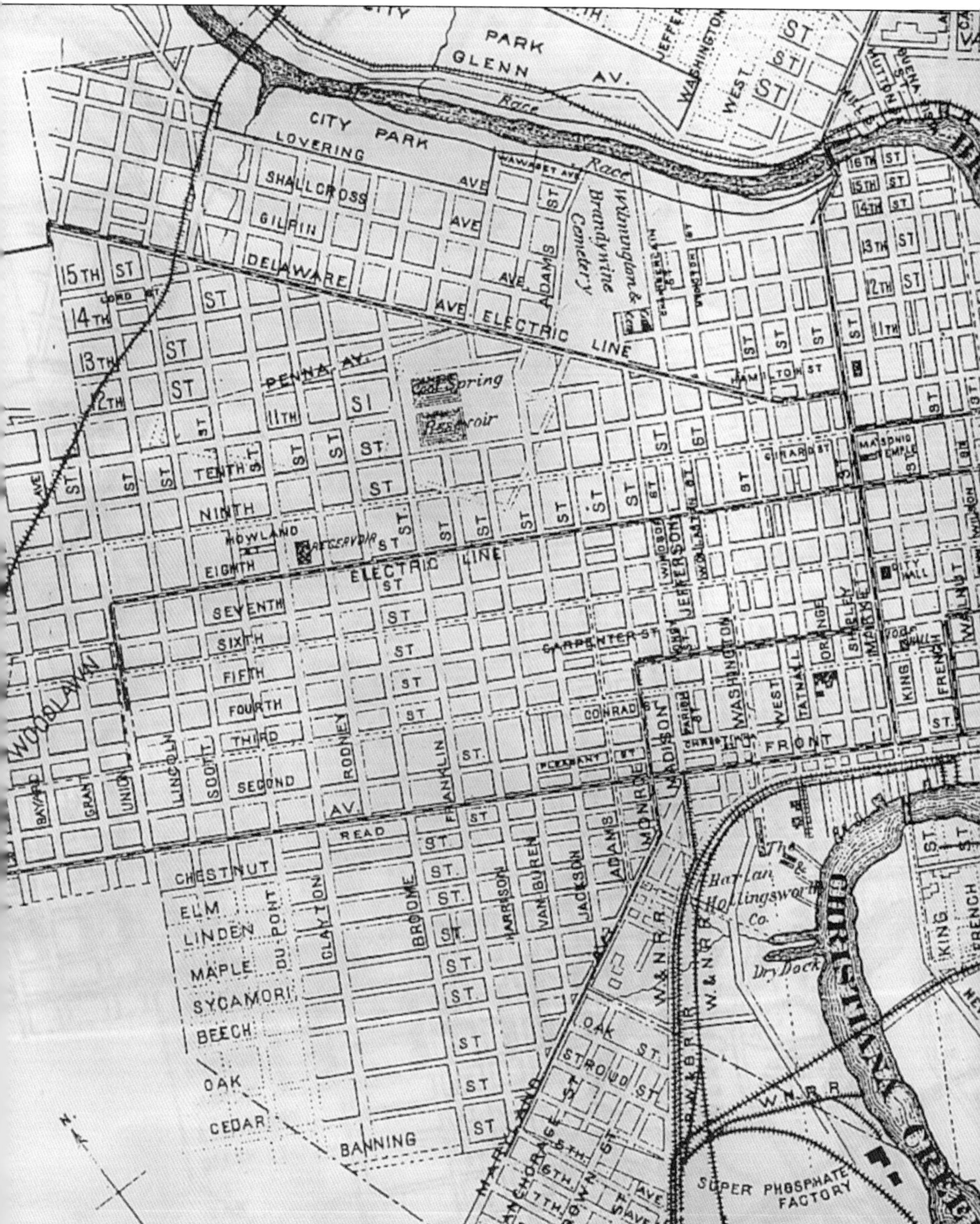

This map of the city of Wilmington appeared in W. Costa's city directory in 1895. Many of the industries and bridges shown in the book appear on this map. Harlan & Hollingsworth, Pusey & Jones, Lobdell Car Wheel, and Jackson & Sharp are clearly marked on the map, for

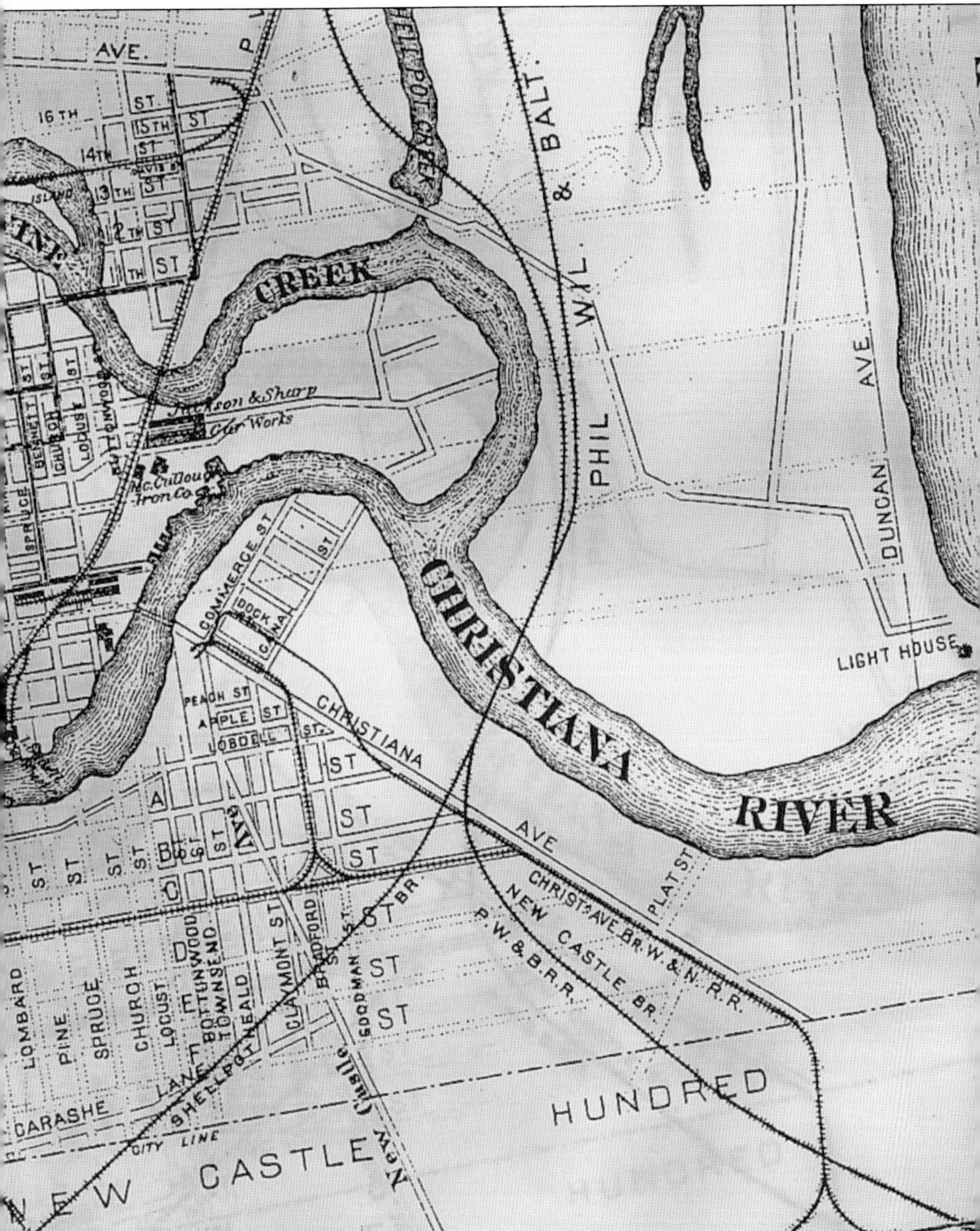

instance. The contours of the river are slightly different from today; Thatcher's Island no longer exists. The course of the rivers and the location of major streets will help to identify the location of many of the buildings shown in the book.

(*cont. from p. 7*) A few daring businesses and organizations saw a future in old buildings such as the Harlan & Hollingsworth office building, the J. Morton Poole building, and others. The city began to polish up some of its park land along the Christina, and recreation came back to the river in the form of Frawley Stadium and several rowing clubs.

As the millennium approaches, more and more activity is coming back to the Wilmington waterfront. The Christina and the Brandywine, which have pumped their life blood into the city for over 350 years, are seeing renewed life themselves. While old buildings take on new lives and modern pioneers try innovative projects along the rivers, there is also a renewed interest in the waterways' past. Exhibition halls, shops, and parks are beginning to blossom along the rivers, and people are beginning to ask, "What was here before? Why didn't we know about the rivers?" This book will answer some of those questions.

Thompson and O'Byrne invite you to explore the Wilmington waterfront with them. They will show you a picture of its past. Based primarily on their research for Project R.O.W., this book is a compilation of photographs and other pictures that tell the story of the city's waterfront. The pictures have come from individual people, the Delaware State Archives, the Historical Society of Delaware, the Hagley Museum and Library, and other sources as indicated in the captions.

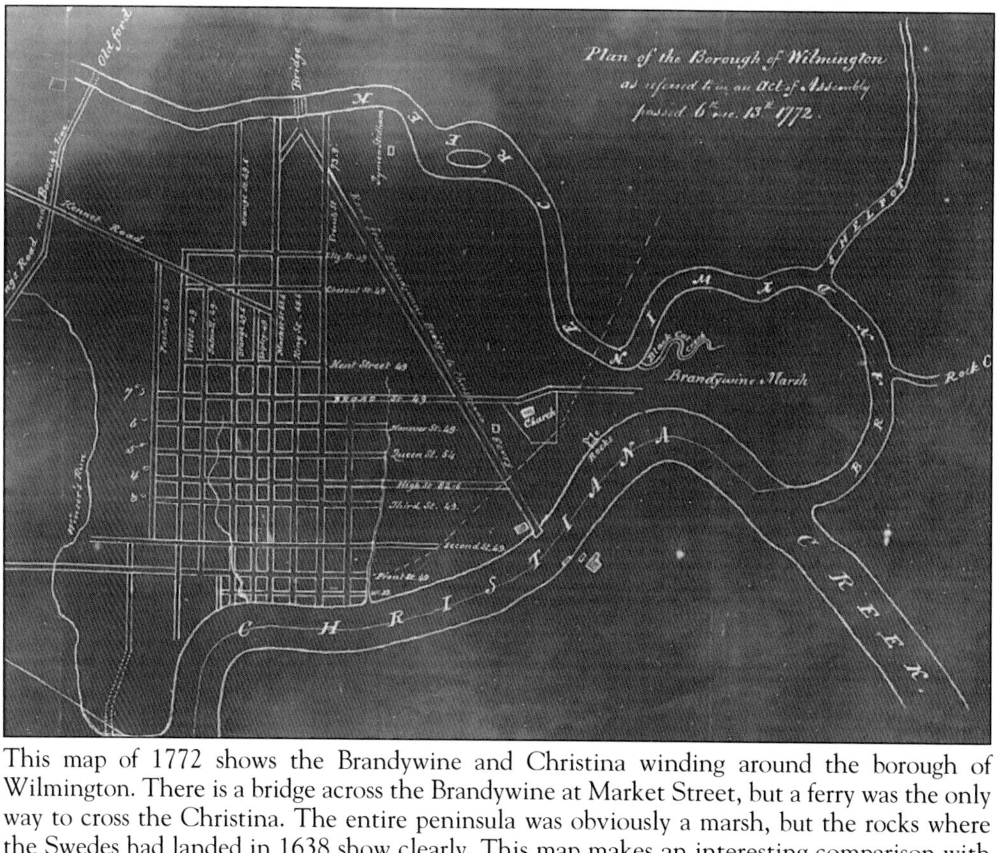

This map of 1772 shows the Brandywine and Christina winding around the borough of Wilmington. There is a bridge across the Brandywine at Market Street, but a ferry was the only way to cross the Christina. The entire peninsula was obviously a marsh, but the rocks where the Swedes had landed in 1638 show clearly. This map makes an interesting comparison with the 1895 map.

One

THE CHRISTINA RIVER

Industrial ghosts haunt the broad and navigable Christina River today as she meanders through Wilmington. From her headwaters near Kemblesville, Pennsylvania, to the Delaware Bay, the river is about 35 miles long. When the Swedes arrived in 1638, they honored this river by naming her for their queen, Christina. Also going by the name Christeen or Christiana and sometimes called creek, the river gave the first European settlers a convenient landing spot, and her marsh-lined banks provided a haven for wildlife and fish.

In the more than three and a half centuries since the Swedish landing, man has put the Christina to work, taking advantage of her deep tidal waters. The river has been the home port for early sailing packets to Philadelphia as well as for the 20th-century Wilson Line steamboats. She still welcomes modern ships from around the world at the Port of Wilmington. The Christina helped Wilmington become the nation's largest builder of iron-hulled ships, and her convenience to rail and water shipping made her an ideal location for manufacturers of iron products, railroad cars, and barges.

The old industries deserted the Christina after World War II, leaving behind crumbling bulkheads, empty buildings, and an inaccessible waterfront. Today, new businesses and public places are beginning to blossom along the Christina, making her a vital part of city life again. Follow the pictures from the city line in a generally downstream direction to the Christina's confluence with the Brandywine. You will see a part of the river's past.

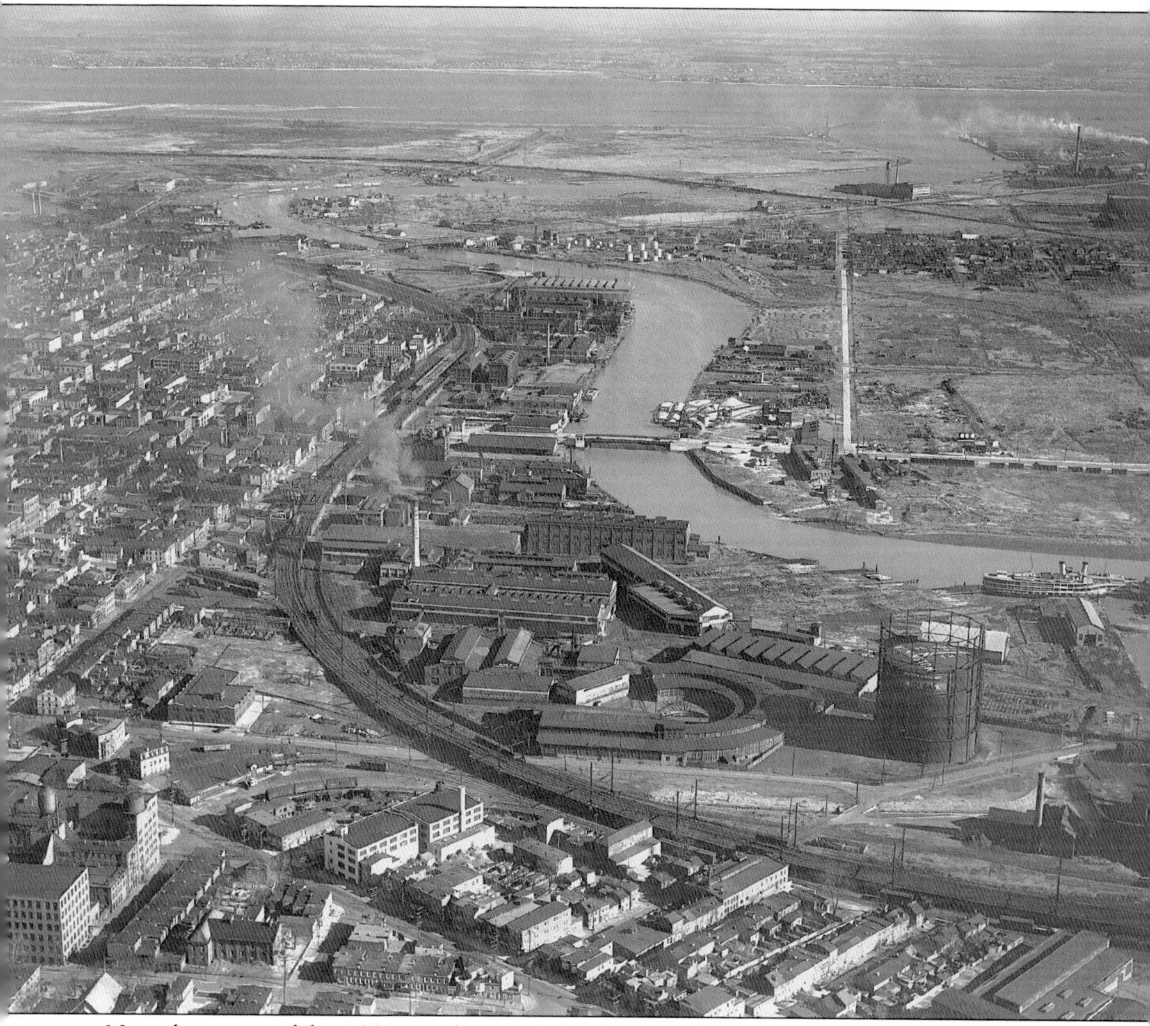

Near the center of this 1931 aerial view of the Christina River is a railroad roundhouse. Harlan and Hollingsworth Company buildings stand on the left side of the river, upstream from the Market Street. bridge. Near the far curve is the enormous Pusey & Jones Company building. Beyond this is the Third Street bridge leading to South Wilmington. The railroad tracks curve parallel to the Christina as it flows out to the Delaware River in the distance. Two steamboats lie at wharves on the center right, and downtown Wilmington sprawls to the left. This photograph shows the Christina in the Depression era between World Wars I and II. (Courtesy of the Hagley Museum and Library.)

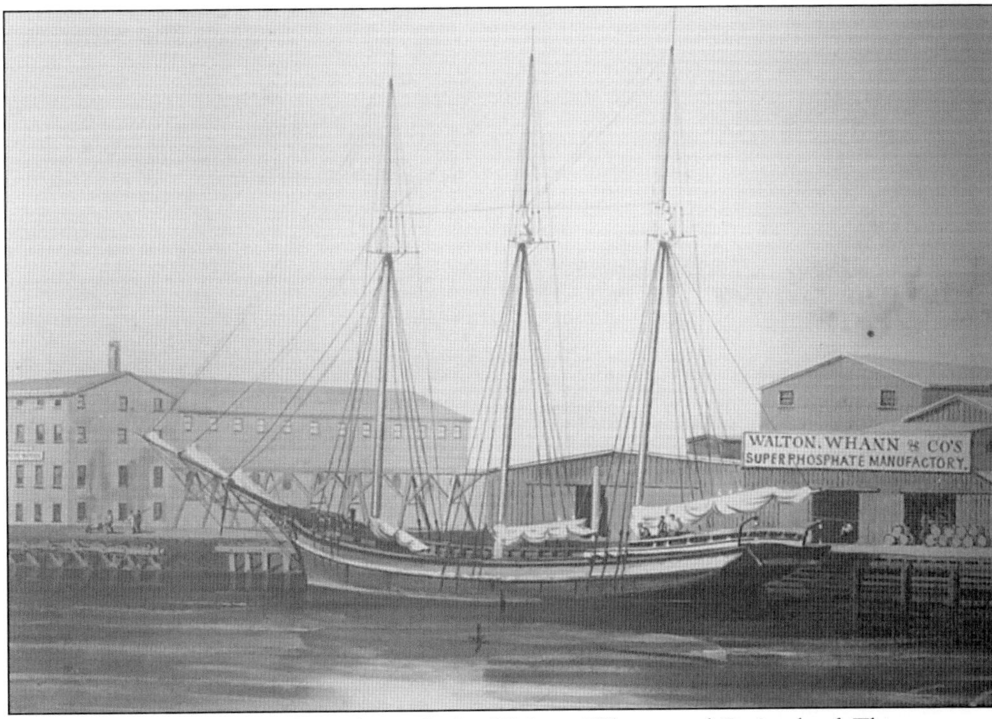

A sailing cargo vessel is tied up alongside the Walton, Whann and Co.'s wharf. This company used bones from meat-packing houses in the western United States and South America to make super phosphate fertilizer. They produced about 100 tons per day at the Wilmington plant, which, by 1893, spread over 6 acres near the city boundary as shown on the map in the introduction. (Courtesy of the Historical Society of Delaware.)

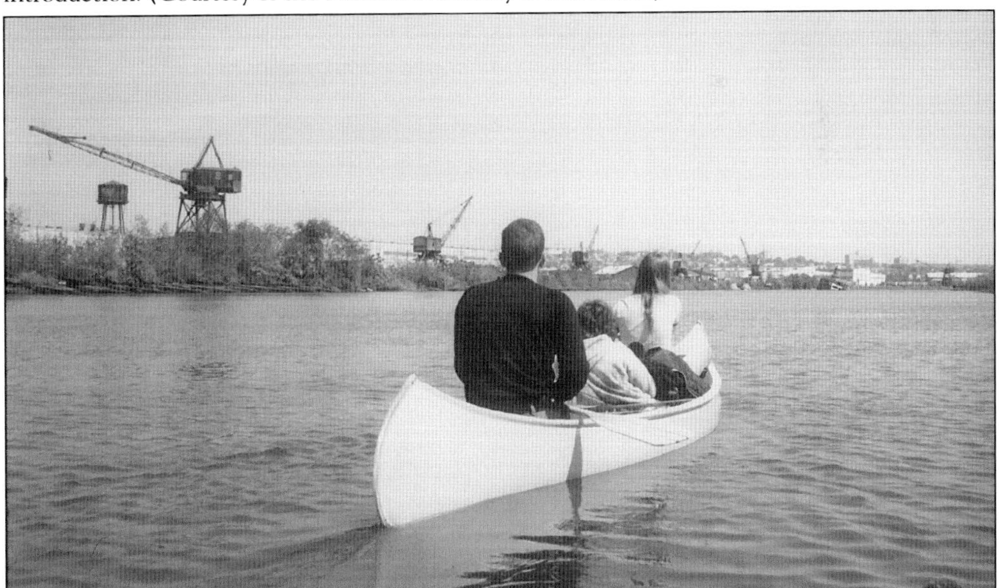

By the 1970s, few of the old industries remained along the Christina River. Here, canoeists paddle quietly over the surface of the broad reaches of the river near the city limits, passing remnants of the industries that once lined the shore.

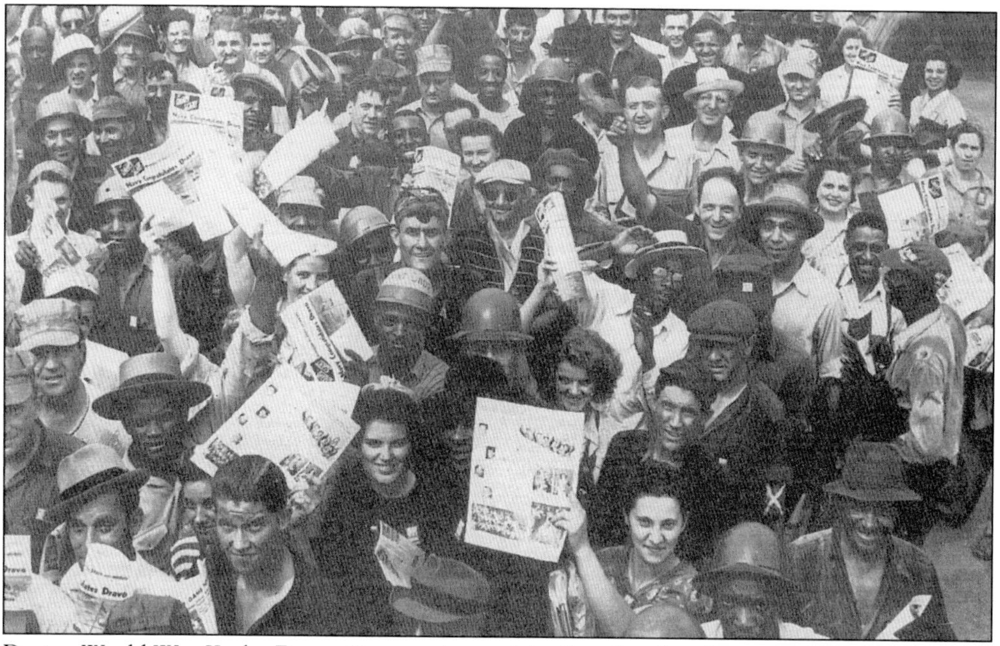

During World War II, the Dravo Corporation, originally a Pittsburgh engineering firm, became the dominant industry on the upper Christina. Men and women put their skills and talents to work building ships at the company yard. Dravo employees participated in company bond rallies, bowling teams, and musical groups. This group is ending their shift just as the plant newspaper, the *Slant*, is being distributed. (Courtesy of the Dravo Corporation.)

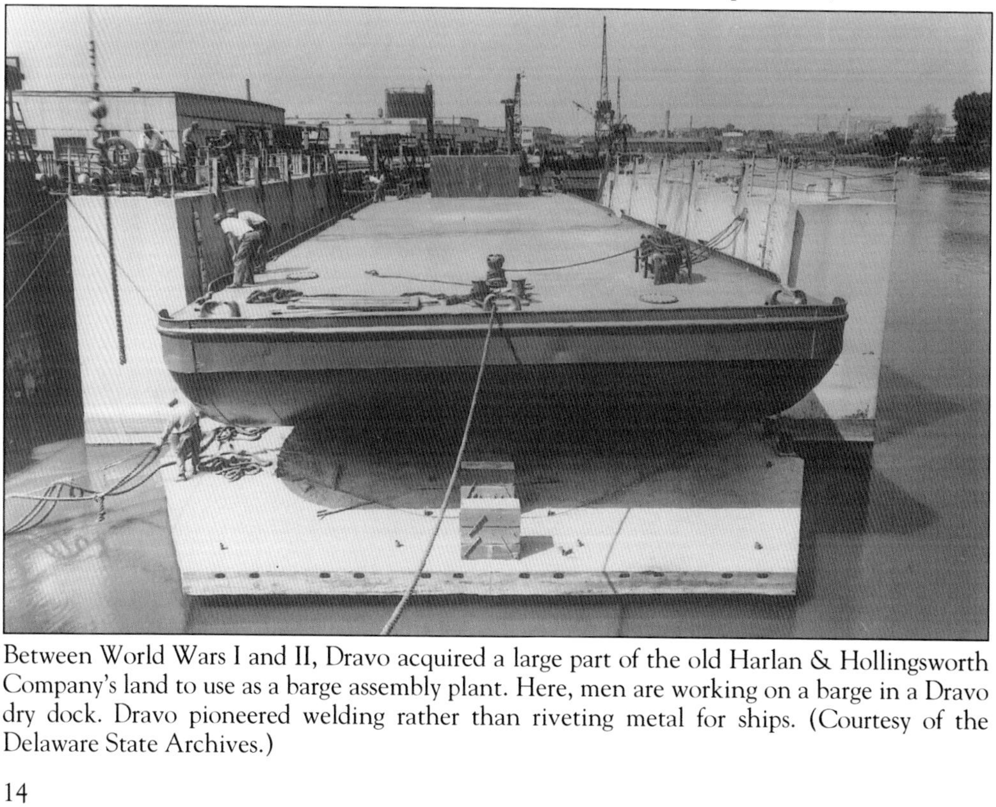

Between World Wars I and II, Dravo acquired a large part of the old Harlan & Hollingsworth Company's land to use as a barge assembly plant. Here, men are working on a barge in a Dravo dry dock. Dravo pioneered welding rather than riveting metal for ships. (Courtesy of the Delaware State Archives.)

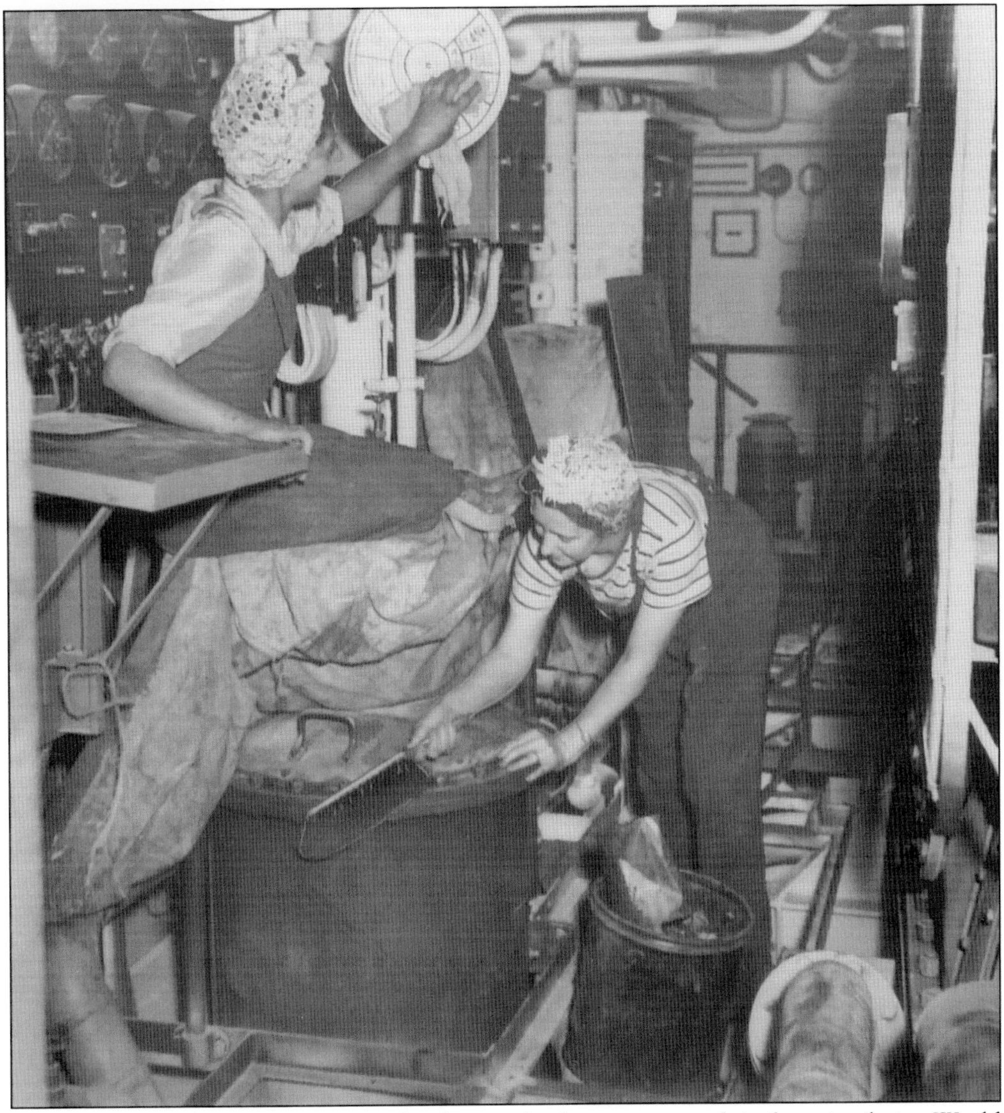

These women at Dravo were among the thousands who went to work in factories during World War II, dispelling any notion that women were unable to do the work traditionally done by men. "Rosie the Riveter" and her sisters across the nation were all a part of the war effort that supplied the materials to fuel the Allied forces in Europe and Asia. In Wilmington, Dravo employed up to 10,500 people during the war years. Other plants in the city also geared up for the war effort, recruiting employees from some distance. The population of Wilmington swelled enough to create a housing shortage, inducing many people to divide their homes into apartments to accommodate the new residents. (Courtesy of the Delaware State Archives.)

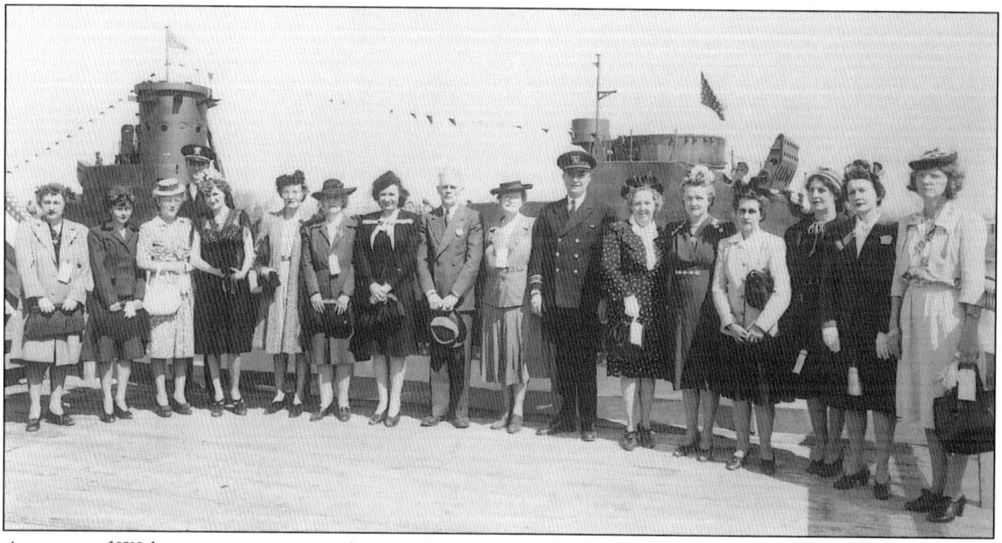

A group of Wilmington women whose sons were serving in the U.S. Navy gathered at the Dravo plant to sponsor the launching of Landing Ship, Medium (LSM) #423 during World War II. Here, they are lined up for a photograph with two naval officers and one other man. The LSM, decorated with pennants, is in the background. (Courtesy of the Delaware State Archives.)

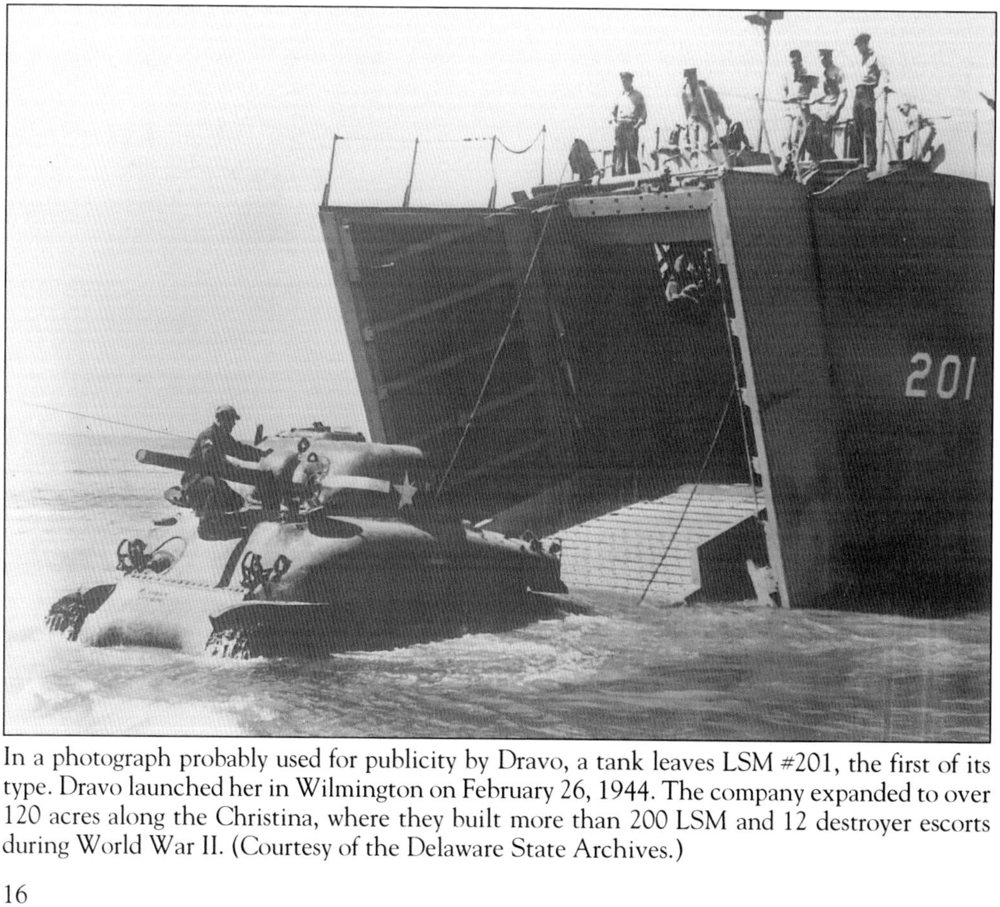

In a photograph probably used for publicity by Dravo, a tank leaves LSM #201, the first of its type. Dravo launched her in Wilmington on February 26, 1944. The company expanded to over 120 acres along the Christina, where they built more than 200 LSM and 12 destroyer escorts during World War II. (Courtesy of the Delaware State Archives.)

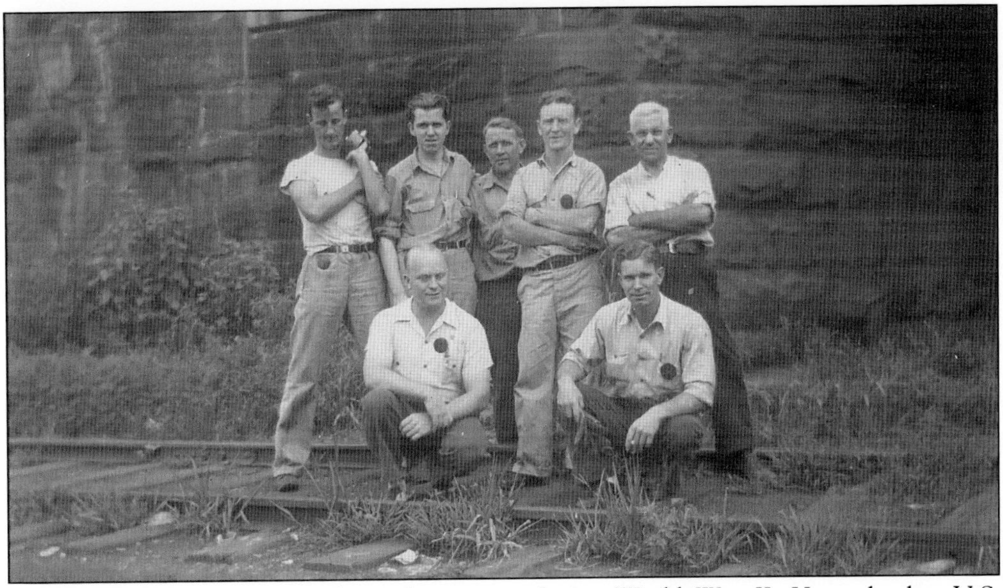

Charles Lavin was a principal naval inspector during World War II. He and other U.S. naval inspectors posed by the railroad viaduct on August 5, 1942. They are, from left to right, as follows: (seated) O. Horlford of Philadelphia and Tom Hefferon of Cleveland; (standing) Fred MacLennan of Wilmington, ? MacDonald of Philadelphia, Steve Bruskey of Philadelphia, Charles Lavin of Chester, Pennsylvania, and A. Ruff of Philadelphia. (Courtesy of Charles Lavin Jr., son of the man in the photo.)

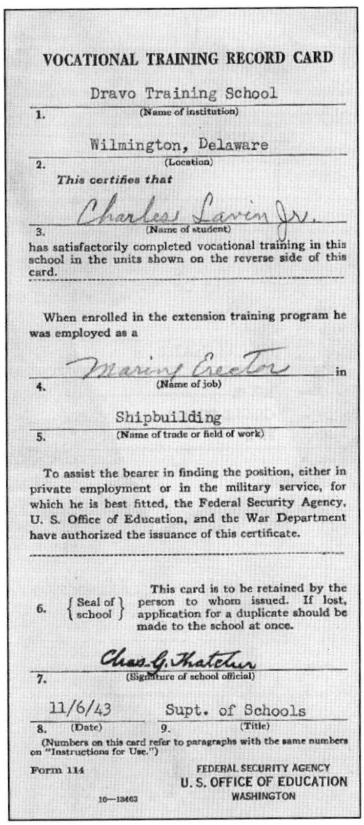

VOCATIONAL TRAINING RECORD CARD

1. Dravo Training School
(Name of institution)

2. Wilmington, Delaware
(Location)

This certifies that

3. Charles Lavin Jr.
(Name of student)

has satisfactorily completed vocational training in this school in the units shown on the reverse side of this card.

When enrolled in the extension training program he was employed as a

4. Marine Erector in
(Name of job)

5. Shipbuilding
(Name of trade or field of work)

To assist the bearer in finding the position, either in private employment or in the military service, for which he is best fitted, the Federal Security Agency, U. S. Office of Education, and the War Department have authorized the issuance of this certificate.

6. { Seal of school } This card is to be retained by the person to whom issued. If lost, application for a duplicate should be made to the school at once.

7. Chas. G. Thatcher
(Signature of school official)

8. 11/6/43 (Date)
9. Supt. of Schools (Title)

(Numbers on this card refer to paragraphs with the same numbers on "Instructions for Use.")

Form 114

10—13463

FEDERAL SECURITY AGENCY
U. S. OFFICE OF EDUCATION
WASHINGTON

Charles Lavin Jr., son of the naval inspector, attended the Dravo Training School as a marine erector. This training record card certified that he had enrolled in additional training while working in shipbuilding. Both Charles Jr. and his twin brother, John, worked for Dravo, installing diesel engines in Destroyer Escorts. (Courtesy of Charles Lavin Jr.)

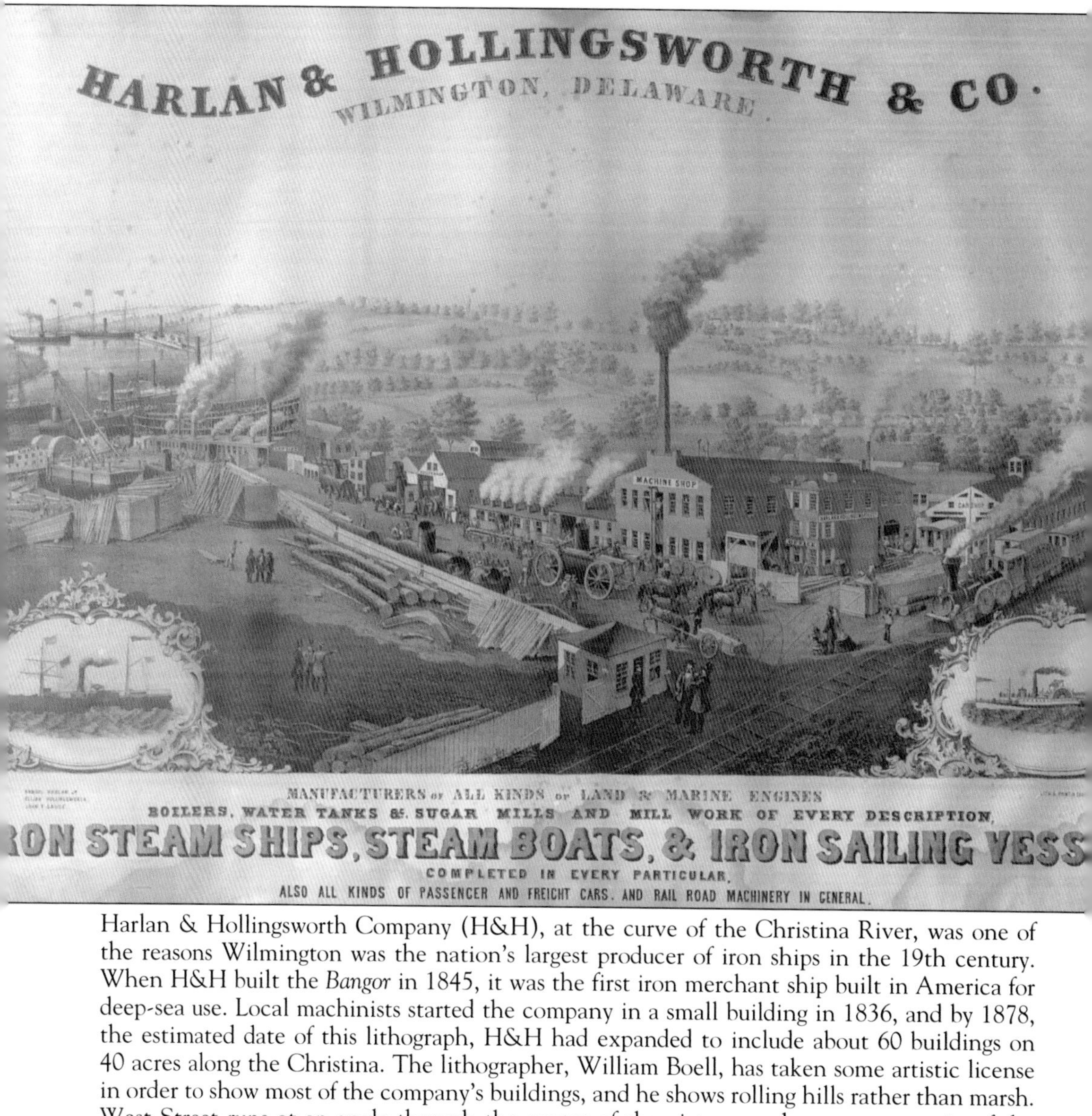

Harlan & Hollingsworth Company (H&H), at the curve of the Christina River, was one of the reasons Wilmington was the nation's largest producer of iron ships in the 19th century. When H&H built the *Bangor* in 1845, it was the first iron merchant ship built in America for deep-sea use. Local machinists started the company in a small building in 1836, and by 1878, the estimated date of this lithograph, H&H had expanded to include about 60 buildings on 40 acres along the Christina. The lithographer, William Boell, has taken some artistic license in order to show most of the company's buildings, and he shows rolling hills rather than marsh. West Street runs at an angle through the center of the picture, and a passenger train of the Philadelphia, Wilmington & Baltimore Railroad heads for town in the lower right. (Courtesy of the Historical Society of Delaware.)

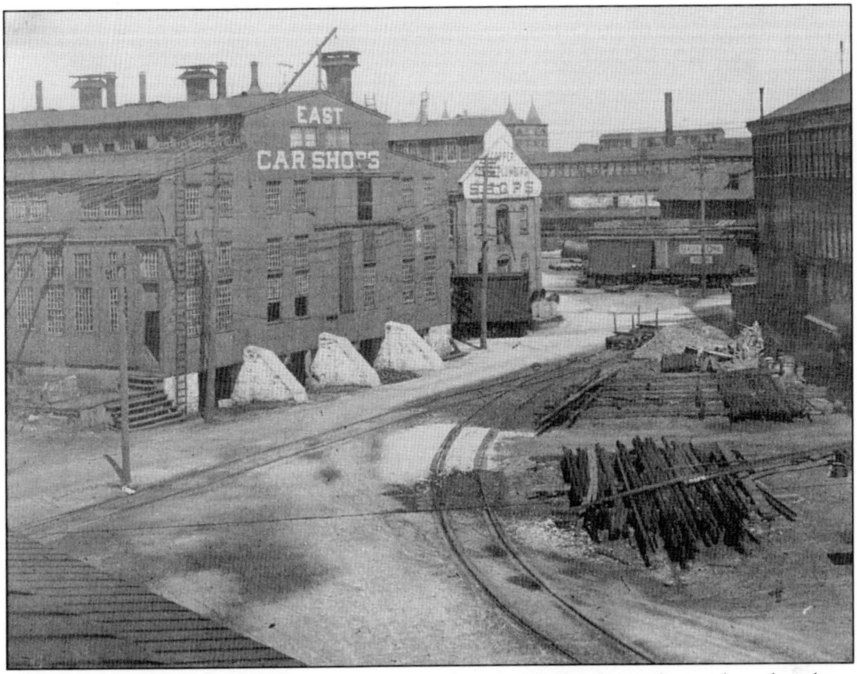

This 1898 photo shows the buildings where Harlan & Hollingsworth produced railroad cars. The overall plant covered more than 70 acres on both sides of the Christina River. With 47 buildings and 3,000 feet of waterfront, the company employed 1,500 people in 1889. The financial panic of 1893, the Spanish-American War, labor problems, and a general move toward trusts and monopolies soon changed the makeup of the company. (Courtesy of the Historical Society of Delaware.)

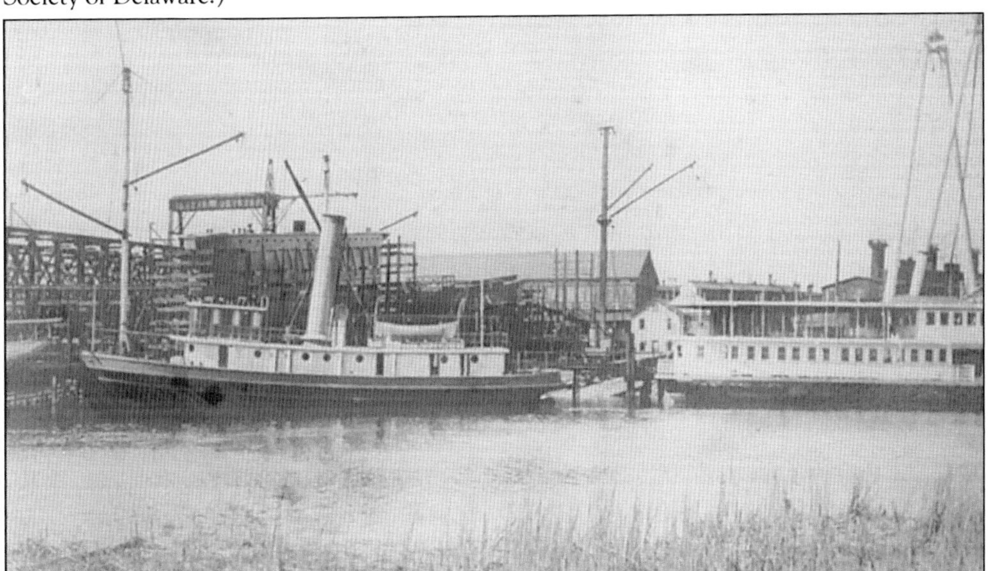

Looking at the Harlan & Hollingsworth area from across the river in 1910, one can see ships, cranes, and industrial buildings. By this time, H&H had become a part of U.S. Shipbuilding, which eventually collapsed and turned its assets, including the Harlan & Hollingsworth plant, over to Bethlehem Steel. (Courtesy of the Historical Society of Delaware.)

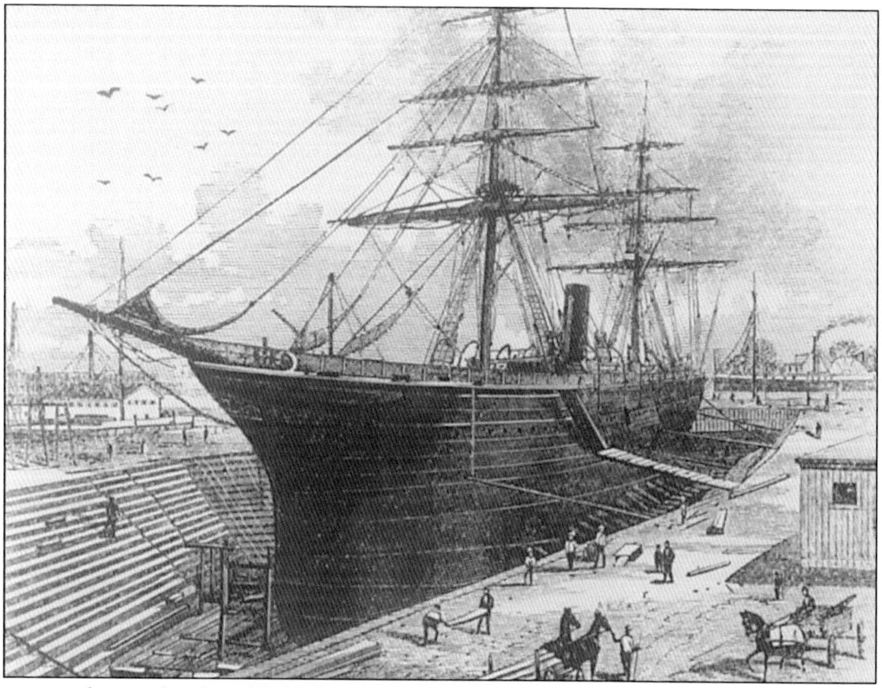

This view is from a book published in 1888 by the Wilmington Board of Trade to promote the city's commercial and maritime advantages. Men are working on a ship in the Harlan & Hollingsworth dry dock. Although the company followed some of the designs of wooden ships, they built only in iron. The wood the men are carrying would have been for the interior and trim. (Courtesy of the Historical Society of Delaware.)

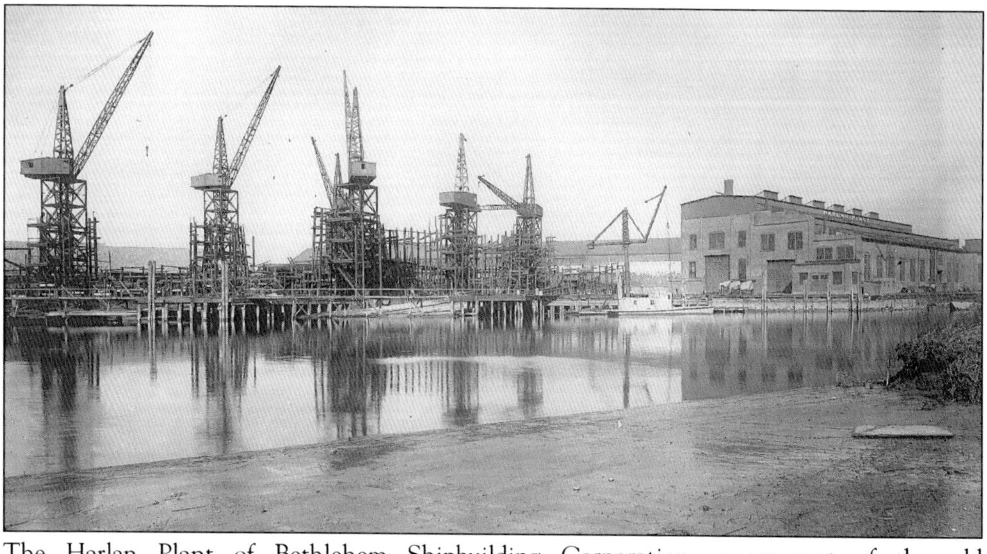

The Harlan Plant of Bethlehem Shipbuilding Corporation, a remnant of the old Harlan & Hollingsworth Company, looked like this in 1925. During World War I, the plant built about 70 vessels and employed nearly 7,500 people in three shifts. When World War II came along, this plant made landing barges, navy ramps, and sheet metal. The building on the right is scheduled to open as a restaurant and nightclub in 2000. (Courtesy of the Delaware State Archives.)

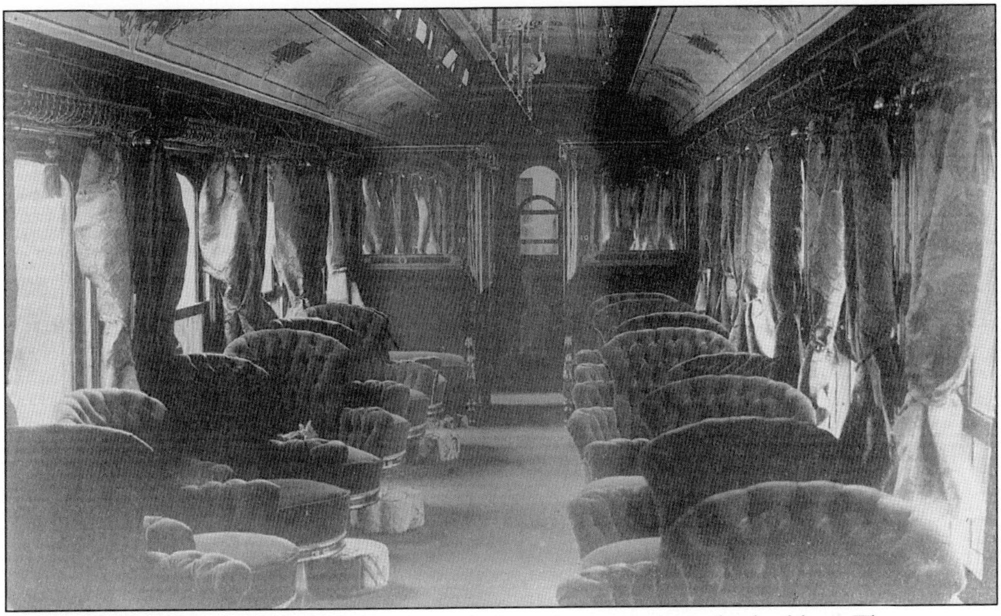

Harlan & Hollingsworth built railroad cars before they went into shipbuilding. The company did all the interior work, including wood trim and upholstery. This parlor car gives some idea of how elaborate that work could be. (Courtesy of the Hagley Museum and Library.)

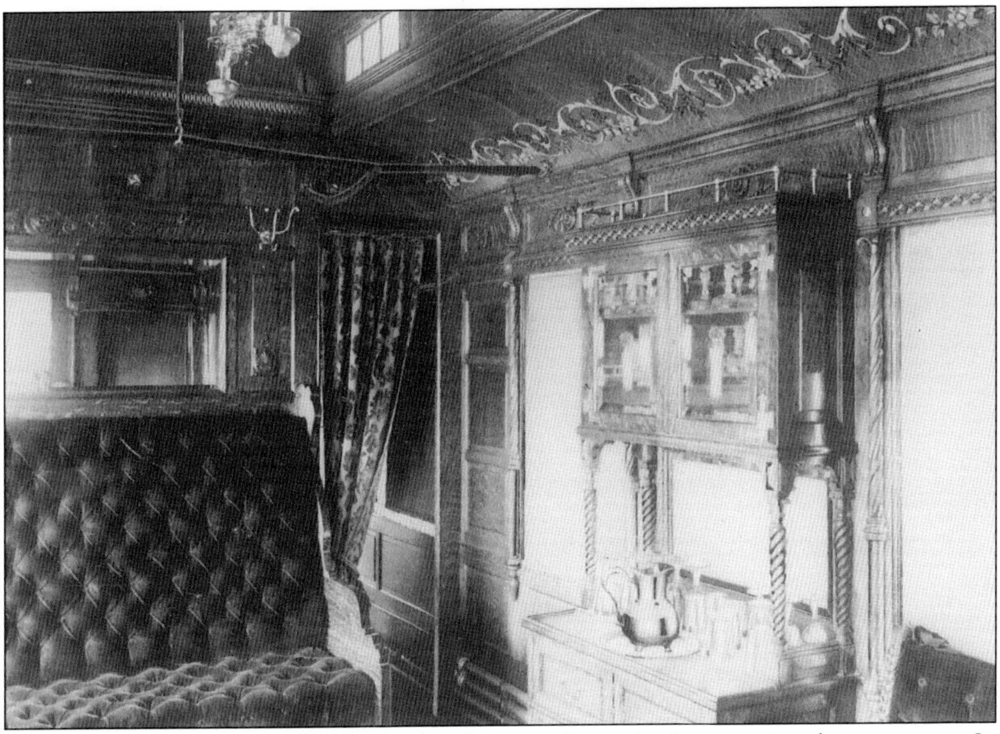

In 1898, Harlan & Hollingsworth put this photograph in a book promoting their company. In the late 19th century, it was not unusual for rich Americans to have their own private railroad cars so that they could travel in the most luxurious way possible at the time. This is a corner of the dining room in a private car. (Courtesy of the Historical Society of Delaware.)

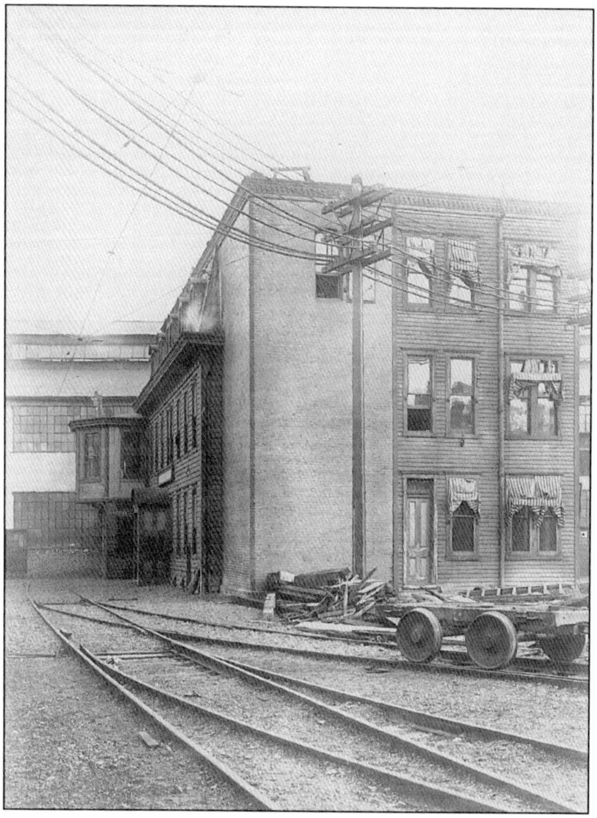

The offices for the Harlan & Hollingsworth Company looked like this in about 1900. This building became inadequate to serve as the company's offices, and the construction of a new office building started in 1910. (Courtesy of the Historical Society of Delaware.)

The new Harlan & Hollingsworth office building went into service in 1912. The building's architectural significance and its historical importance in Wilmington qualified it for listing in the National Register of Historic Places in 1979. The company 100 South West Street Associates, owned by Lammot Copeland Jr. and his family, purchased the building in 1991 and renovated it, making it once again a viable asset on the Wilmington waterfront. (Courtesy of the Hagley Museum and Library.)

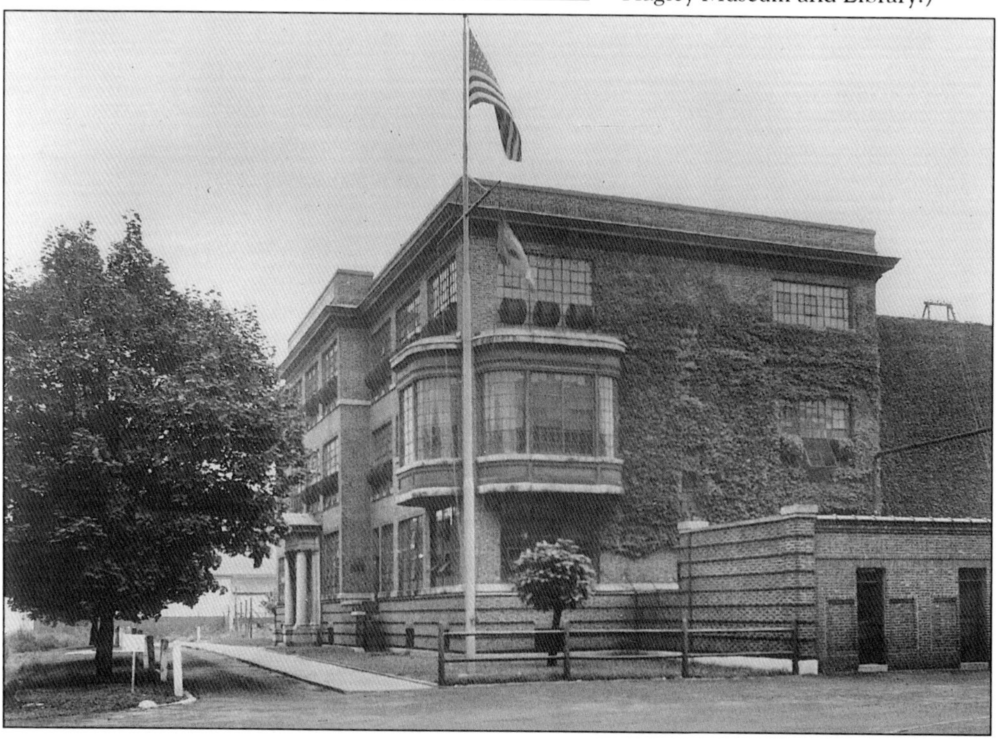

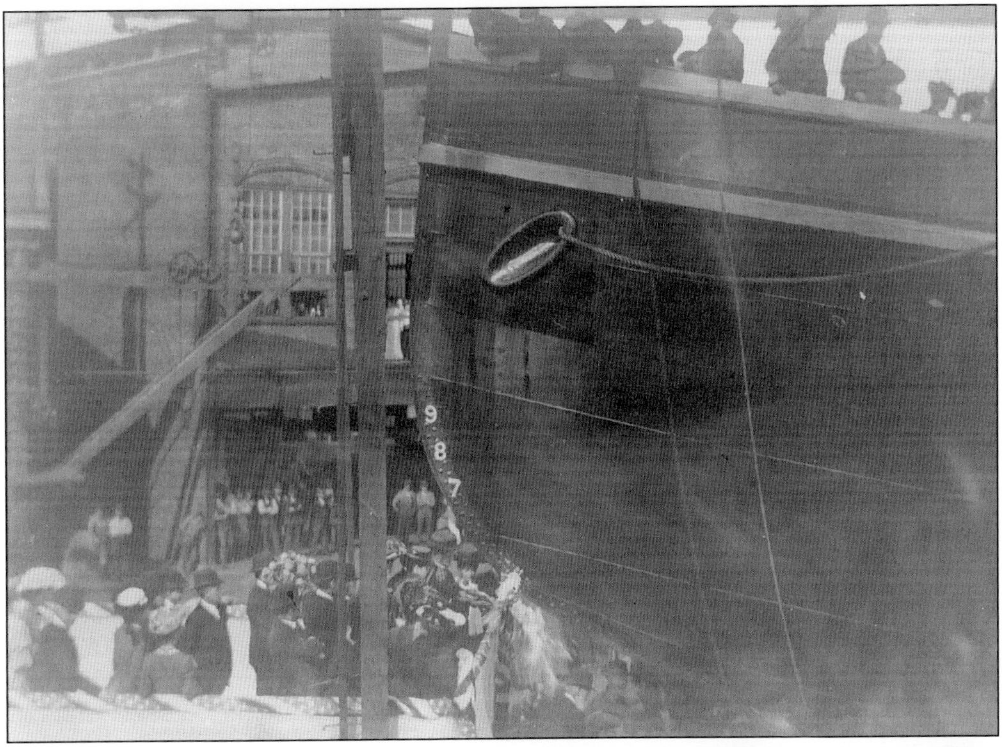

A ship launching in the 1890s always brought a crowd to the Christina riverfront. The owner of a new boat and guests watched at close range while the sponsor smashed a bottle of champagne over the bow. H&H employees in the background admire the results of their work while more onlookers peer over the bow at the action below. (Courtesy of the Historical Society of Delaware.)

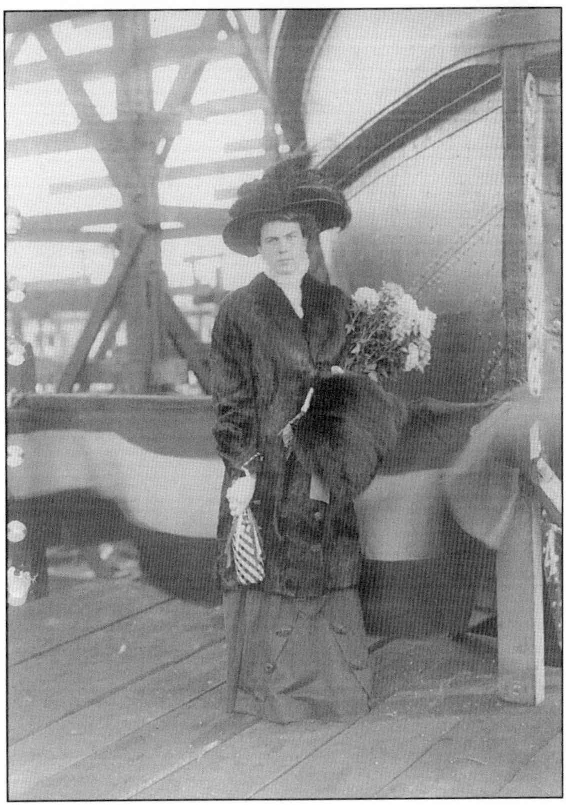

This young woman is prepared to launch a boat at the Harlan & Hollingsworth Company in the late 1890s. She wears her fur coat with matching muff and hat and carries a bouquet of chrysanthemums for this gala occasion. In her right hand, she carries a bottle of champagne, which she hopes will break as she strikes her first blow against the bow. (Courtesy of the Historical Society of Delaware.)

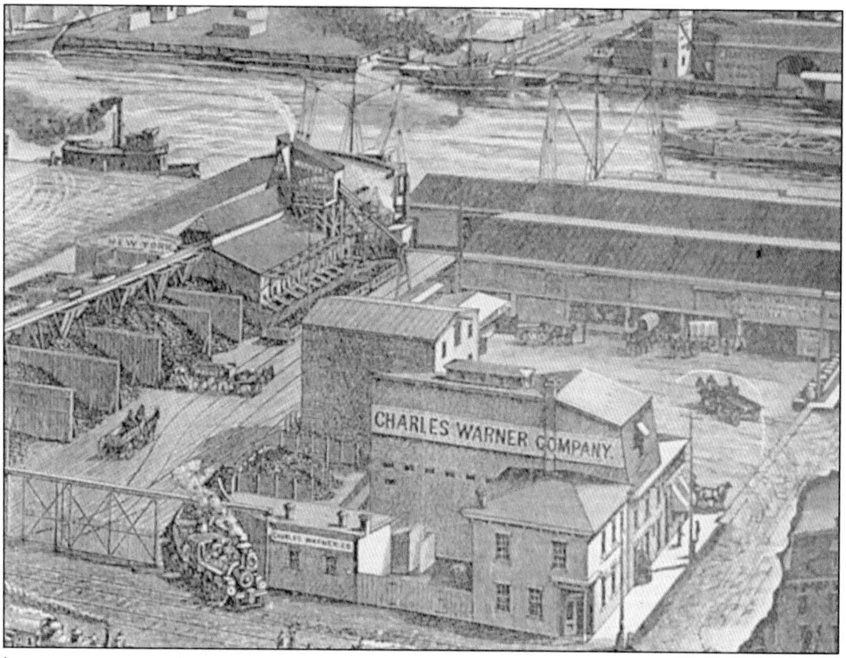

For well over a century, the name Warner was a presence along the Christina River. In 1794, John and William Warner, Quaker brothers, formed a partnership that prospered and grew through many generations. By 1888, the company operated steamers to Philadelphia and New York from its wharves at Market Street on the Christina. Warner eventually expanded its coal and other operations to both sides of the river. (Courtesy of the Historical Society of Delaware.)

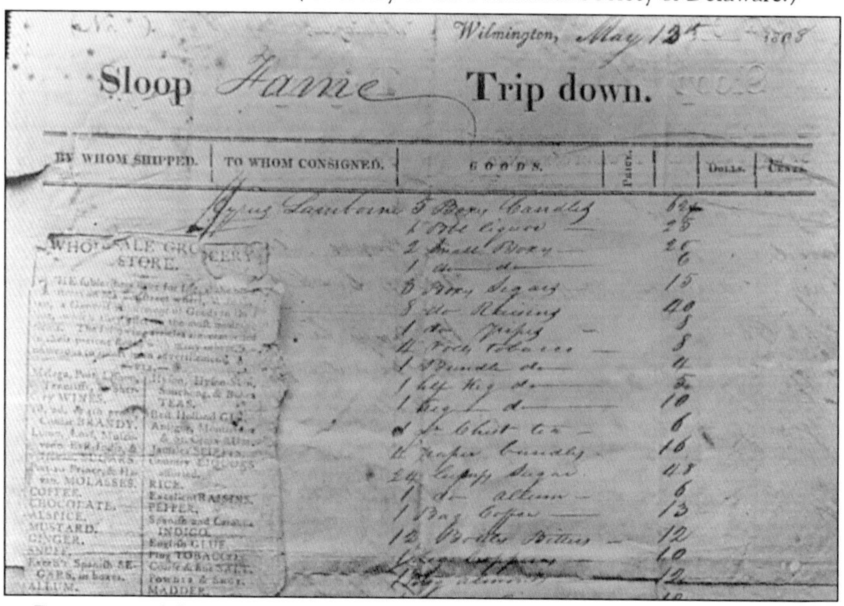

The sloop *Fame*, one of the Warner sailing vessels, made regular trips between Wilmington and Philadelphia starting in 1808. The vessel's manifest of May 12, 1808, lists freight that included candles, liquor, cigars, raisins, tobacco, sugar, and coffee. On this same trip, the *Fame* carried 304 empty kegs for the du Ponts, who were already in business on the Brandywine. (Courtesy of the Delaware State Archives.)

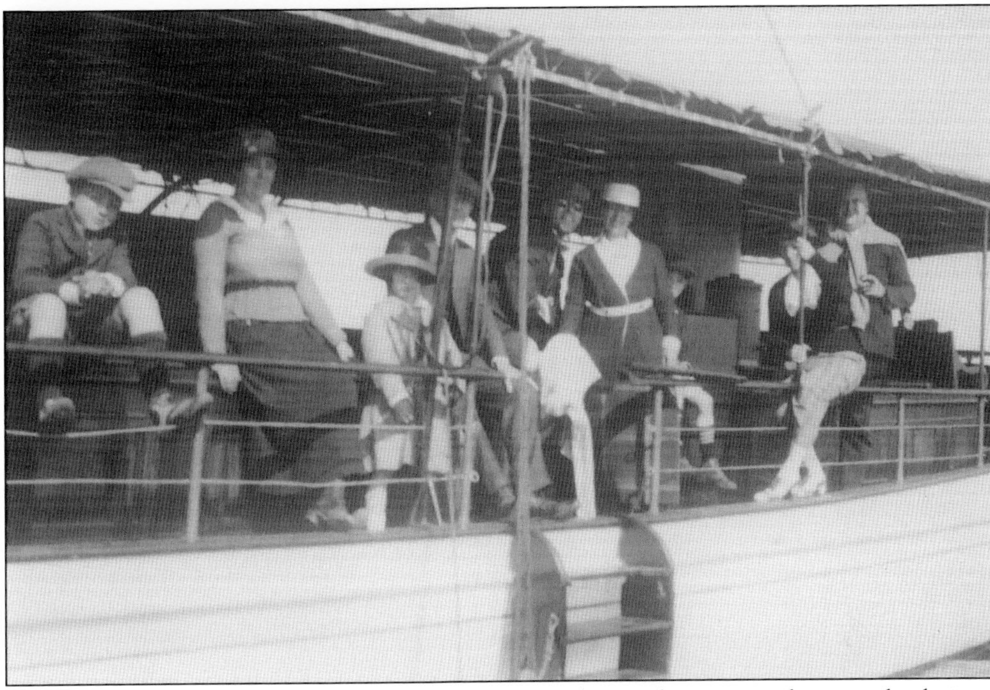

Quaker families in Wilmington tended to join together in business and personal relations, so it is not surprising that Alfred D. Warner married Emmalea Pusey, a leader in local civic and philanthropic affairs. The Quaker preference for a quiet life did not exclude recreation altogether, and here is a group aboard the Warner-Pusey yacht, *Bellerton*. (Courtesy of the Historical Society of Delaware.)

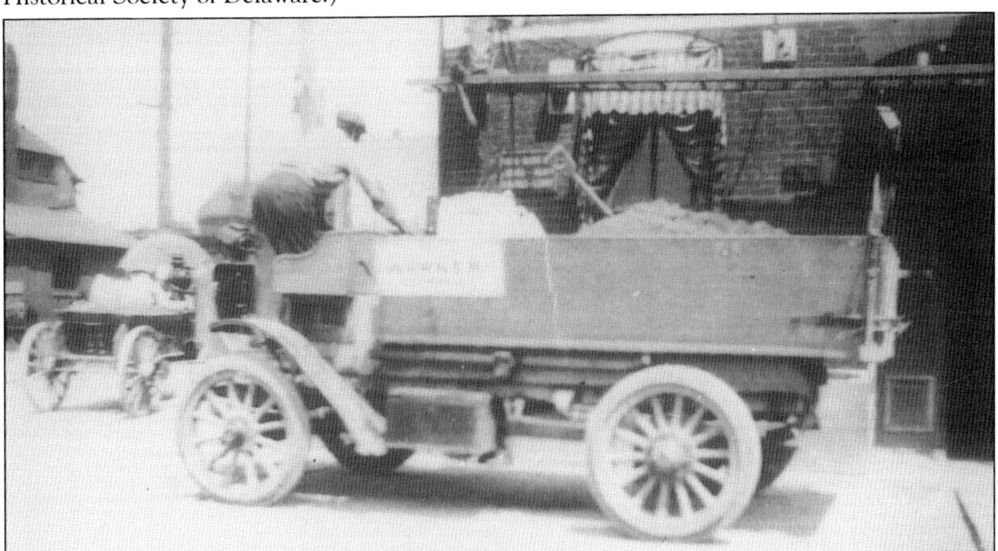

In the early 20th century, as Warner expanded into concrete, sand, and gravel, trucking became important. Here is one of the early trucks in a fleet that would grow to about 200. Although the company moved its headquarters to Philadelphia in the 1920s, it kept an office for some time at its old location near the foot of Market Street in Wilmington. (Courtesy of the Historical Society of Delaware.)

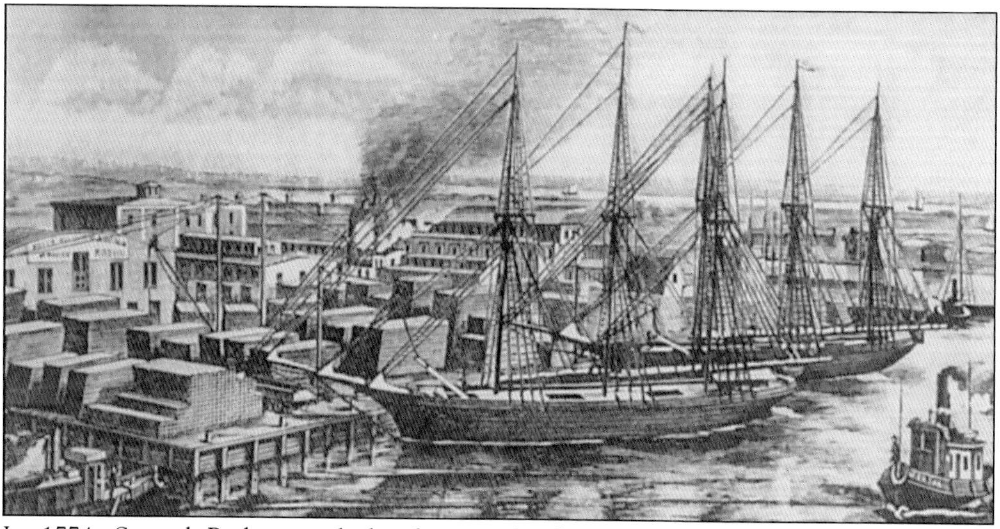

In 1774, Samuel Bush started the first regular boat service between Wilmington and Philadelphia with the sloop *Ann*. By the late 1880s, as shown above, the company had become G.W. Bush & Sons and had a lumber and coal business as well as a steam freight line. (Courtesy of the Historical Society of Delaware.)

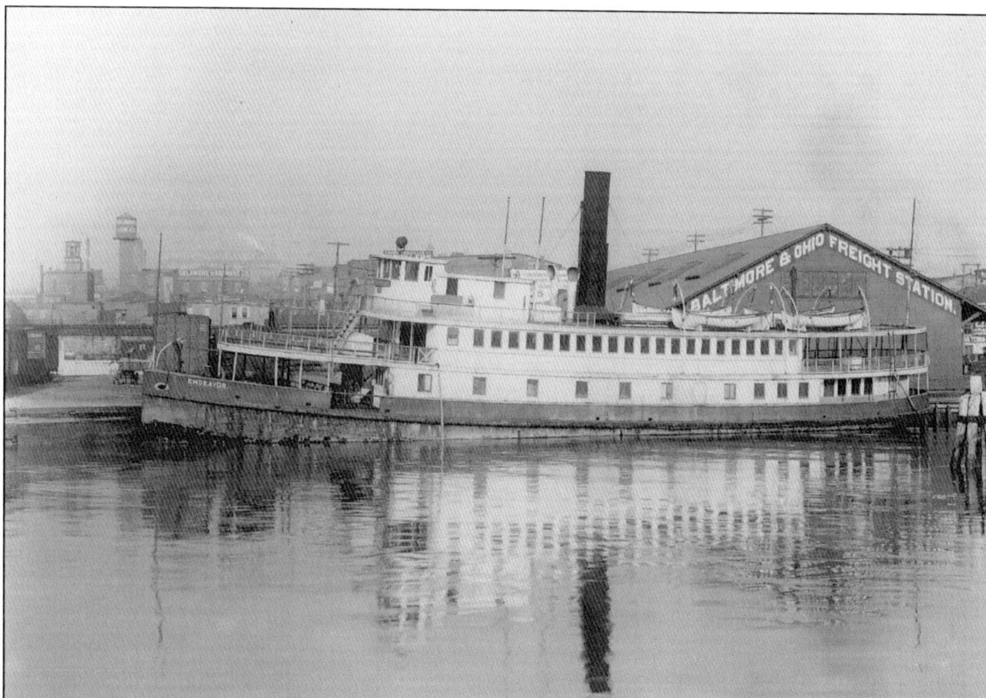

The ship *Endeavor* is docked in front of the Baltimore & Ohio (B&O) Freight Station at 101 South Market Street. H. Rushworth took this photograph from the south side of the Christina, probably in the 1930s. (Courtesy of the Historical Society of Delaware.)

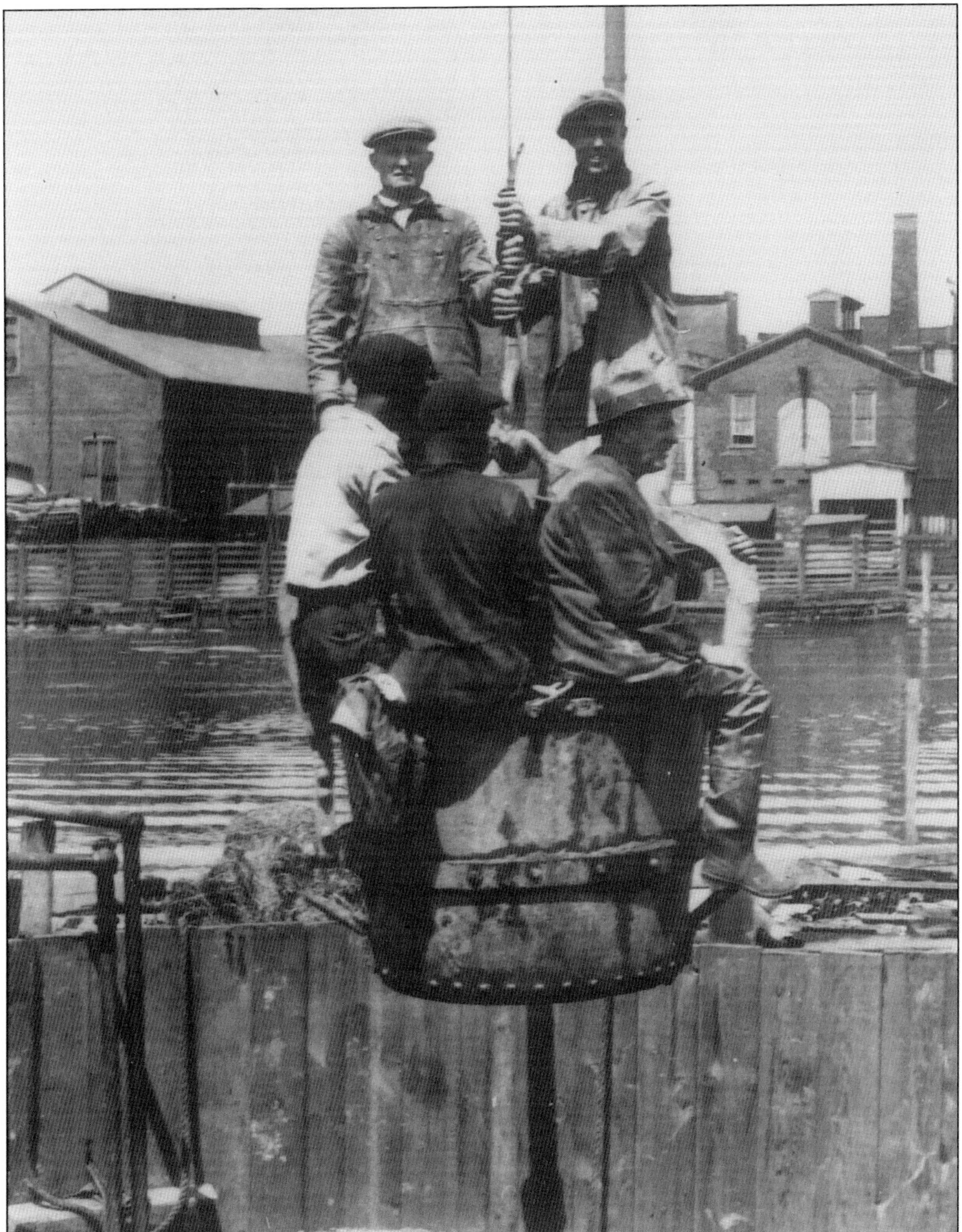

These five men look nonchalant as they take precarious positions to head underground to work on the tunnel under the Christina. It is doubtful that this method of descent would meet modern safety requirements. The tunnel is at the foot of Orange Street, and this view is from the south side of the river facing north and slightly upstream. The Wilmington Board of Water Commissioners took this photo as one of a series during the 1931 construction of a tunnel to hold pipes carrying drinking water to the south side of the river. The Orange Street tunnel carried a 16-inch main. Eventually, there was a need for an additional tunnel near the Third Street bridge that held a 20-inch main. (Courtesy of the Delaware State Archives.)

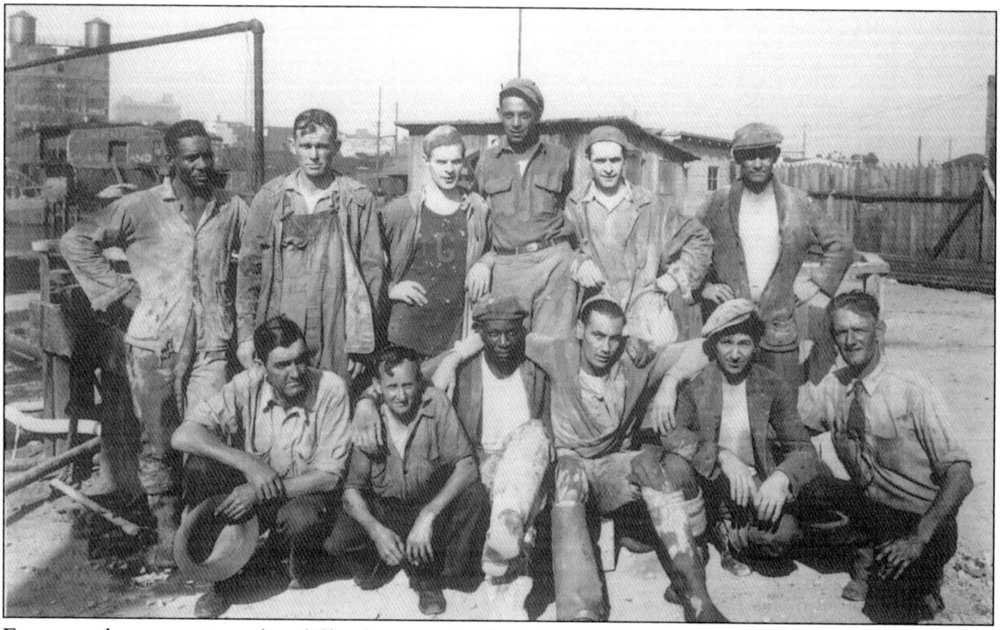

Few people appreciate the difficulty involved in providing the conveniences they take for granted today—a clean supply of drinking-water, for instance. On September 9, 1931, these men were just coming off the 8 a.m. to 4 p.m. shift while digging the tunnel that would pass under the Christina River at Orange Street. (Courtesy of the Delaware State Archives.)

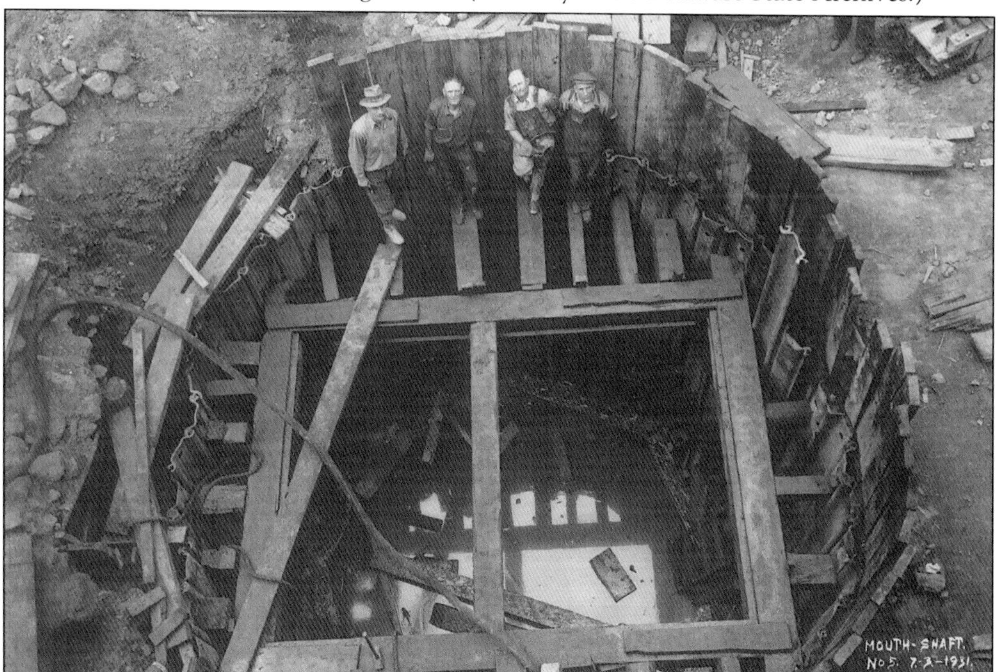

Looking into the mouth of the Orange Street tunnel shaft gives some idea of how difficult it was to build a tunnel under the Christina River in 1931. These four workers seem to be totally at ease as they pose on planks stretching across the edges of the shaft. (Courtesy of the Delaware State Archives.)

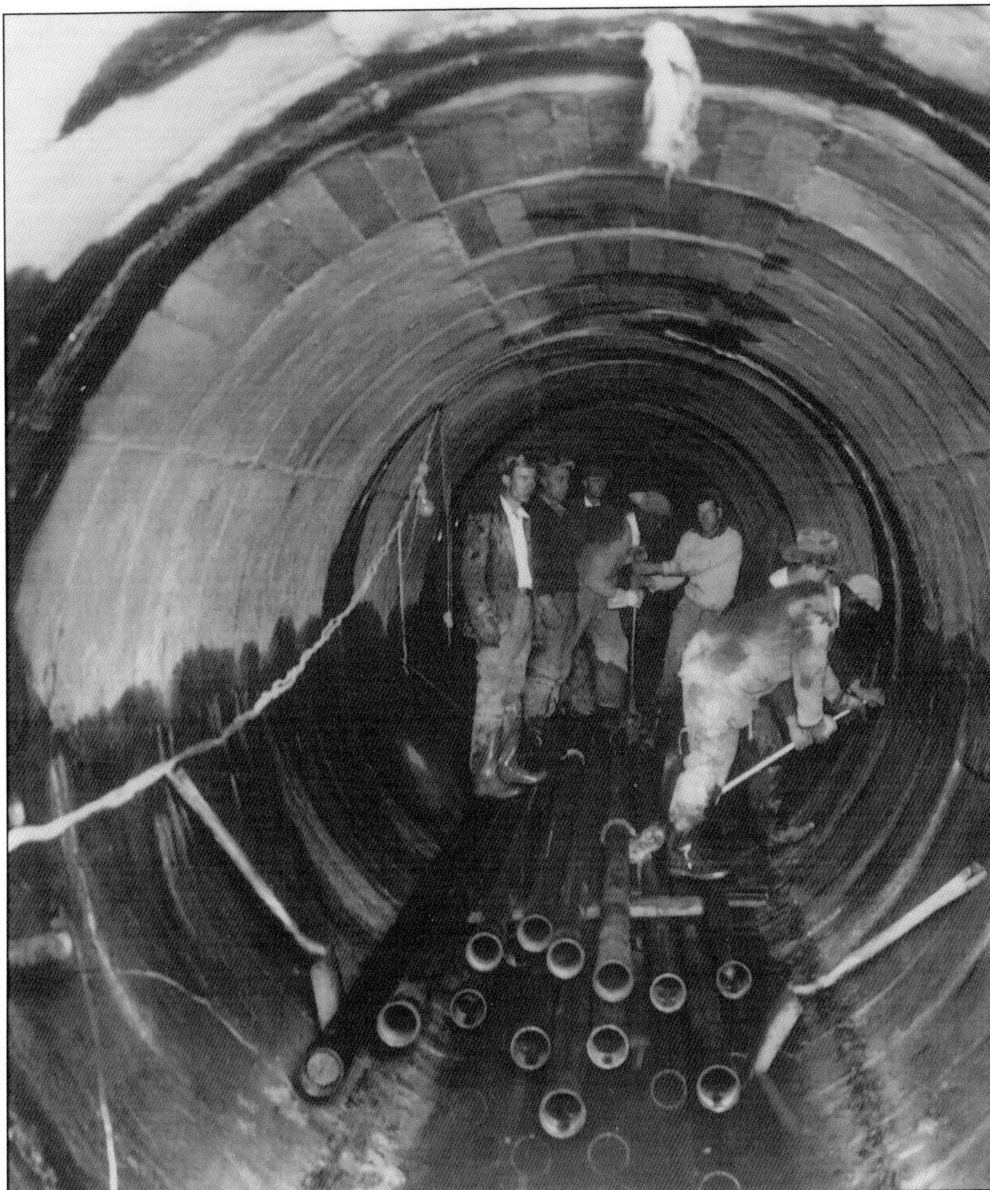

A crew is setting the telephone ducts in the Christina River Tunnel in November 1931. While the main purpose of the tunnel is to carry a 16-inch water main that supplies drinking water to South Wilmington, it is evident from the size of the men standing inside the tunnel there is space for much more than one water pipe. The intention at the time of construction was to carry cables and wires. Today the extra room is used for telecommunications, and the water department rents space in the tunnel for modern technological uses. (Courtesy of the Delaware State Archives.)

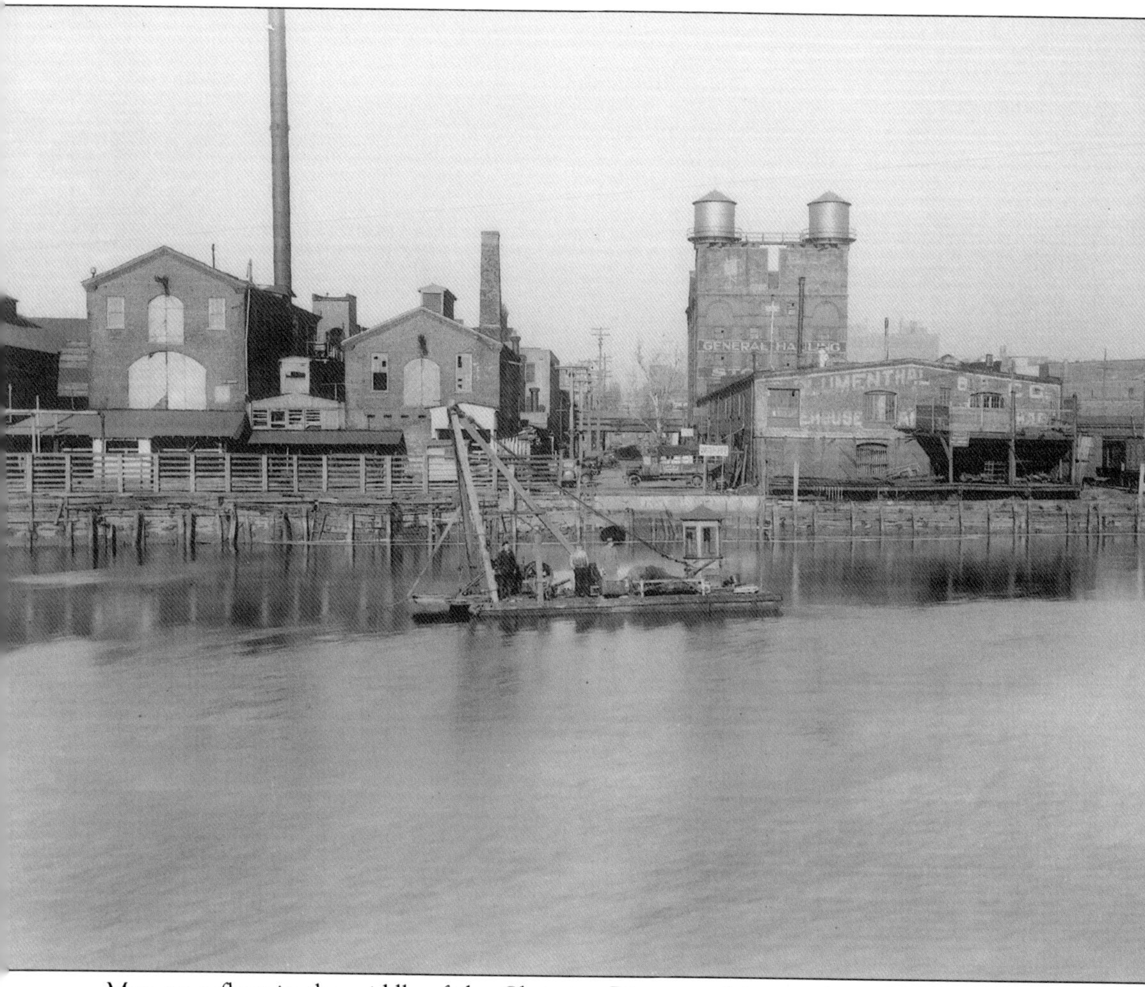

Men on a float in the middle of the Christina River are doing work in connection with the Wilmington Water Department. The Kent Building, dating from about 1885, stands in the right background at the foot of Orange Street. It has been a warehouse for most of its 100-plus years. Ownership passed from its builder, D.H. Kent, to the Chorman Warehouse business in the 1890s and to the Byrd Transfer Company in the 1920s. The long, low building that extends from the Kent Warehouse to the river was a warehouse for the Blumenthal Leather Company at the time of this photograph. In the left background are the buildings of J. Morton Poole, a company that made metal rollers for manufacturers of paper and textiles in Wilmington and elsewhere. This highly specialized company was known around the world and received a reward for excellence at the 1878 Exposition in France. (Courtesy of the Delaware State Archives.)

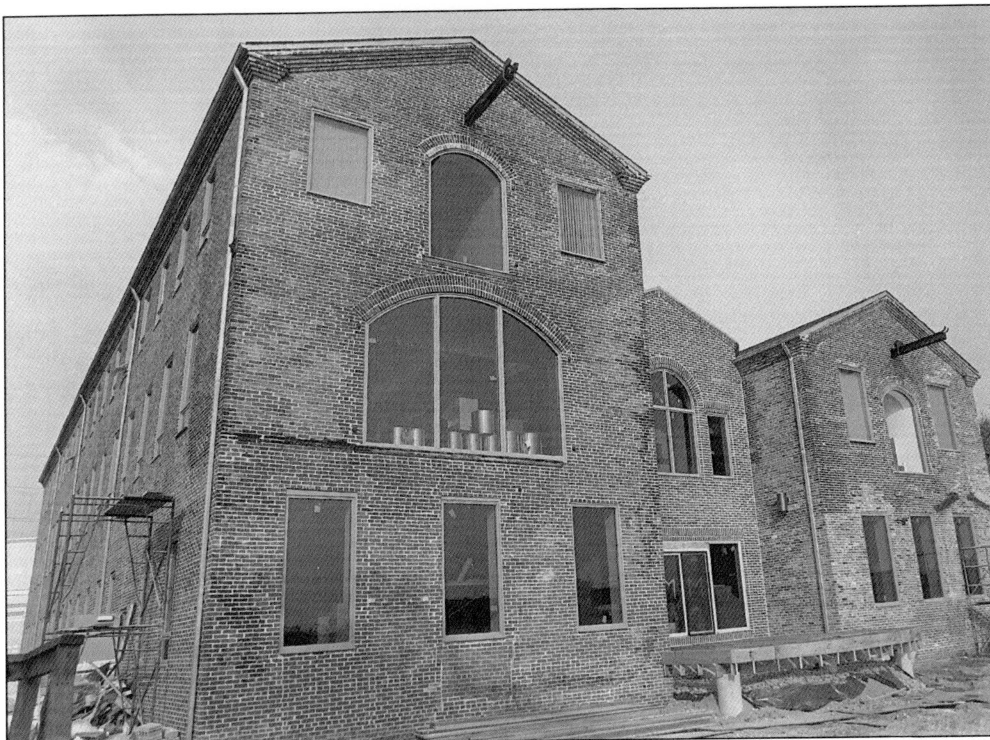

In 1984, the architectural firm of Moeckel Carbonell Associates began renovation of the J. Morton Poole buildings. Renovation, which was under way in the picture, included removing masonry from the arched windows and other openings. Today, the building is an attractive feature on the Christina waterfront. (Courtesy of Moeckel Carbonell Associates.)

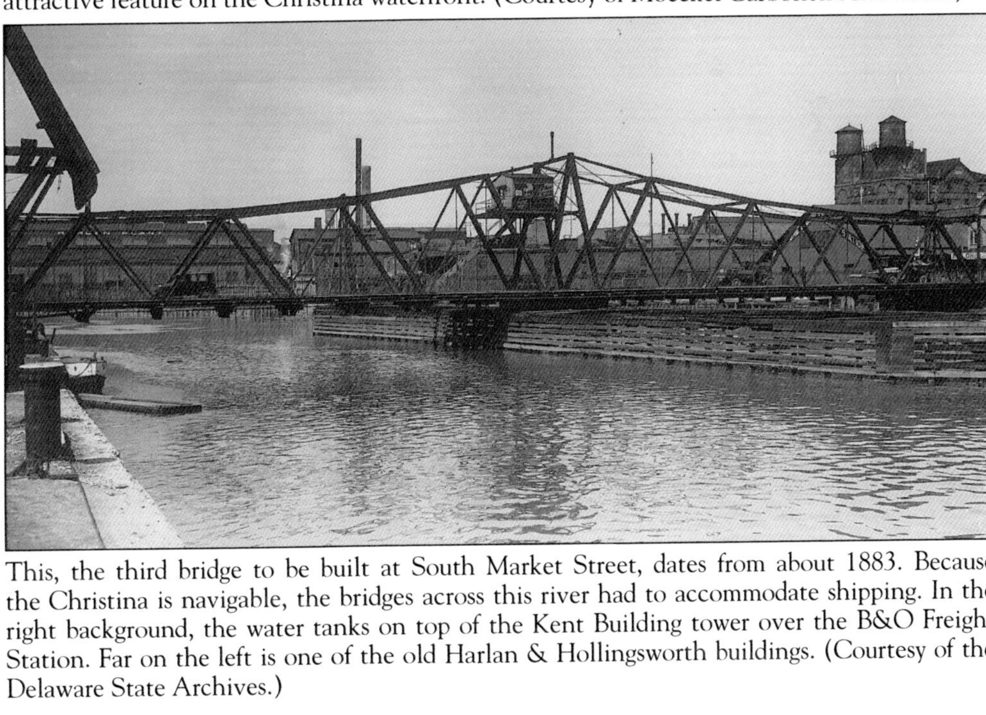

This, the third bridge to be built at South Market Street, dates from about 1883. Because the Christina is navigable, the bridges across this river had to accommodate shipping. In the right background, the water tanks on top of the Kent Building tower over the B&O Freight Station. Far on the left is one of the old Harlan & Hollingsworth buildings. (Courtesy of the Delaware State Archives.)

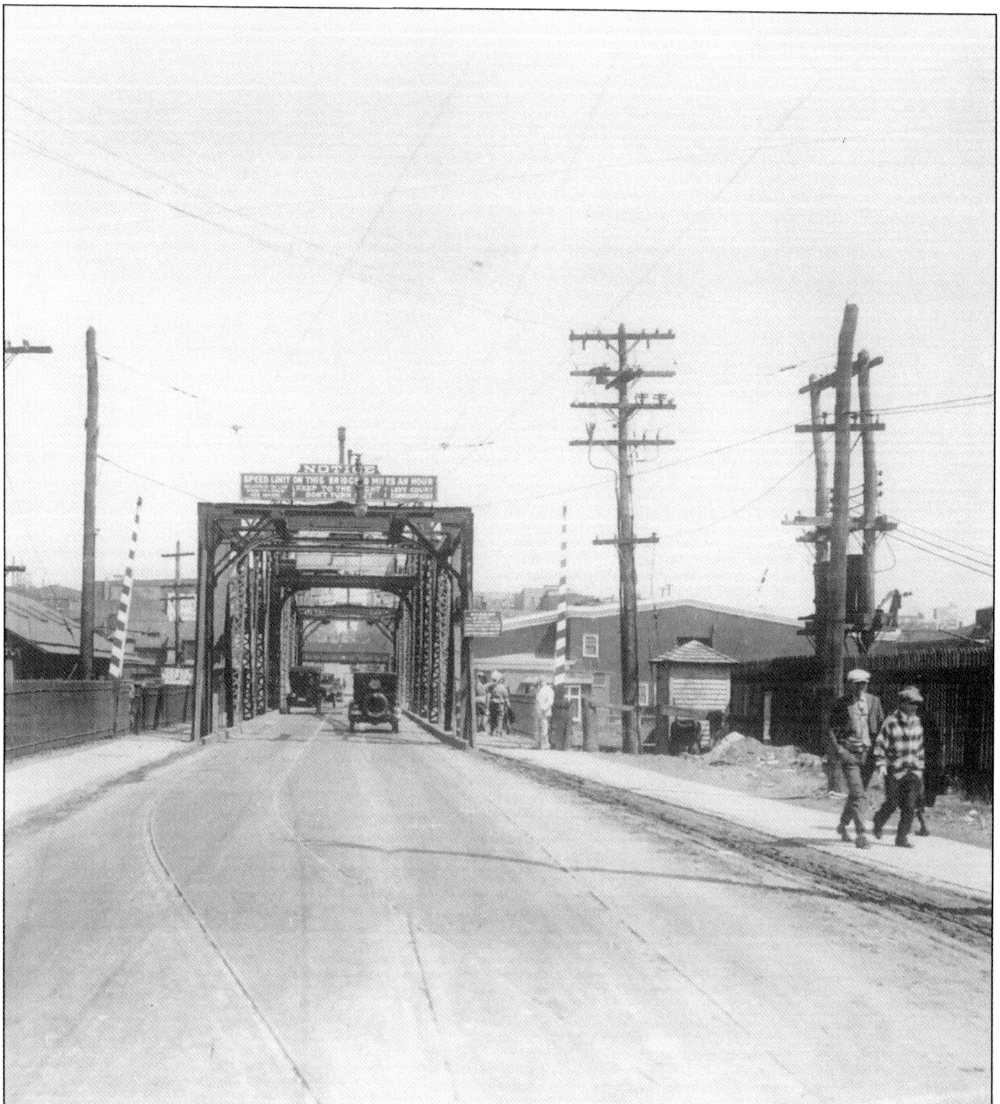

In 1926, when this picture was taken, the old Market Street bridge's days were nearly over, for there were plans for a new bridge. Here, looking north toward Wilmington, a large "Notice" outlines the rules for using the bridge, which no longer required a toll for passage. The bridge was a necessity for the businesses operating on both sides of the Christina, as well as for automobiles traveling north and south in Delaware. (Courtesy of the Delaware State Archives.)

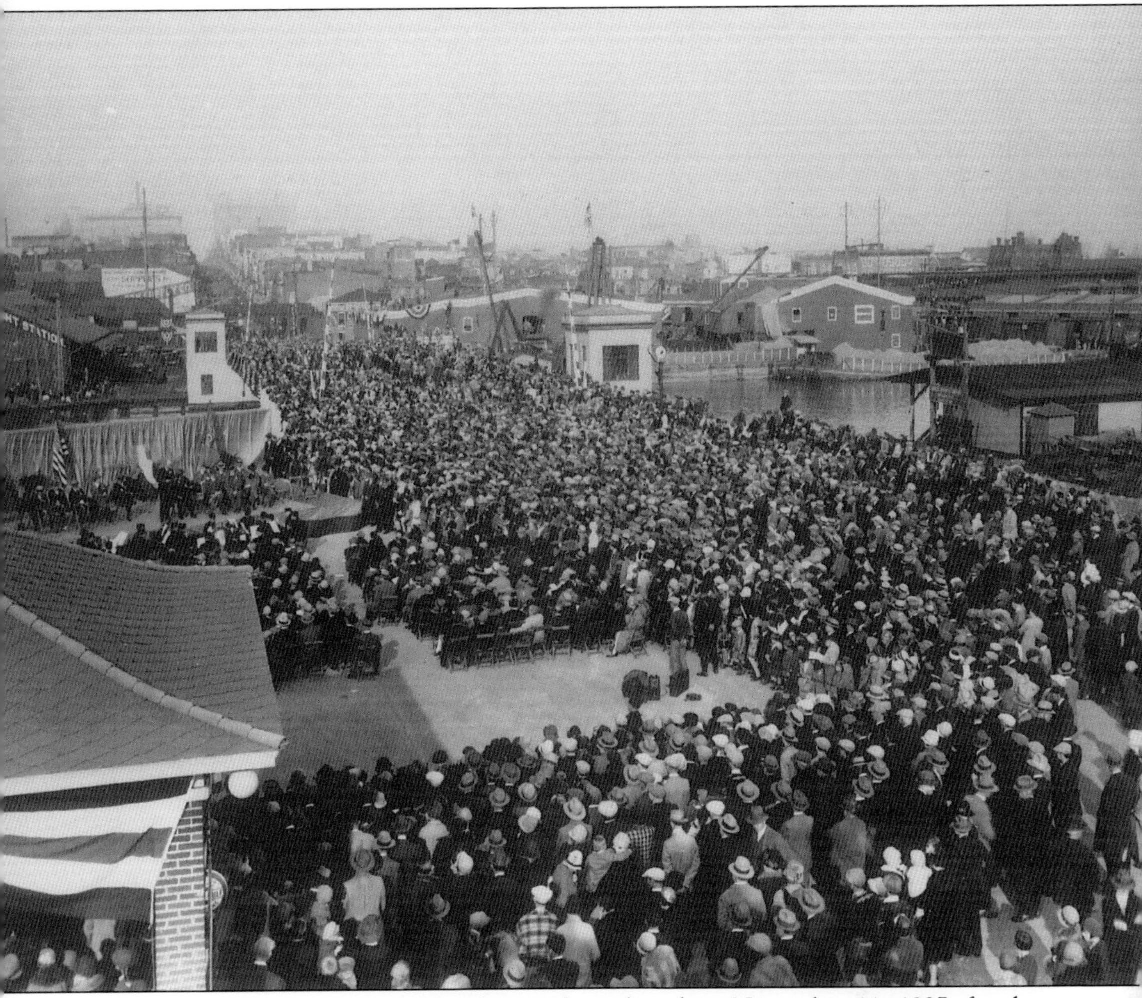

A crowd, appearing to number in the thousands, gathered on November 11, 1927, for the dedication of the new Market Street bridge across the Christina River. In this view, looking north from the south end of the bridge, it looks as though extra space has been added to accommodate the crowd and the speakers. According to one source, the bridge cost about half a million dollars, a minuscule amount by late-20th-century standards. Since shipbuilding was still an important industry on the Christina, the new bridge was of the bascule type that could be raised to allow the passage of large vessels. (Courtesy of the Delaware State Archives.)

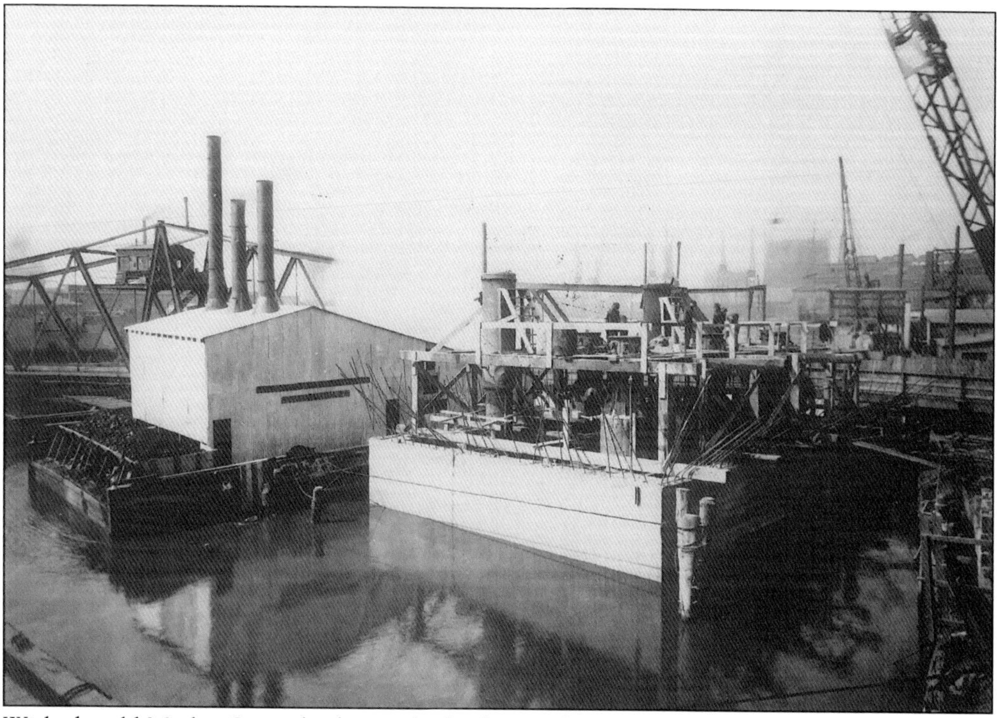

With the old Market Street bridge in the background, men are at work on the new bridge on March 16, 1927—only nine months before its completion. An air plant on a float allowed work on the north caisson. (Courtesy of the Delaware State Archives.)

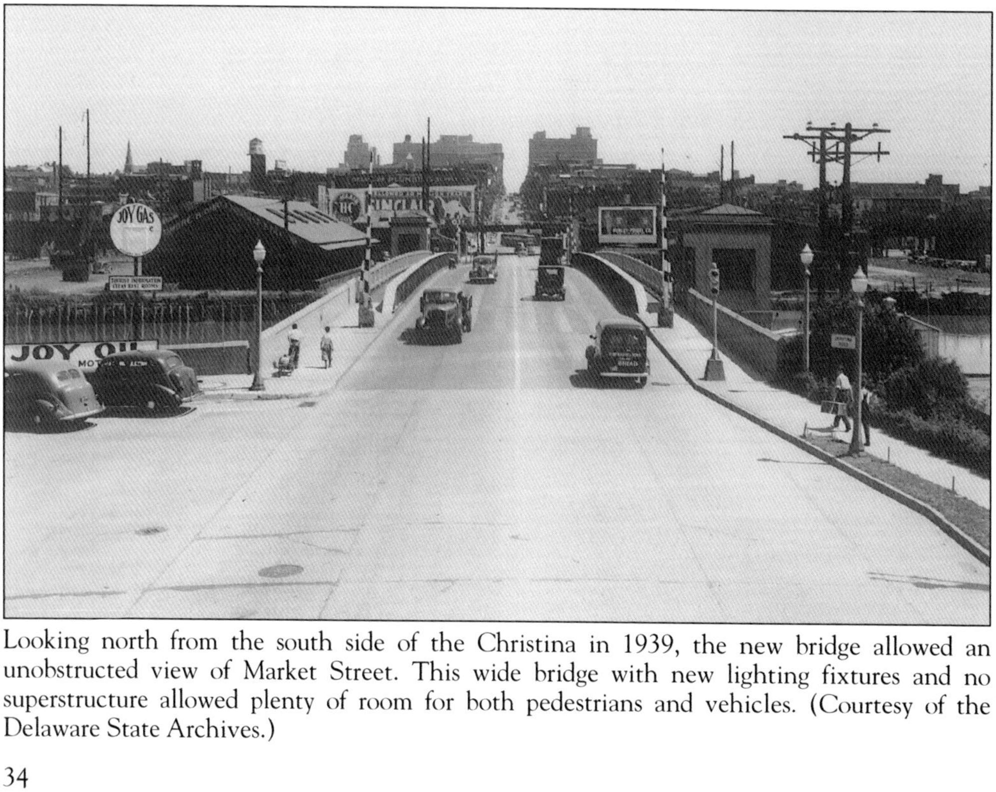

Looking north from the south side of the Christina in 1939, the new bridge allowed an unobstructed view of Market Street. This wide bridge with new lighting fixtures and no superstructure allowed plenty of room for both pedestrians and vehicles. (Courtesy of the Delaware State Archives.)

The U.S. Coast Guard cutter *Mohawk* was one Wilmington-built ship that came back to the city to spend part of her retirement. The shipbuilding firm of Pusey & Jones launched her on the Christina River on October 23, 1934. After the United States declared war against Germany in 1941, the *Mohawk* hunted enemy submarines, escorted convoys, and rescued survivors from the ocean. (Courtesy of Malcolm Mackenzie.)

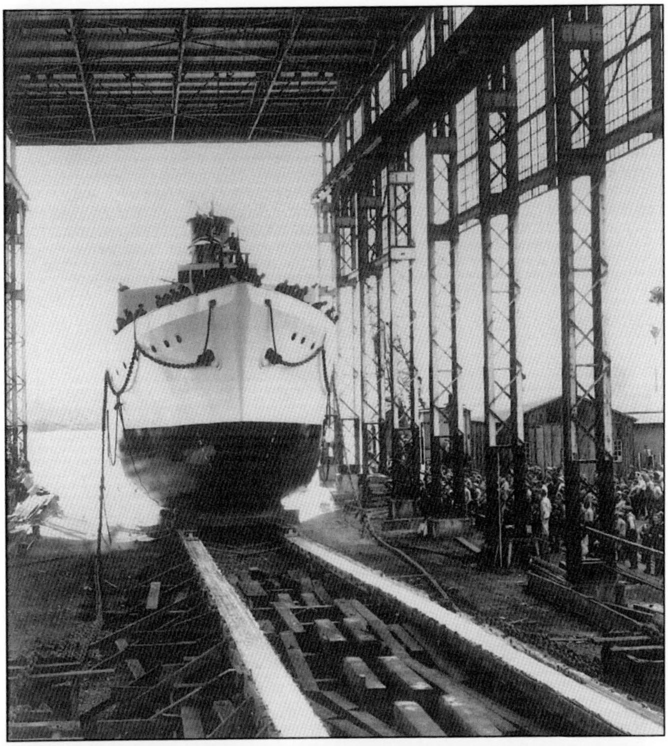

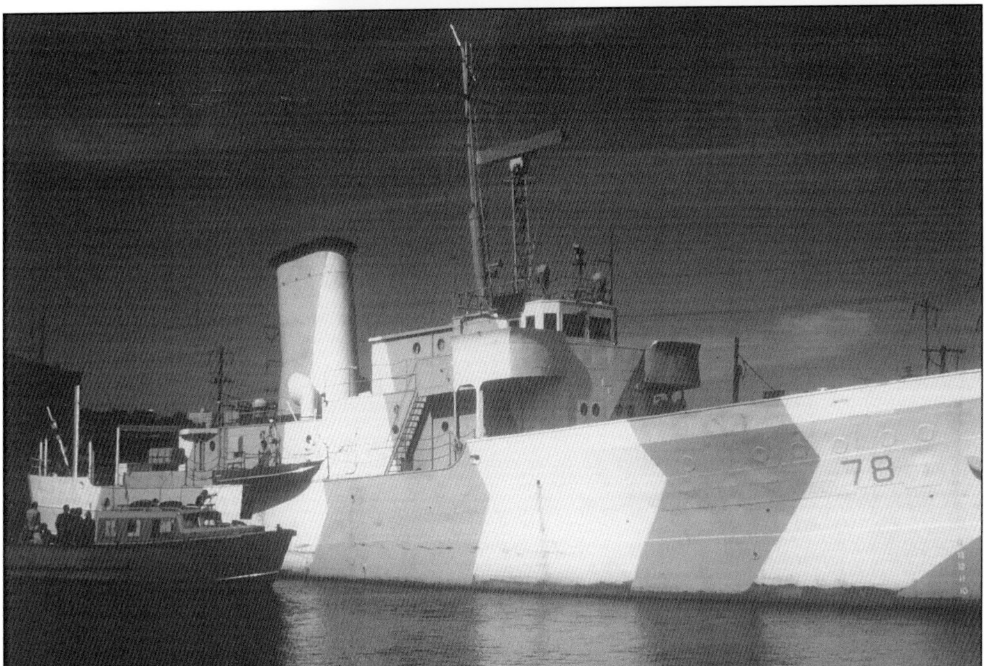

After World War II, the *Mohawk*, renamed the *Philadelphia*, became an offshore headquarters for Delaware pilots who escorted ships through the Delaware Bay. When that service ended, Charles Weymouth and other volunteers brought her back to Wilmington in hopes of restoring her. Here she is in 1981 at the foot of King Street.

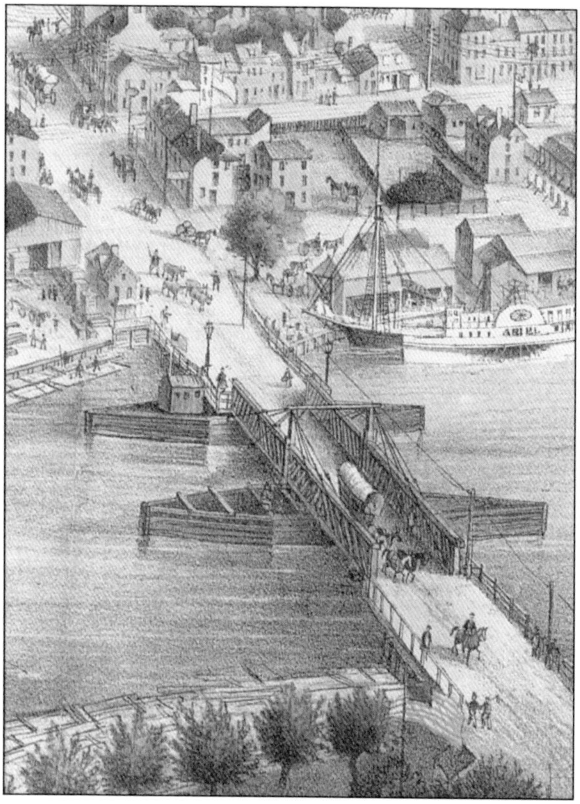

A section of the *Birds Eye View of Wilmington*, published by Sachse & Co. in 1864, shows the Market Street bridge when it was the only bridge across the Christina before and during the Civil War. The bridge played a role in the Underground Railroad when Harriet Tubman led groups of slaves over it on their way to freedom. (Courtesy of the Historical Society of Delaware.)

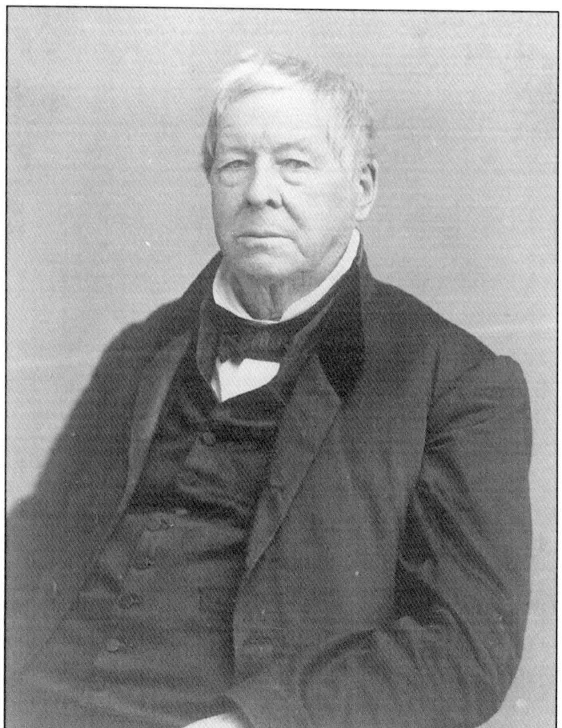

Thomas Garrett, Wilmington's most famous Quaker abolitionist, lived in the area today known as Quaker Hill. Garrett was a "station master" on the Underground Railroad and assisted up to 2,000 runaway slaves as they passed through Wilmington on their way to Pennsylvania and further north. Garrett helped Tubman, a "conductor" on the Underground Railroad, on at least eight of her journeys. (Courtesy of the Historical Society of Delaware.)

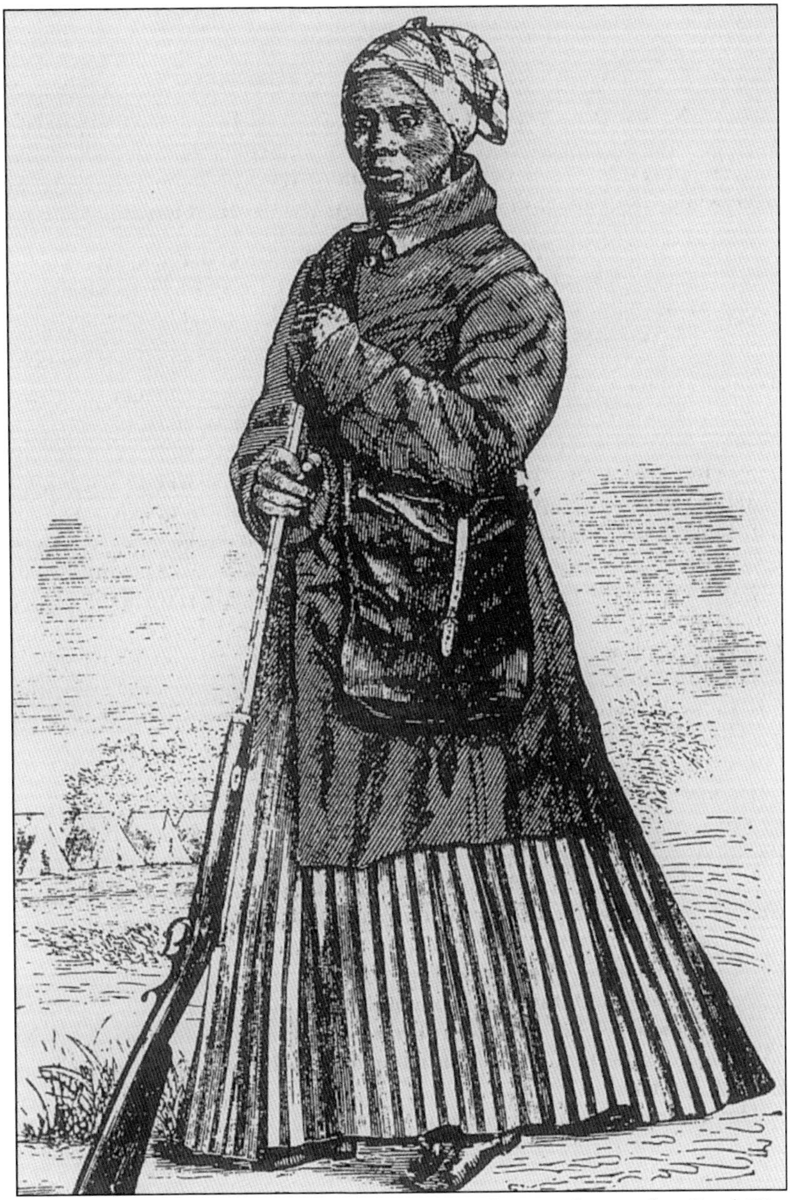

This engraving, showing Harriet Tubman as a scout and nurse during the Civil War, appeared in 1869 in a book by Sarah Bradford. Tubman was born a slave about 1820 near Cambridge, Maryland. Her determination to be free, her personal bravery, and her concern for her fellow slaves made her a strong leader in the Underground Railroad, through which she probably rescued about 300 slaves. In Wilmington, she worked closely with Thomas Garrett. On one trip, for instance, Tubman hid her group of slaves in South Wilmington while Garrett sent two wagons over the Market Street bridge. Garrett loaded the wagons with straw and bricklayers who appeared to be heading for a day's outing. On the return trip, Tubman and her runaways hid underneath the straw while the bricklayers shouted and laughed as though they had been celebrating all day. Both Tubman and Garrett were called "Moses" by their admirers because they led so many people out of slavery. It is fitting that the Tubman-Garrett Riverfront Park on the Christina River now pays tribute to them. (Courtesy of the Historical Society of Delaware.)

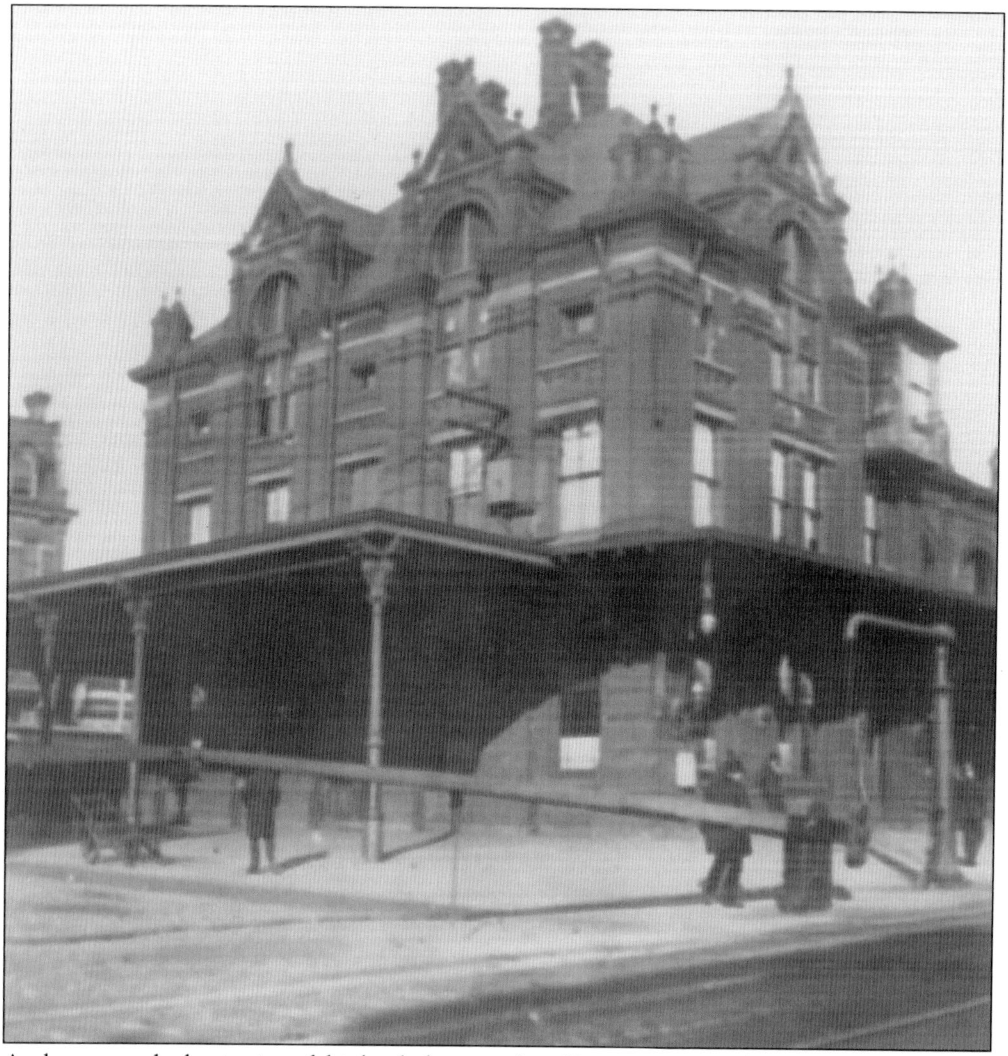

As the map at the beginning of this book shows, railroad lines crisscrossed Wilmington at an early date and were as much of a boon to industrial development as the city's rivers. The Philadelphia, Wilmington and Baltimore (PW&B) Railroad had followed the large curve of the Christina River since the 1830s. After gaining control of the PW&B in 1881, the Pennsylvania Railroad built an elaborate new station at Front and King Streets. As this picture taken in about 1900 shows, the tracks were at grade level in front of the station. Passengers gathered on the platform and could easily step into the path of an oncoming train. Carts and wagons in the street crossed the tracks unless the long wooden arm in the foreground of the picture made them stop. This station was in use for only a little over 20 years. (Courtesy of the Delaware State Archives.)

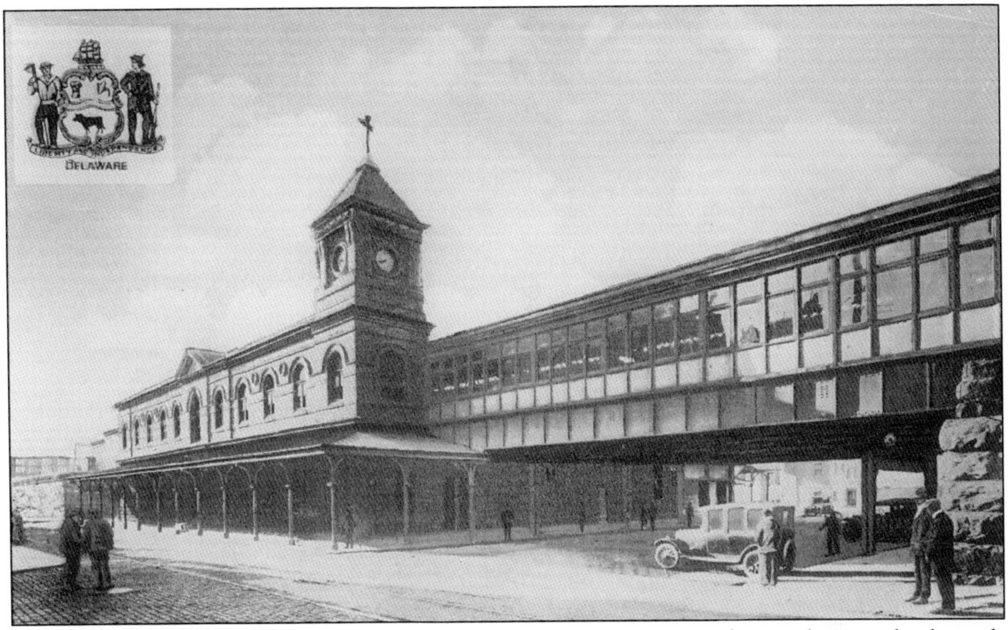

As train travel increased, the Pennsylvania Railroad made plans to elevate their tracks through Wilmington and to construct a new depot in 1905. This postcard view shows the new station, a design of the Philadelphia architectural firm of Furness, Evans and Company. Frank Furness was one of the leading architects of the day, and the station was eventually listed in the National Register of Historic Places. (Courtesy of the Hagley Museum and Library.)

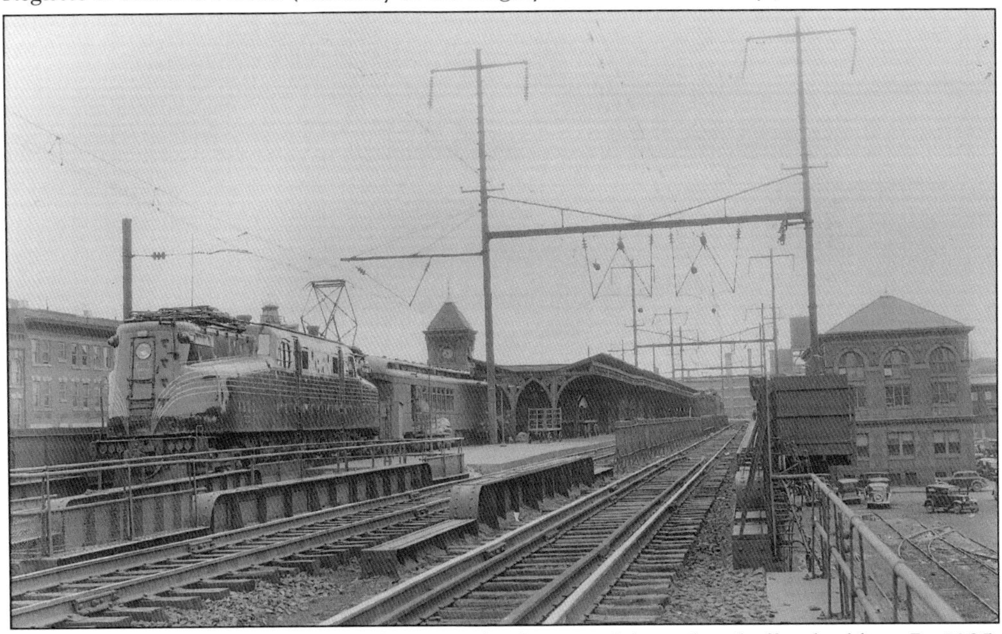

Elevation of the tracks placed them between the depot and the railroad office building. By 1935, the Pennsylvania Railroad electrified the line, and "streamlined" locomotives and trains came into use, permitting through service between Washington and New York via Wilmington. The GG-1 model locomotive, shown here with its five narrow stripes, was a Raymond Loewy design. (Courtesy of the Hagley Museum and Library.)

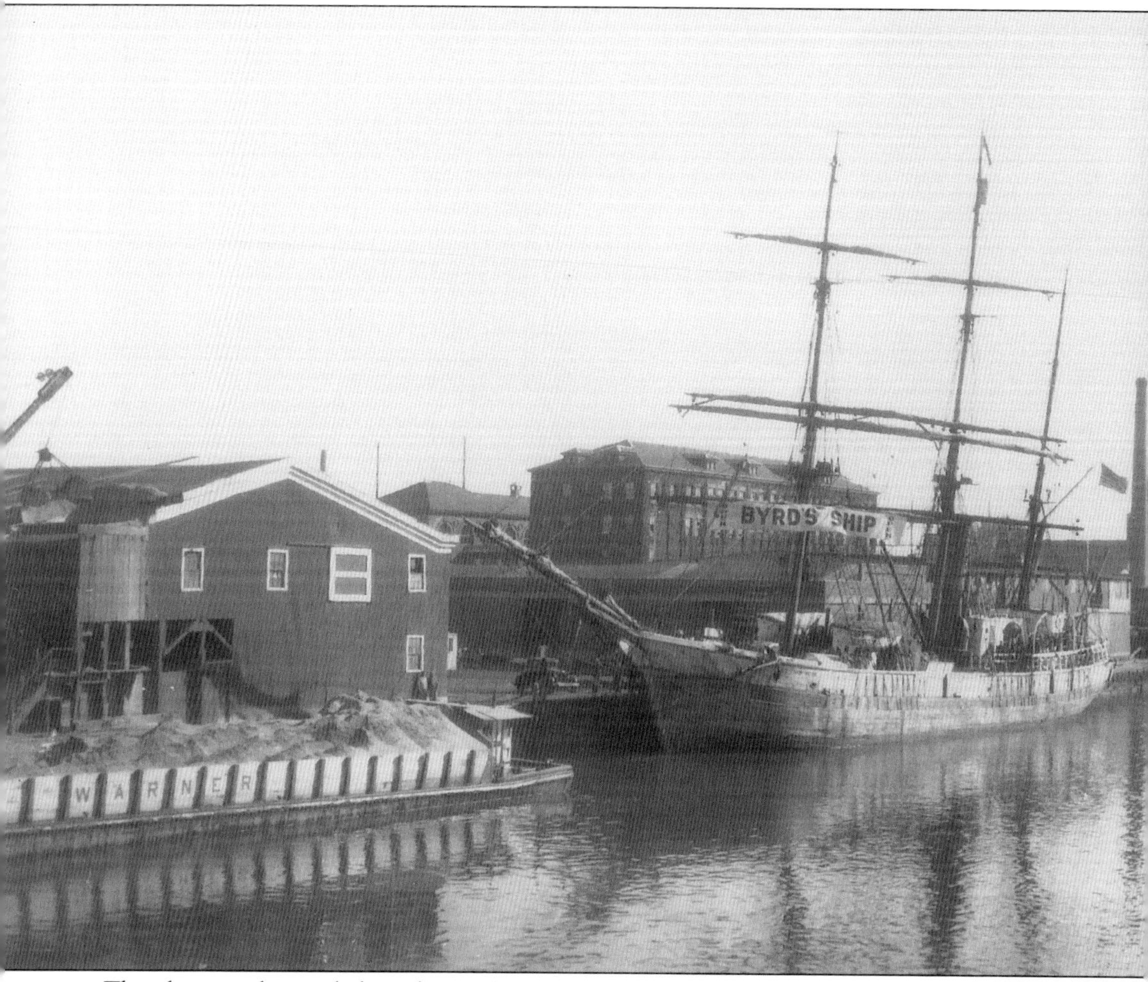

This photograph, entitled simply "Byrd's Ship," is presumably the ship of Admiral Richard E. Byrd, the famous Antarctic explorer. The large banner proclaiming its title makes it obvious that people were supposed to notice it. This three-masted sailing ship is tied up alongside the north bank of the Christina near the railroad office building in the background. To the left is one of the many signs for the Warner Company. This is one of hundreds of photographs taken by Frank R. Zebley of Wilmington, who recorded buildings, events, and people as a permanent record. (Courtesy of the Delaware State Archives.)

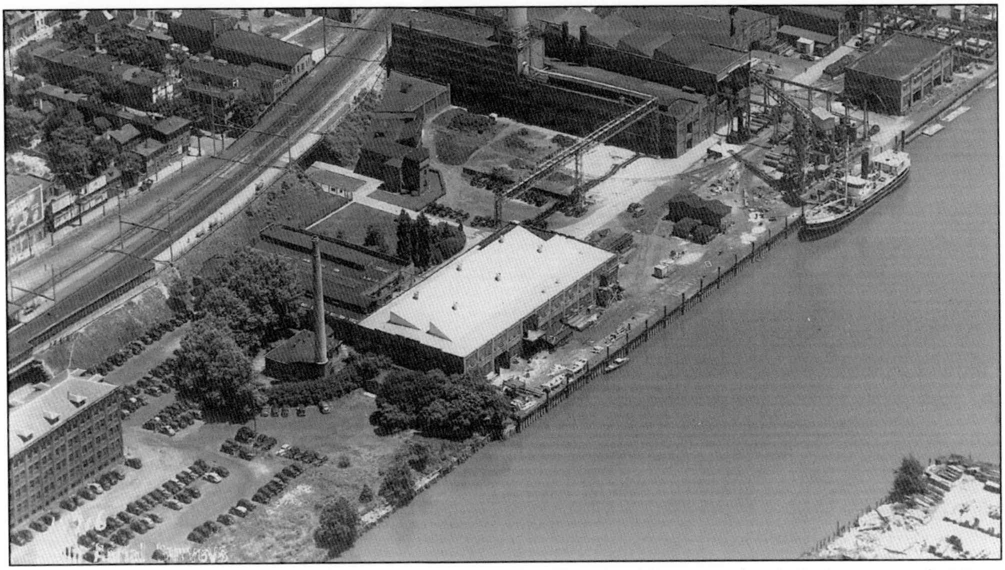

This 1939 aerial photograph shows the railroad office building in the left foreground. Note that the tracks are elevated and that there is no bridge across the Christina. The Pusey & Jones Company is in the upper right. (Courtesy of the Hagley Museum and Library.)

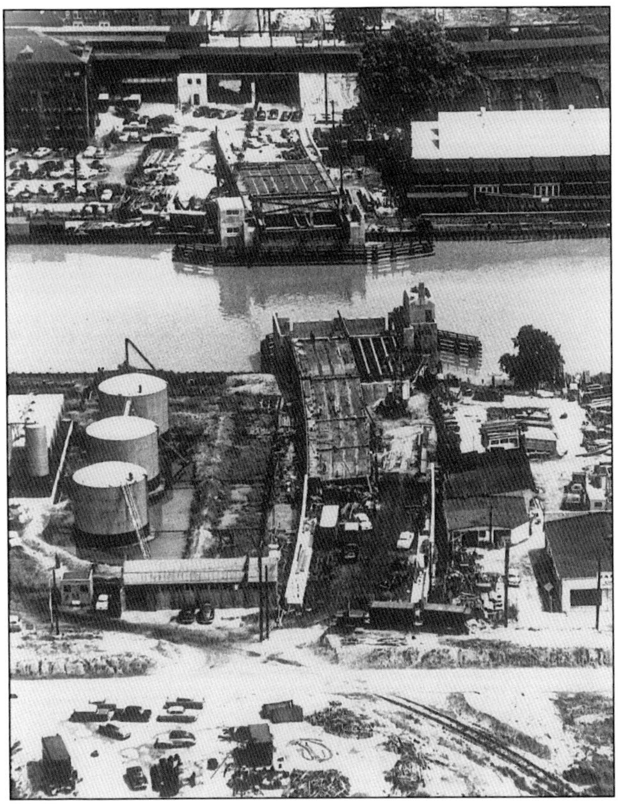

By the 1950s, there was need for another bridge across the Christina, and here is the Walnut Street bridge under construction. In this scene, snow covers the cars in the railroad office building parking lot on the upper left, and the elevated railroad track is visible in the background. (Courtesy of the Delaware State Archives.)

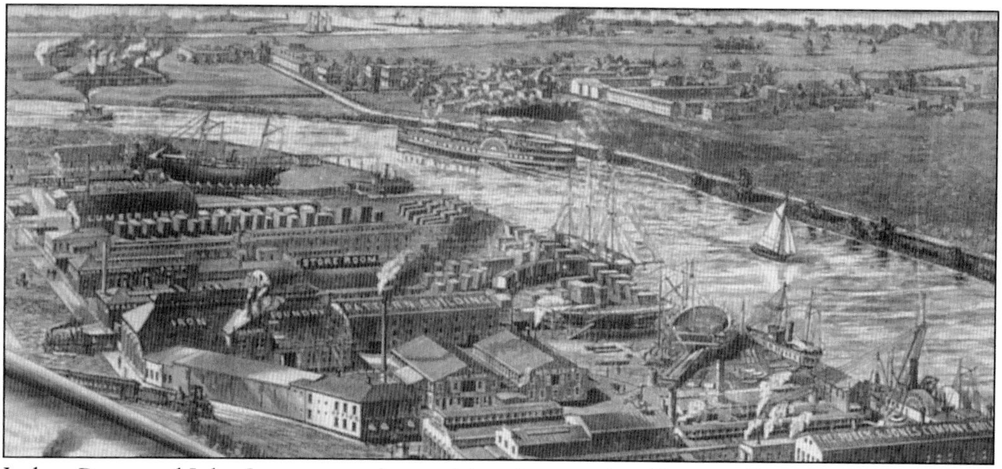

Joshua Pusey and John Jones opened a machine shop on the Christina River in 1848 and built their first iron vessel, the side wheeler, *Flora McDonald,* in 1853. By 1890, the Pusey & Jones Company plant, shown here, covered over 7 acres, and the company had become one of the four largest iron shipbuilders in the nation. (Courtesy of the Historical Society of Delaware.)

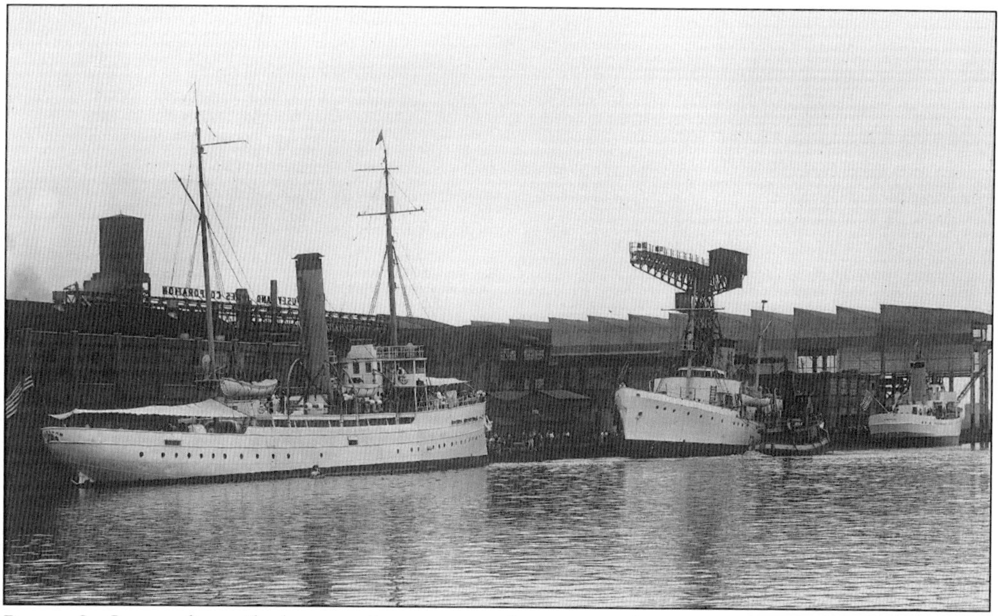

Pusey & Jones diversified over the years and continued to operate until 1960. During the late 19th century, it was the combination of Pusey & Jones with their competitors, Harlan & Hollingsworth, that made Wilmington the largest producer of iron vessels in the United States. Here, boats are tied up near one of the firm's 20th-century buildings with its distinctive jagged roof. (Courtesy of the Delaware State Archives.)

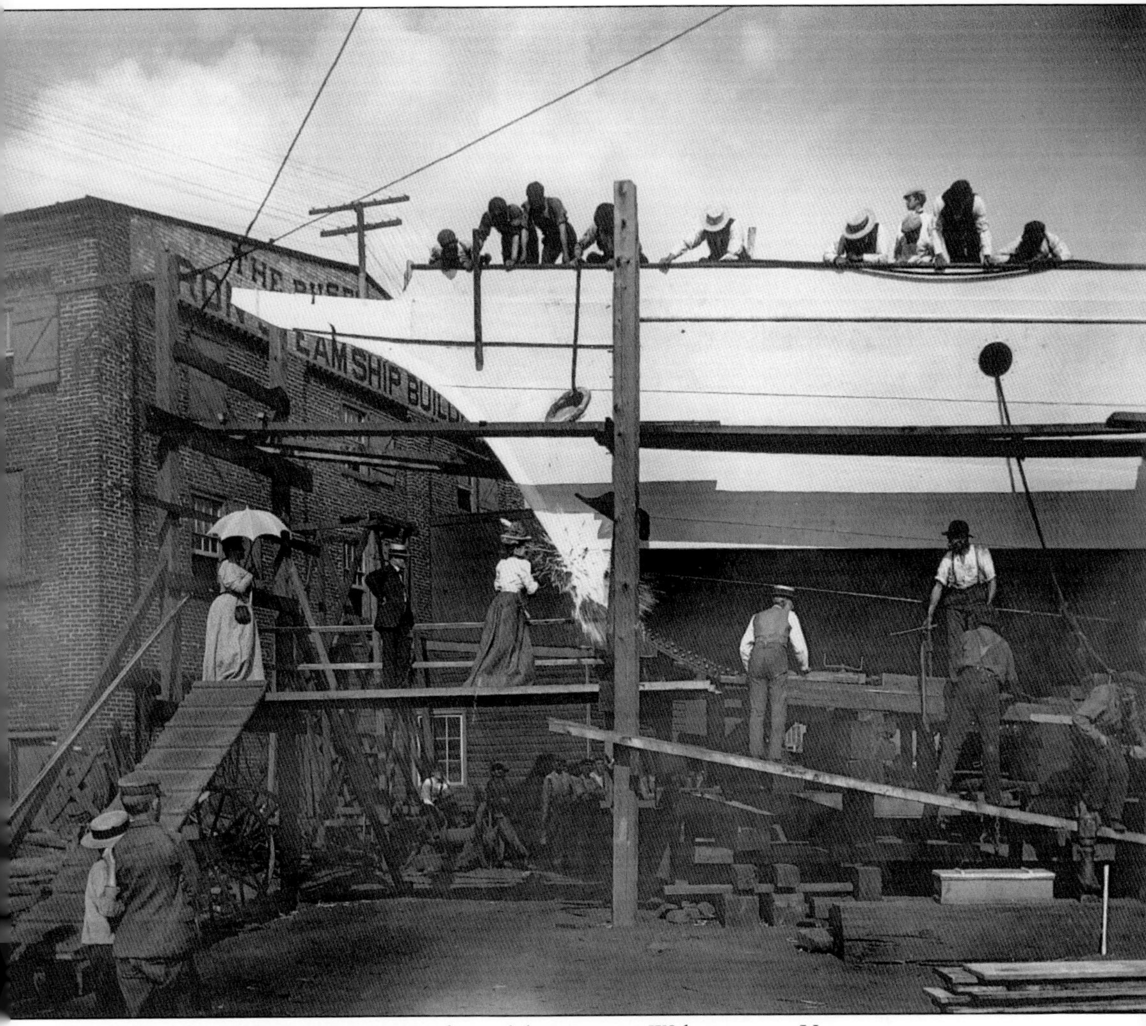

Every ship launching was a cause for celebration in Wilmington. Here, a young woman successfully smashes her champagne bottle over the bow of the private yacht *Kismet* while men and women look on from the deck of the boat and from the launching platform. This christening took place on June 14, 1899, and the *Kismet* was only one of many private yachts built by Pusey & Jones. The company then employed nearly 900 people and also made heavy tools, iron and brass castings, engines and boilers, and machinery for paper, sugar, powder, and cotton mills. Pusey & Jones also made the anchors for the cables for the Brooklyn Bridge. (Courtesy of the Hagley Museum and Library.)

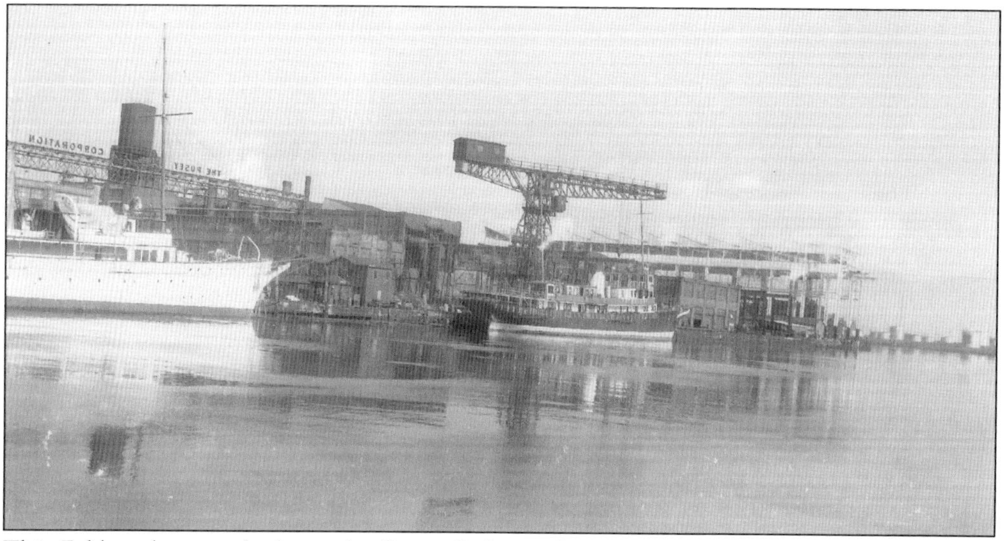

This Zebley photograph shows the Pusey & Jones Corporation's giant crane looming above boats tied up at their riverfront. The smaller, older buildings are between the two boats, while the newer jagged-roofed building looms in the background. The Wilmington Youth Rowing Association and University of Delaware Rowing Team now use the low brick building as their boathouse. (Courtesy of the Delaware State Archives.)

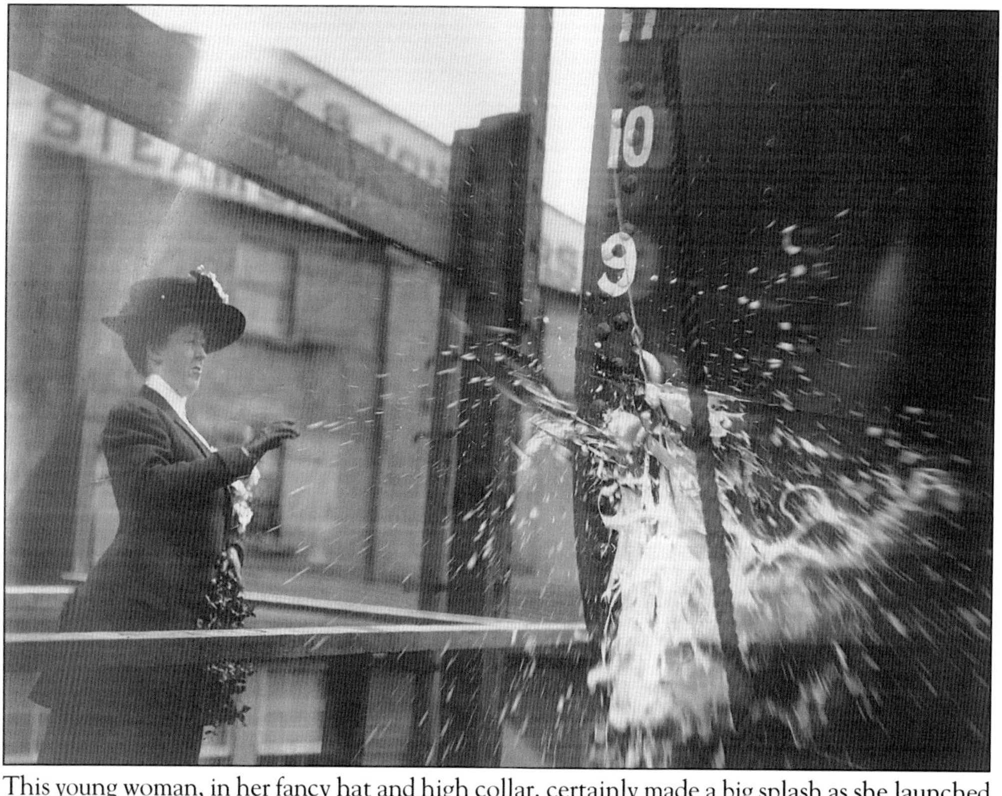

This young woman, in her fancy hat and high collar, certainly made a big splash as she launched a tug boat on April 23, 1910, at the Pusey & Jones yard. The large numbers are the depth markers on the bow of the boat. (Courtesy of the Hagley Museum and Library.)

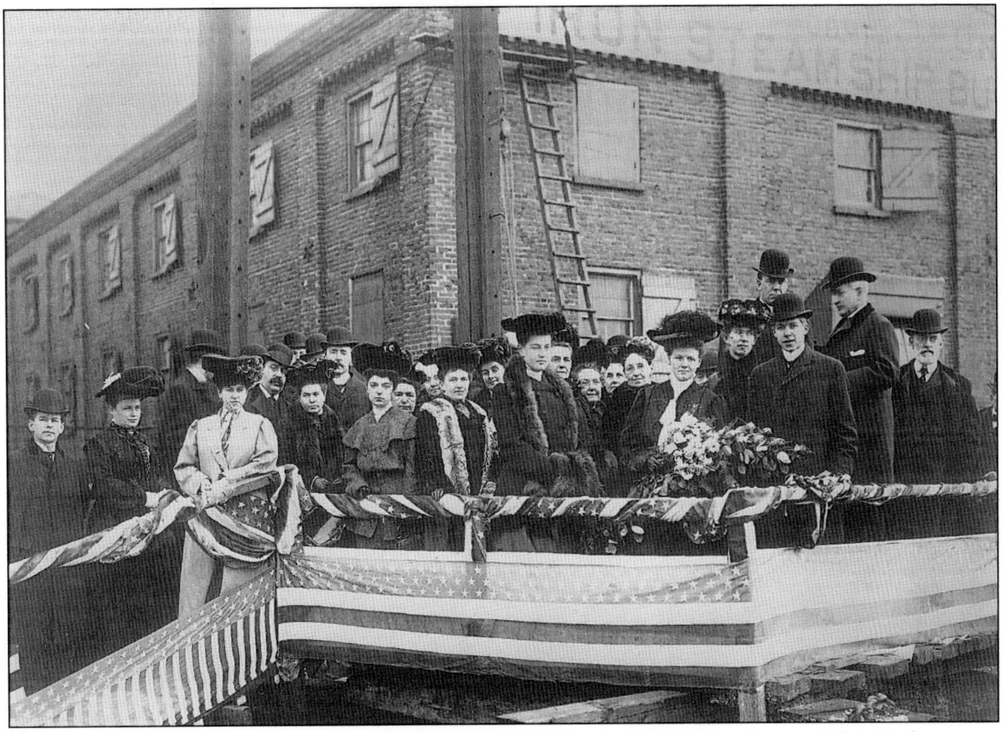

A small crowd is gathered on the platform for the January 1905 launching of the *Ordnance* at the Pusey & Jones yard. Anne Savery Thayer stands on the bunting-draped platform holding a large bouquet. The group surrounding her includes her husband, Horace H. Thayer, who stands at her side wearing a derby (Courtesy of the Hagley Museum and Library.)

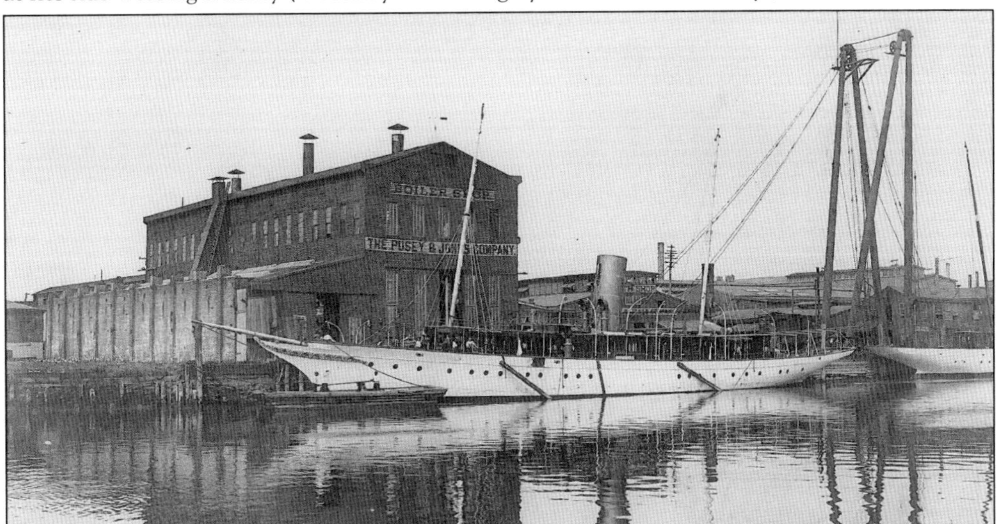

Here, the 177-foot yacht, *Viking*, is tied up in the Christina River in 1909 before she leaves the yard to have her masts stepped. Pusey & Jones was one of the largest iron shipbuilders in the nation, but surely the success of the America's Cup yacht, *Volunteer*, which they built in 1887, enhanced their reputation for building luxury yachts. (Courtesy of the Hagley Museum and Library.)

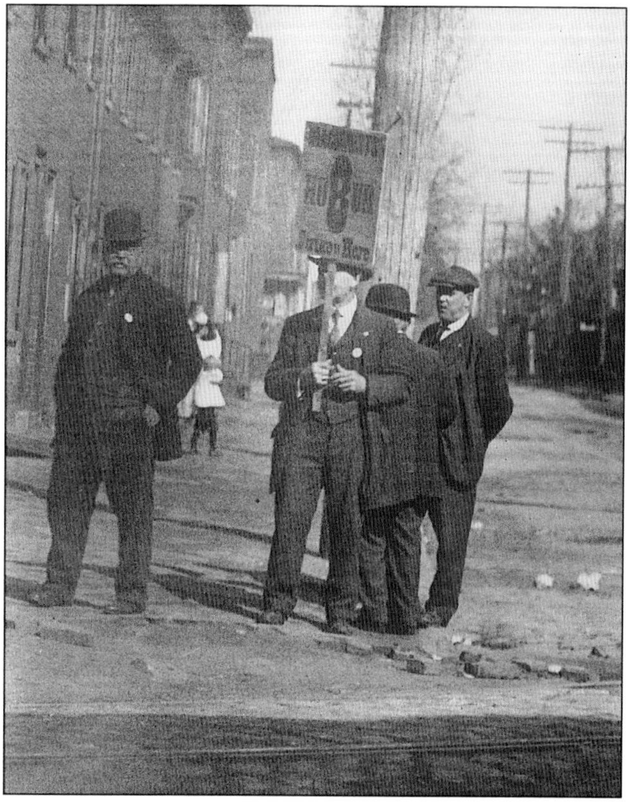

It took thousands of workers to man Wilmington's industries, and they would not always agree with management. Machinists had gone on strike against Wilmington industries in 1901 to gain a nine-hour day. In this photograph of October 28, 1915, machinists are striking against the Pusey & Jones Company to demand an eight-hour day. (Courtesy of the Hagley Museum and Library.)

The Christina River is navigable and sheltered. It is not surprising that the Menhaden fishing fleet from Lewes came to Wilmington and tied up at the Pusey & Jones wharf to seek protection from a hurricane in 1954. (Courtesy of the Delaware State Archives.)

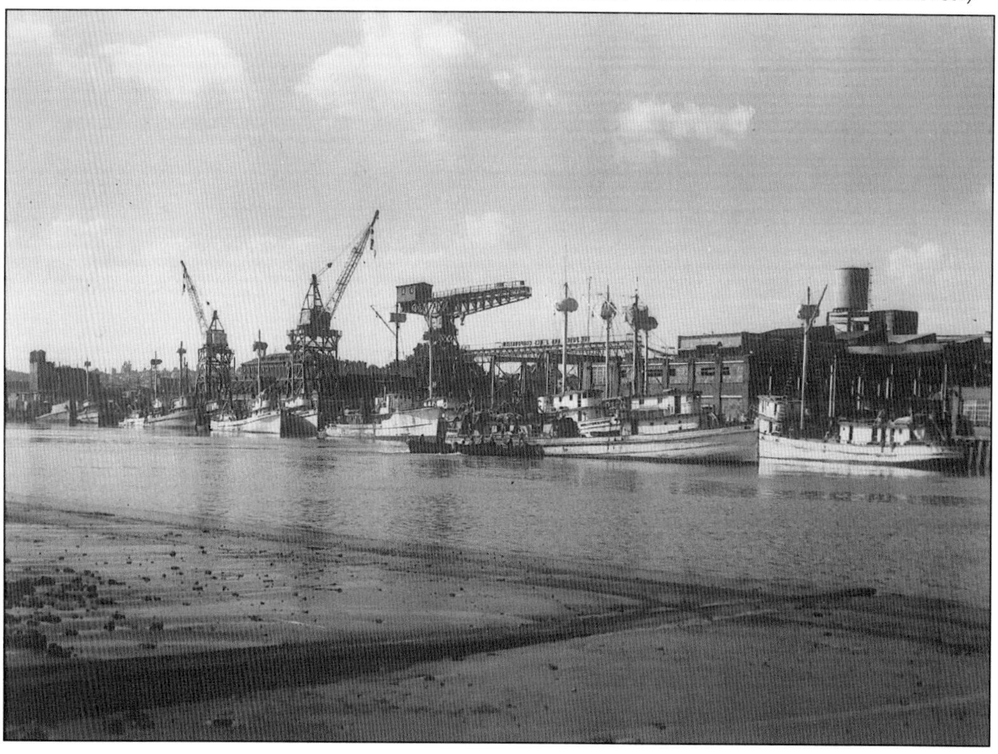

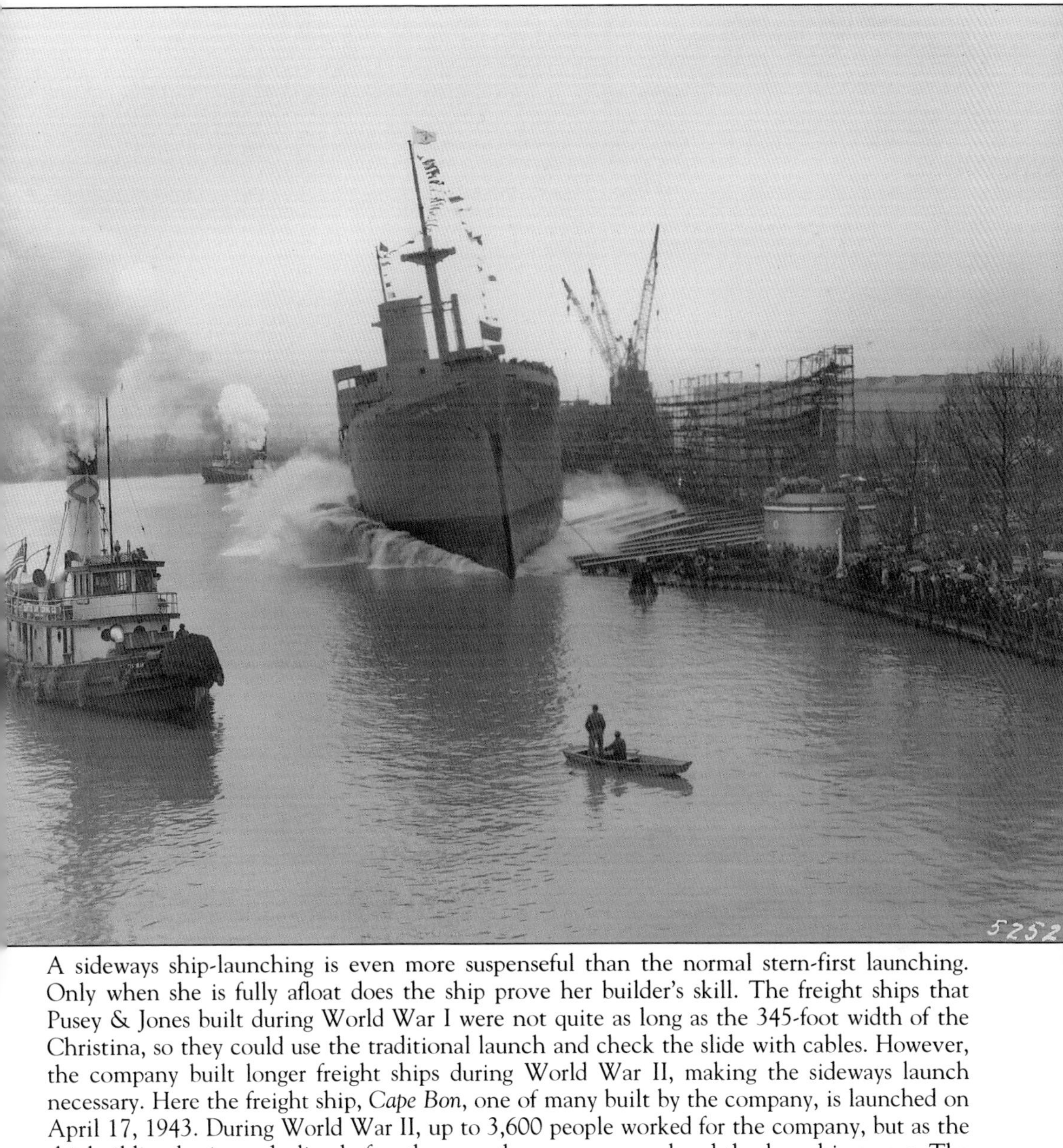

A sideways ship-launching is even more suspenseful than the normal stern-first launching. Only when she is fully afloat does the ship prove her builder's skill. The freight ships that Pusey & Jones built during World War I were not quite as long as the 345-foot width of the Christina, so they could use the traditional launch and check the slide with cables. However, the company built longer freight ships during World War II, making the sideways launch necessary. Here the freight ship, *Cape Bon*, one of many built by the company, is launched on April 17, 1943. During World War II, up to 3,600 people worked for the company, but as the shipbuilding business declined after the war, the company enclosed the launching ways. The area became a metal fabrication shop until 1960 when the company closed. (Courtesy of the Hagley Museum and Library.)

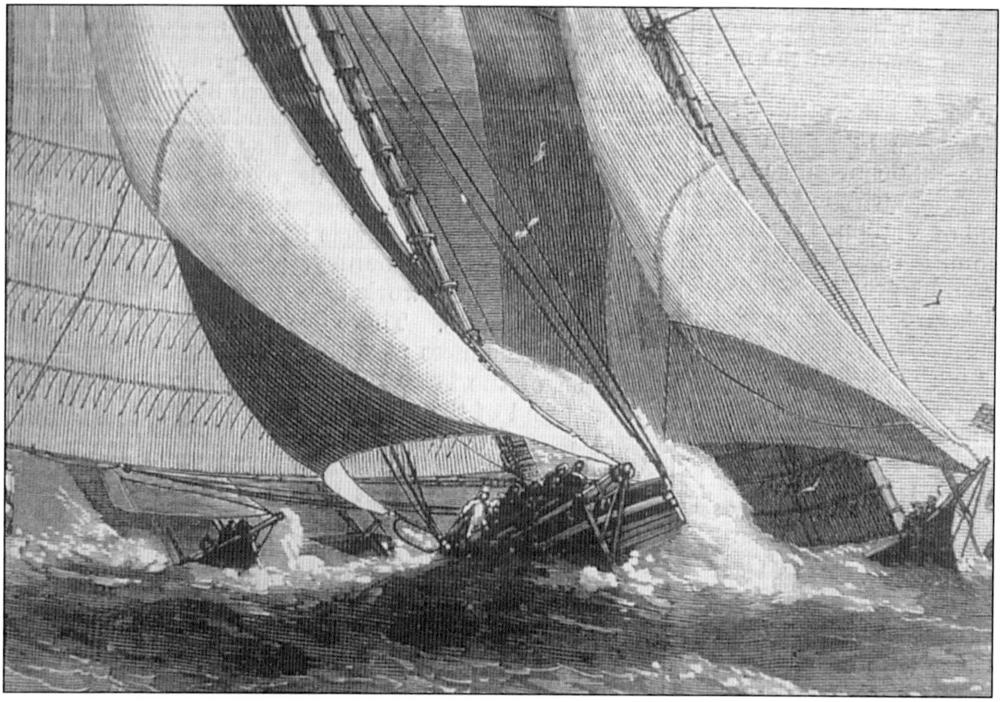

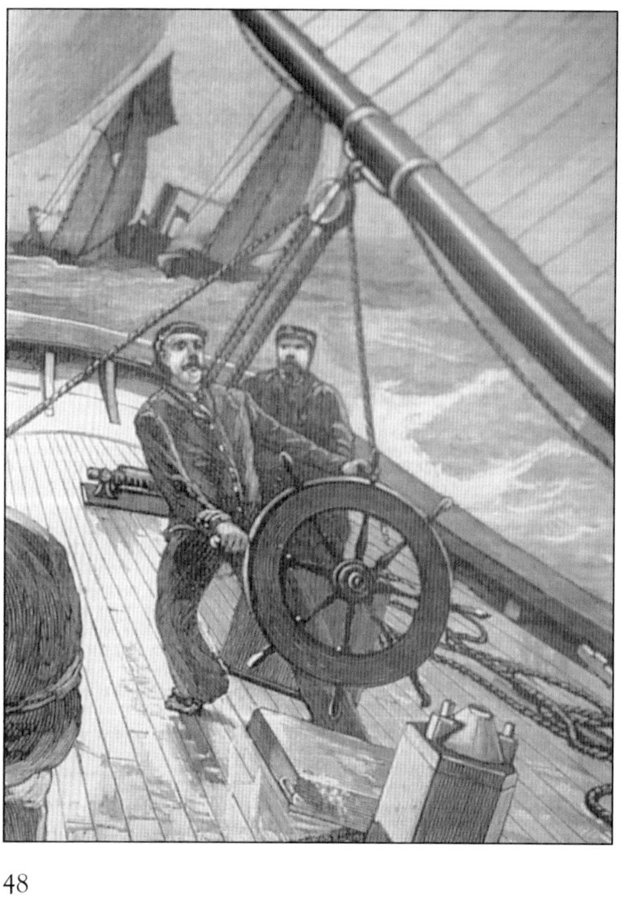

It is hard to believe that over 100 years ago thousands of Wilmingtonians felt that they had a part in the America's Cup races and waited anxiously for the results of the most famous sailing races of all. The *Mischief*, the first iron yacht to compete in the races, was built in 1879 by Harlan & Hollingsworth and is in the lead in this illustration from *Harper's Weekly*, which reported the details of the race.

The Mischief was 61 feet long, and her mast was longer. She made history for iron-hulled yachts. She was the second to be built in America and the first to be used in the America's Cup races. The "Iron Pot," *Mischief's* nickname, triumphed in the 1881 races. Those who waited at home for the results could only imagine the scene on board as being like this illustration from *Harper's Weekly*.

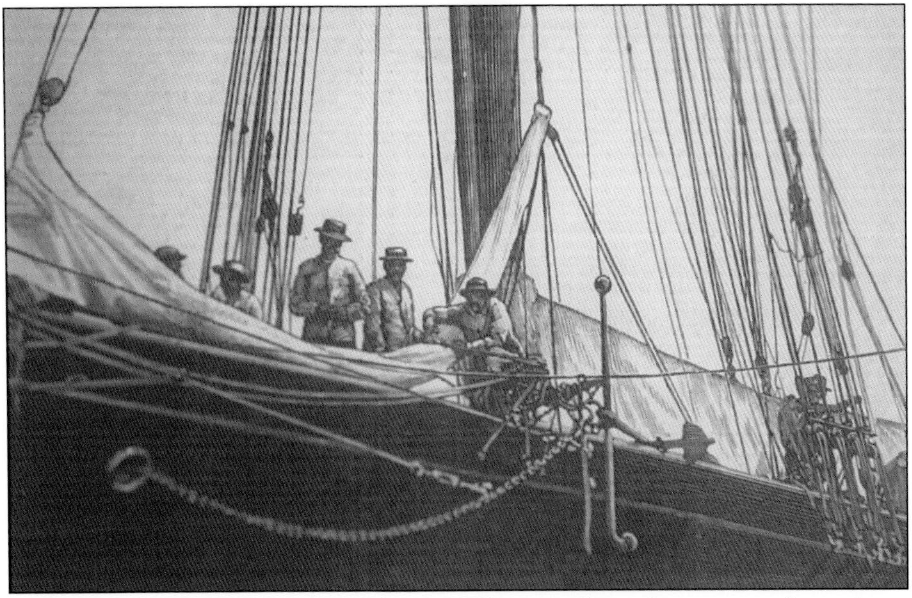

Success in the races of 1881 brought Harlan & Hollingsworth another contract for an America's Cup yacht of iron in 1885. This was the 85-foot compromise sloop *Priscilla.* The Wilmington newspapers carried the story of her construction and launching in the Christina River. *Harper's Weekly* gave her national coverage and showed her here in New York having her sails fitted.

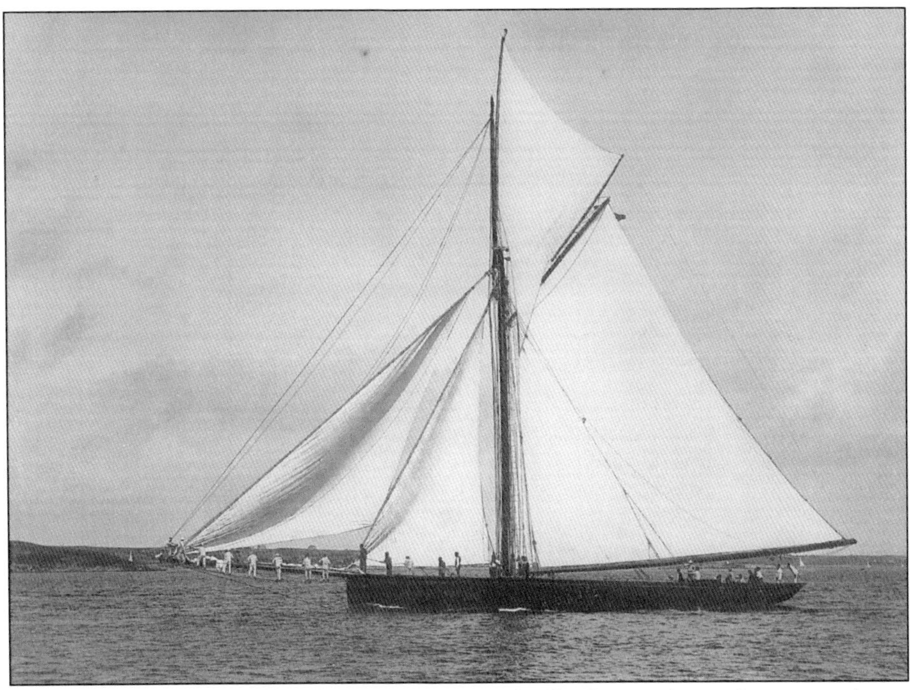

Priscilla, shown here under full sail, was not to triumph. She lost in the trials to a wooden yacht, the *Puritan*, sponsored by a Boston group. The Wilmington press reported the disappointing details of the races to its readers. *Priscilla's* quest for the cup was over. She underwent alterations, served as a private yacht for some time, and wound up as a Bahamian mail boat in the 1930s.

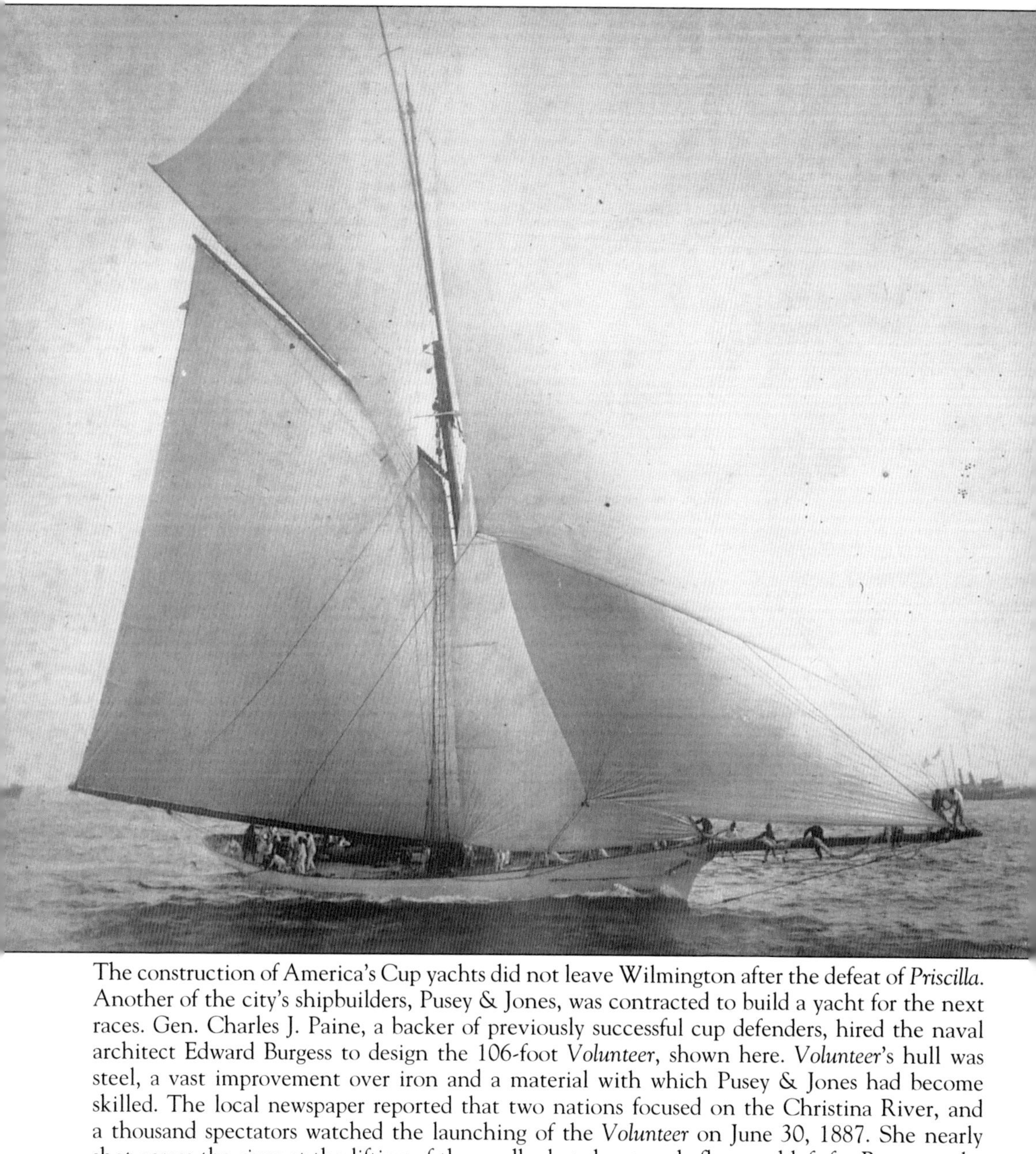

The construction of America's Cup yachts did not leave Wilmington after the defeat of *Priscilla*. Another of the city's shipbuilders, Pusey & Jones, was contracted to build a yacht for the next races. Gen. Charles J. Paine, a backer of previously successful cup defenders, hired the naval architect Edward Burgess to design the 106-foot *Volunteer*, shown here. *Volunteer*'s hull was steel, a vast improvement over iron and a material with which Pusey & Jones had become skilled. The local newspaper reported that two nations focused on the Christina River, and a thousand spectators watched the launching of the *Volunteer* on June 30, 1887. She nearly shot across the river at the lifting of the cradle, but she stayed afloat and left for Boston to be fitted for spars and sails. Going into the races, *Volunteer* carried over 9,000 square feet of sail. She was a dramatic sight, and her races created even more excitement in Wilmington than her launching. (Courtesy of the Hagley Museum and Library.)

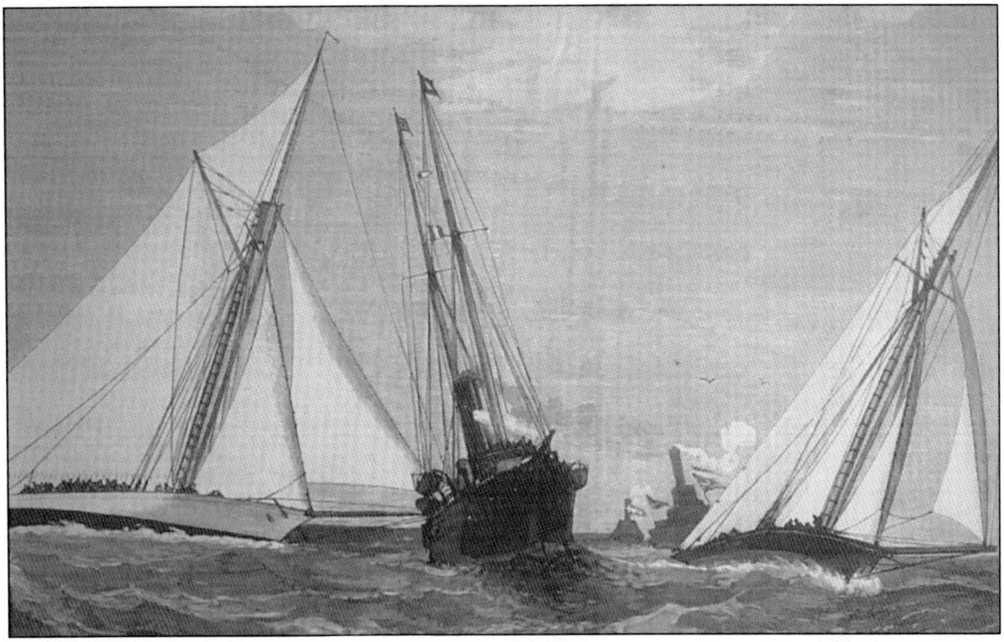

Another *Harper's Weekly* illustration shows *Volunteer* competing against the British boat, *Thistle*. *Volunteer* won, and Charles Pusey of Pusey & Jones, who had gone to New York to see the races, sent a simple wire message to the Wilmington newspaper after the first race: "Hurrah, Hurrah, Hurrah." According to the newspaper, thousands of excited people waited for the results of the race.

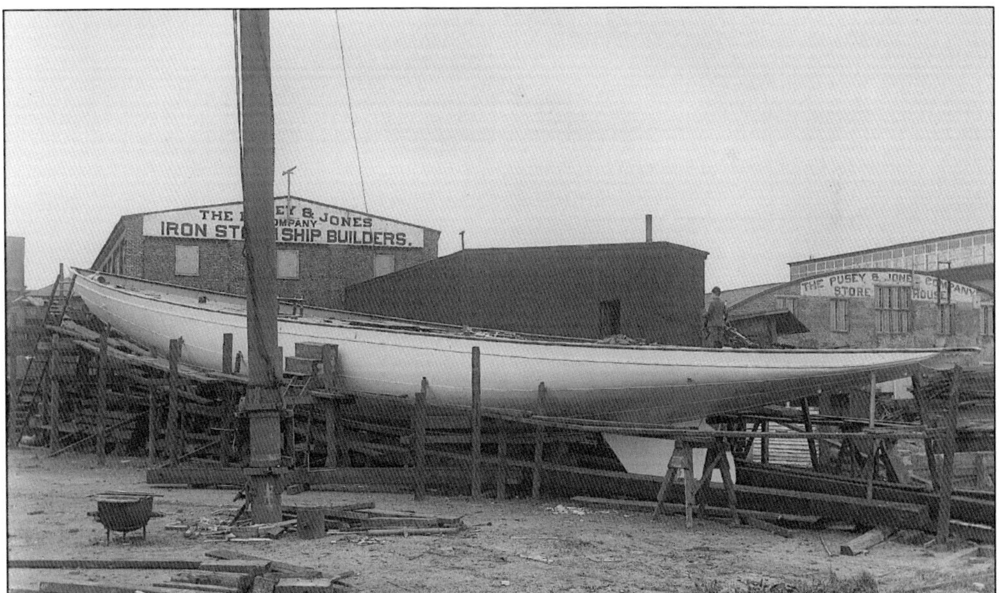

After *Volunteer's* victory, Paine contracted to build another steel America's Cup yacht. *Pilgrim*, shown here at the Pusey & Jones yard, was a 120-foot-long sloop and attracted a crowd of 500 to her launching on June 12, 1893. Her fans at home were disappointed when they learned that she had lost in the trials and would not make it to the big race. She was Wilmington's last America's Cup yacht. (Courtesy of the Hagley Museum & Library.)

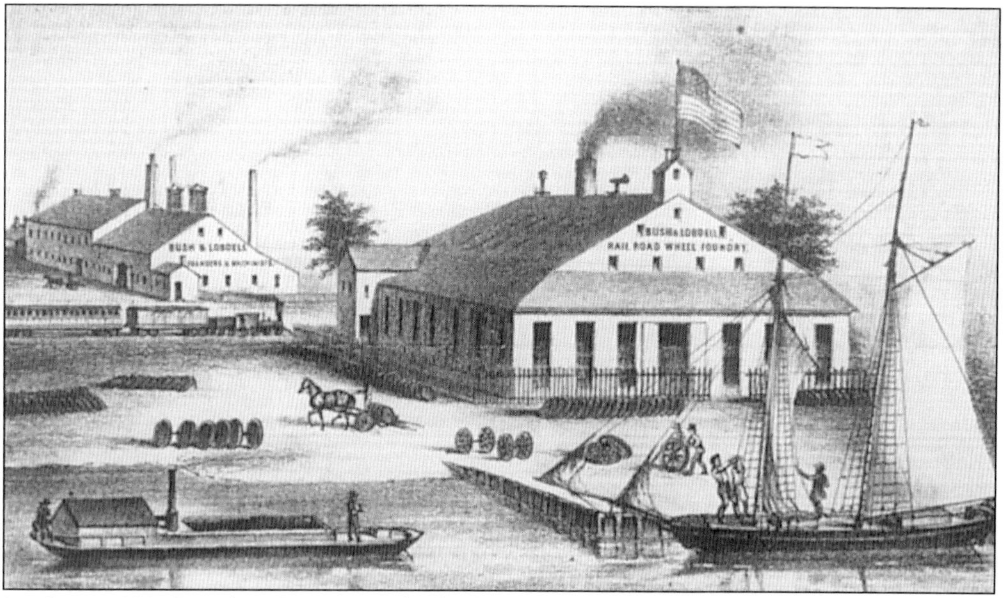

In about 1830, Jonathan Bonney and Charles Bush started making machinery castings and railroad car wheels at Second and Lombard Streets. George Lobdell soon joined the firm and became the head of it. In 1844, according to a company history, they moved to the banks of the Christina, as shown in this illustration from a company catalog. Eventually, they moved further downstream nearer the port. (Courtesy of the Historical Society of Delaware.)

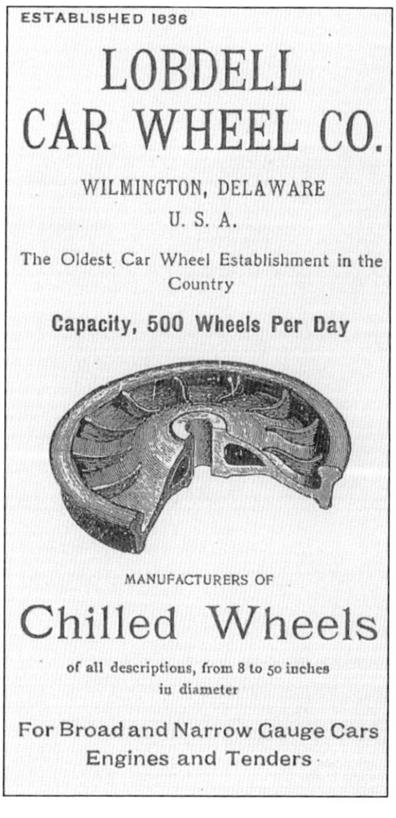

The Lobdell Car Wheel, which evolved from Bush and Lobdell, boasted that it could make 500 chilled, cast-iron wheels per day. The company did make a few other products. Even today, the name Lobdell is still visible on many of Wilmington's storm sewer covers, a last reminder of a once-great industry. This ad appeared in a book about the Harlan & Hollingsworth Company in 1898. (Courtesy of the Historical Society of Delaware.)

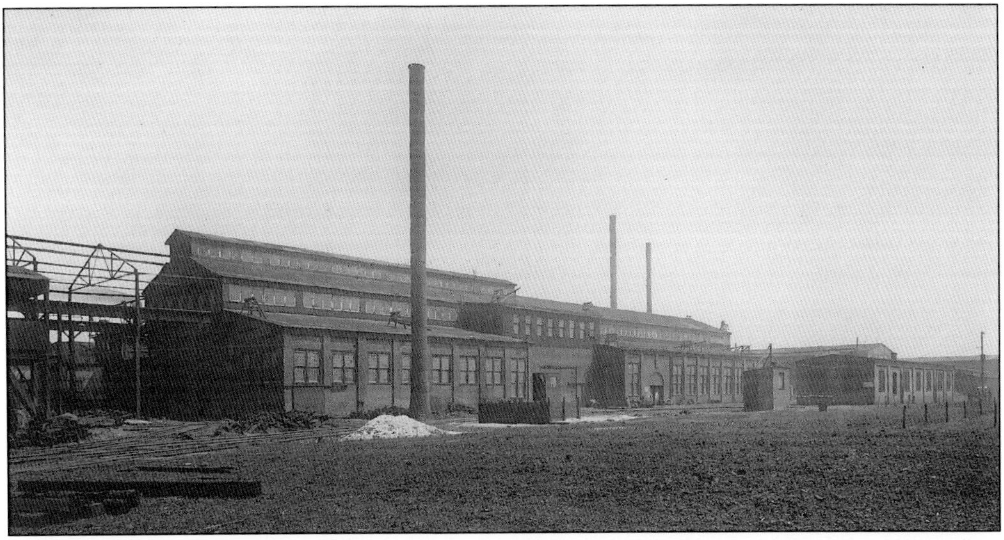

The Lobdell Car Wheel Company is downstream from Pusey & Jones, as shown on the map in the introduction. By 1912, over 300 people worked at the plant, turning out wheels for railroad cars, street cars, mine cars, and other uses. The company continued to profit through the First World War. In 1926, when this photograph was taken, Lobdell was in a decline from which it never recovered. (Courtesy of the Delaware State Archives.)

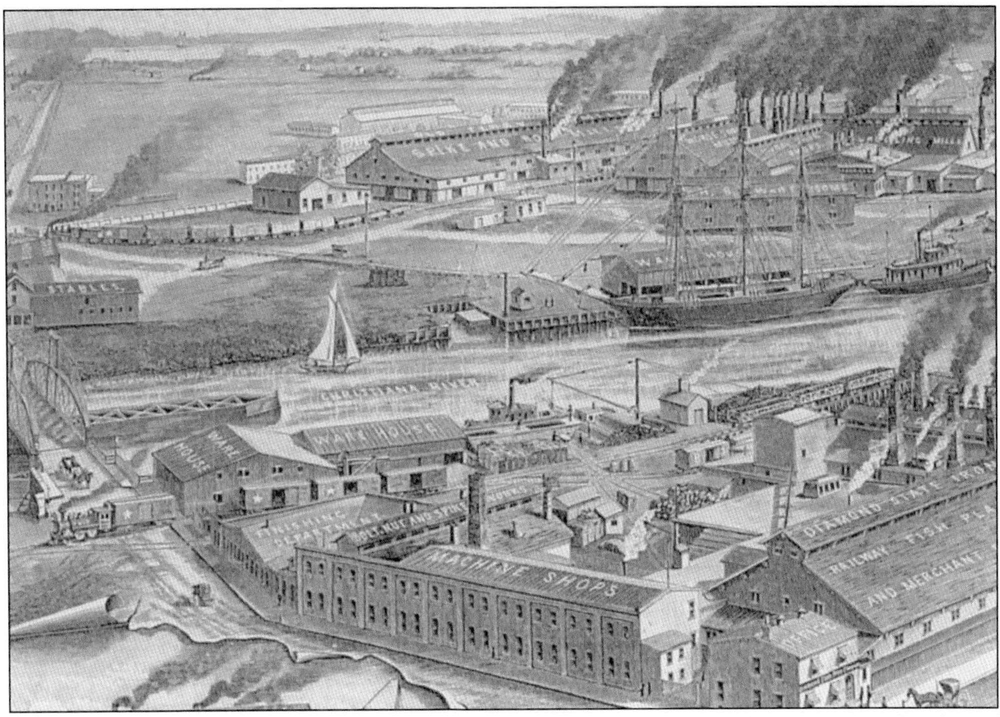

Today, the black smoke pouring out of its stacks would not add to the promotional value of this picture of the Diamond State Iron Co. The company started operations in 1853 on Church Street making bar iron, and it was the first incorporated manufacturer in Delaware. By 1891, Diamond State Iron employed 600 people and had expanded to the south side of the old Third Street bridge. (Courtesy of the Historical Society of Delaware.)

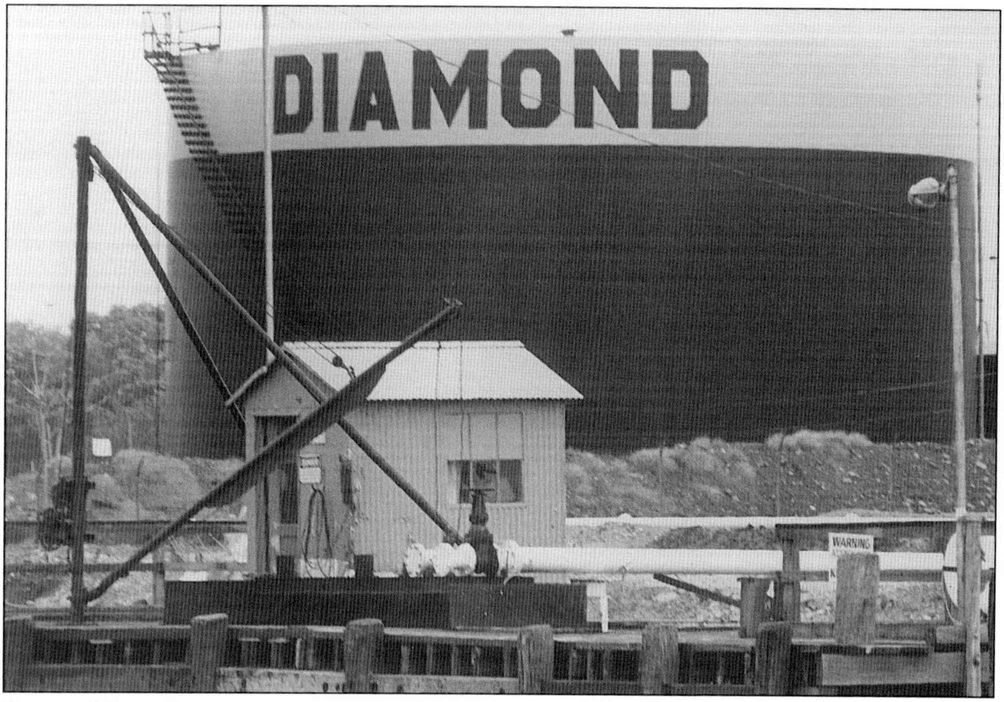

Diamond State Iron went into receivership in 1907 and eventually liquidated all its properties. However, the name Diamond continued to loom over the south bank of the Christina for some time because the area became a tank farm for Diamond State Oil as shown in this 1970s photo. (Courtesy of the Wilmington Department of Parks and Recreation.)

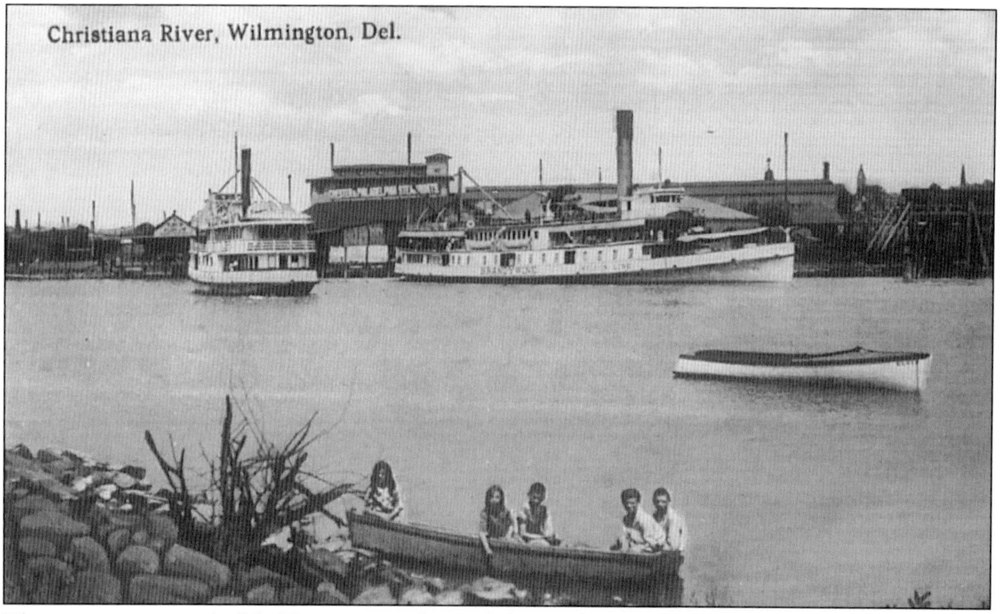

This picture postcard of children in a rowboat while another small boat is moored a short distance away is evidence of some recreational use of the Christina River in the early 20th century. This view is taken from the south bank of the river looking upstream at Wilson Line Steamers. (Courtesy of the Hagley Museum and Library.)

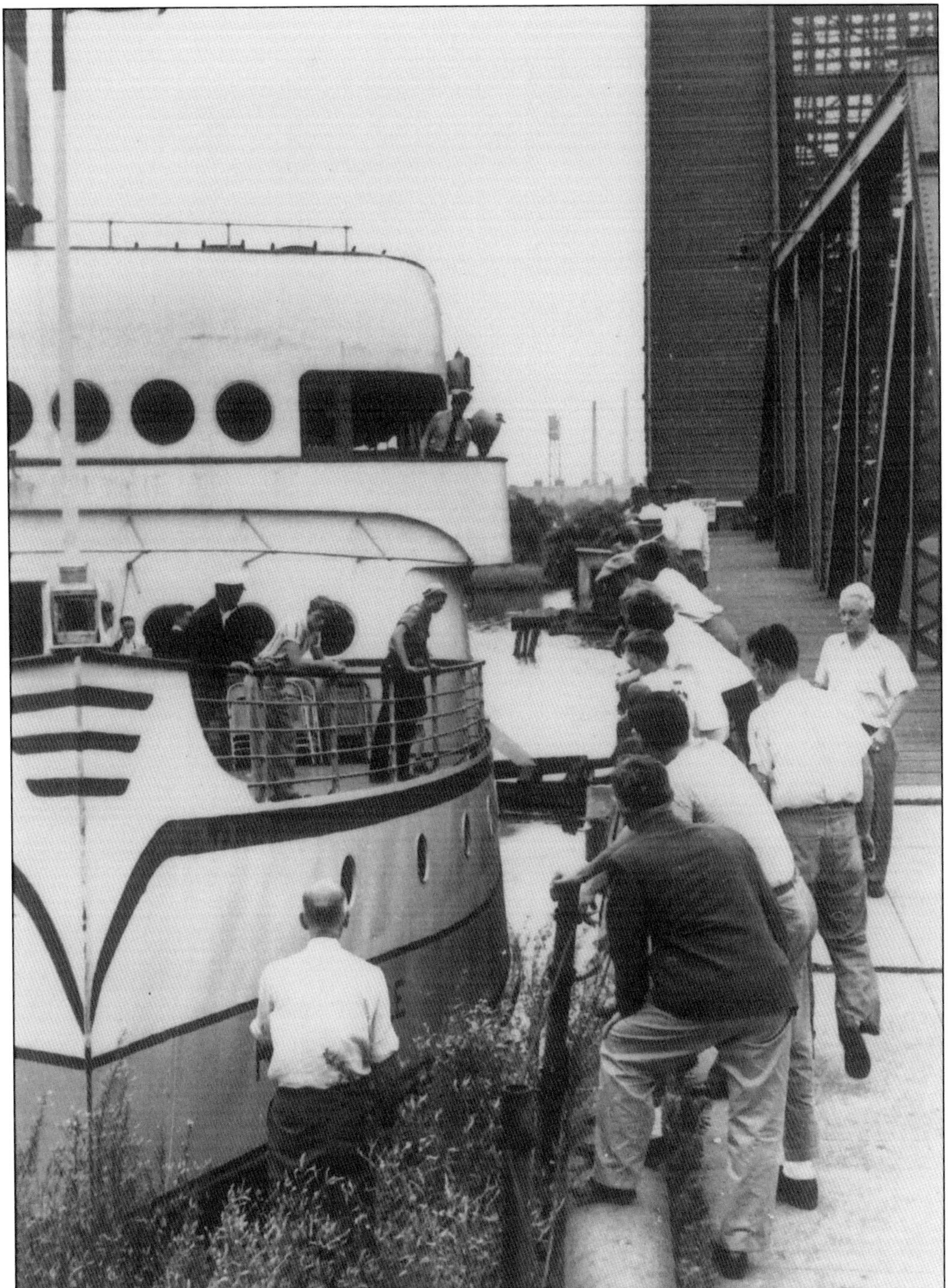

On July 6, 1949, a Wilson Line steamer hit the Third Street bridge. Here you can see onlookers watching from the bridge as well as Wilson Line employees studying the problem from two decks of the ship. The bridge is open, of course, and the steamer is out of service for the time being. This was a big inconvenience during the hot Wilmington summer. (Courtesy of the Delaware State Archives.)

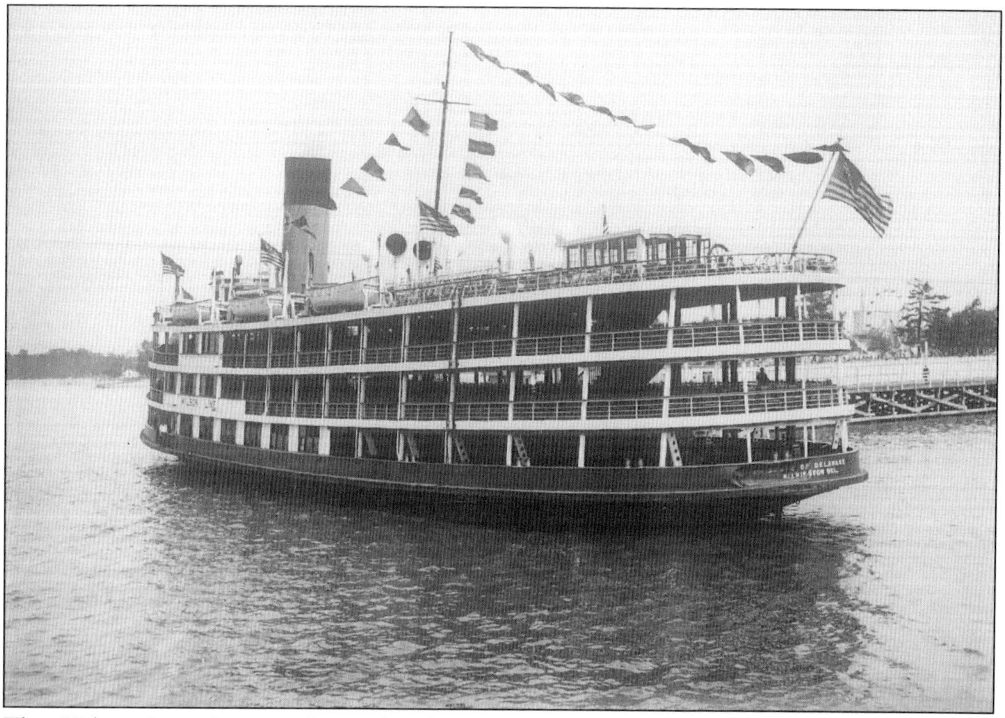

The Wilson Line Steamer *State of Delaware* regularly sailed from the Christina River to Philadelphia and Riverview Beach, across the Delaware River in New Jersey. In this picture, she is bedecked with flags as she nears the dock at Riverview, identified by the Ferris wheel in the background. (Courtesy of the Historical Society of Delaware.)

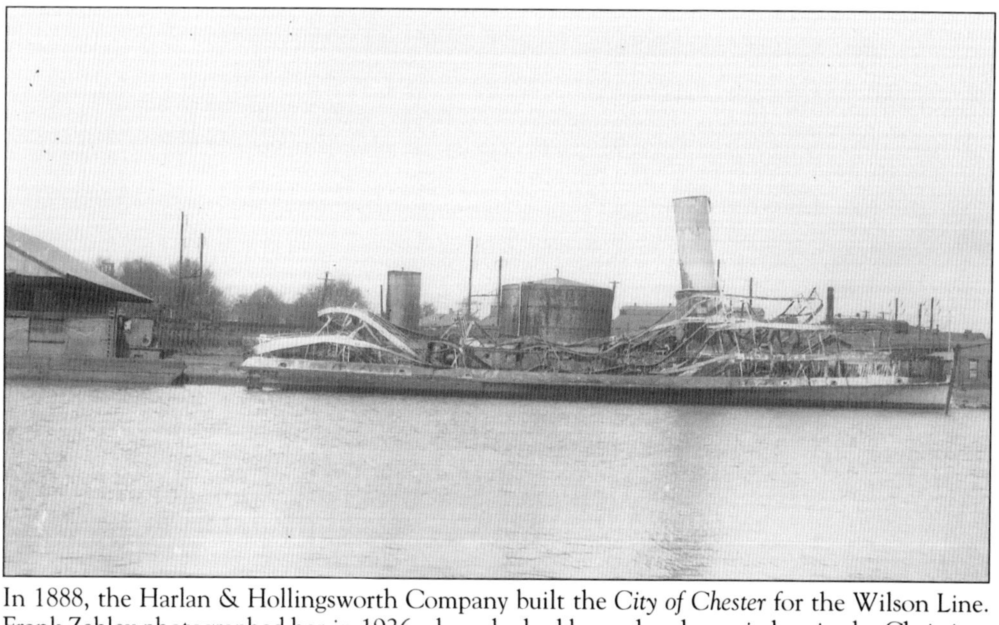

In 1888, the Harlan & Hollingsworth Company built the *City of Chester* for the Wilson Line. Frank Zebley photographed her in 1926 when she had burned and was tied up in the Christina. (Courtesy of the Delaware State Archives.)

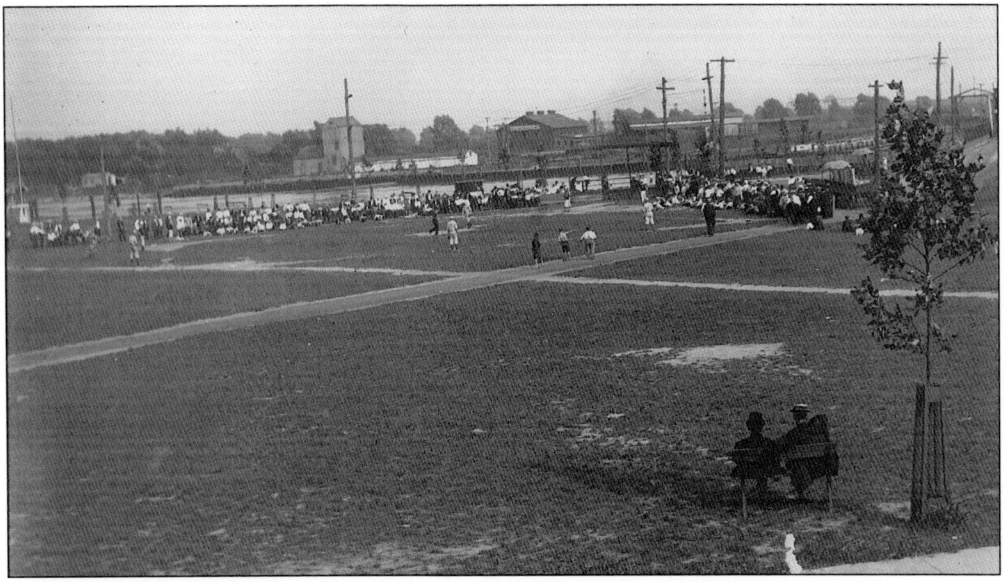

The city leased land for Christina Park in 1908 and laid out a baseball field the following year. In 1914, the county condemned part of this land for approaches to a new bridge. At the same time, the city acquired additional land that became the major portion of today's park. This 1911 photo shows a small crowd gathered to watch a baseball game in the park. (Courtesy of the Wilmington Department of Parks and Recreation.)

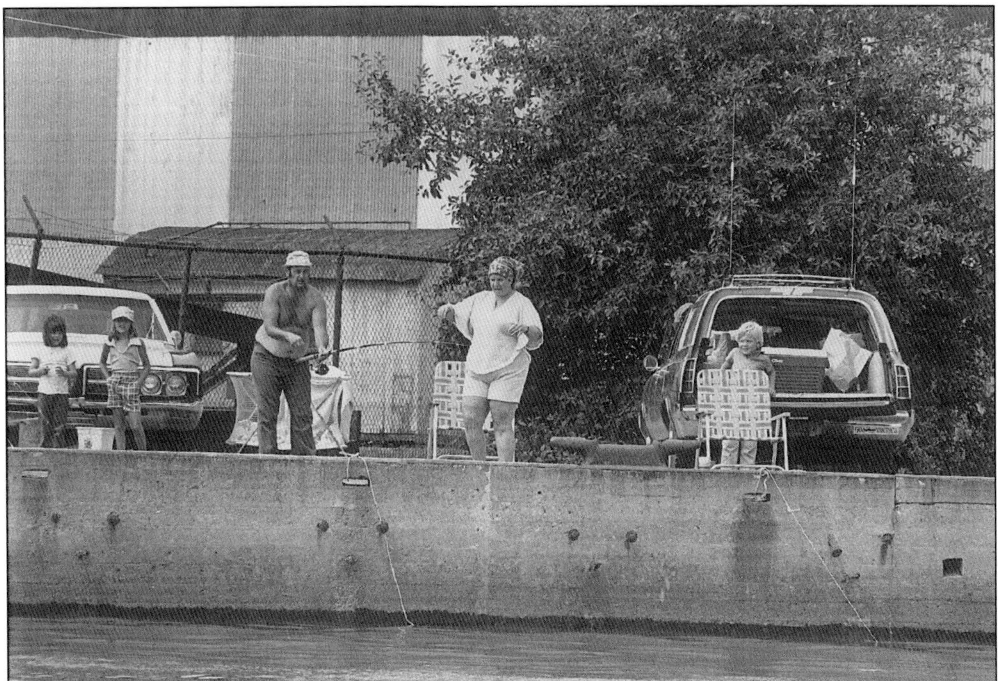

Wilmington residents have used the city's rivers for recreation of different kinds, but fishing has always been popular. This 1970s photograph by David W. Allen shows a family enjoying fishing from the north bank of the Christina at the present Christina Park at the junction of Church and Front Streets. (Courtesy of the Wilmington Department of Parks and Recreation.)

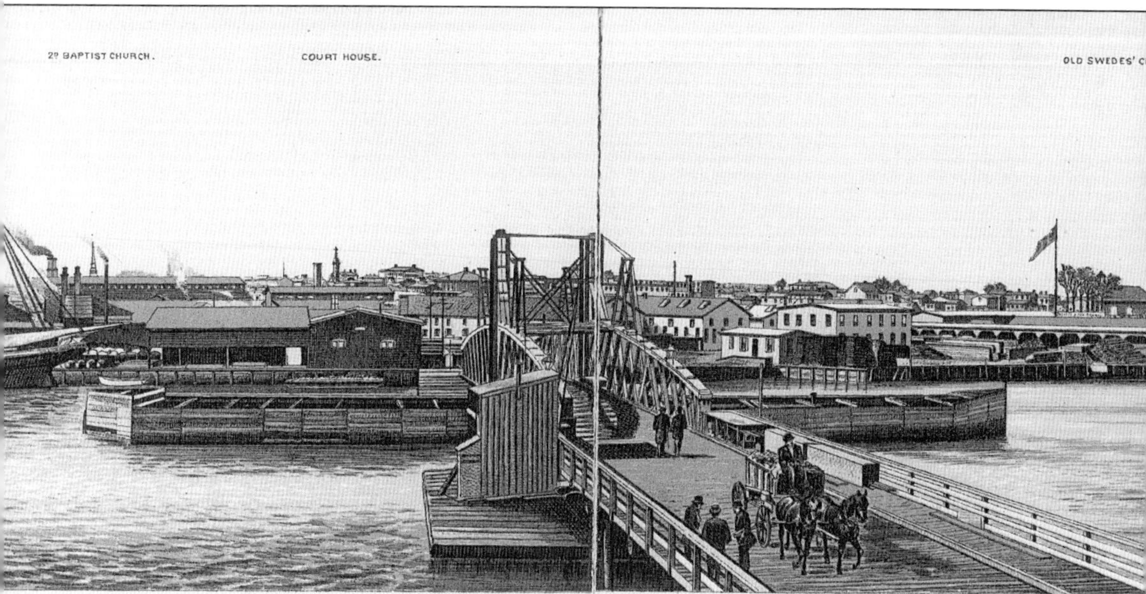

VIEW FROM 3º STREET BRIDGE, CHRISTIANA RIVER.

In 1883, Witteman Brothers of New York City published an album containing this view of Wilmington from the Third Street bridge. The notations pointing out the Second Baptist Church, the courthouse, and Old Swedes Church provide some orientation as to how the city looked at that time from the south side of the bridge. Prior to 1867, when the Delaware State legislature authorized this bridge, there had been a ferry across the river here. The original ferry was established in the late 17th century and connected a road from the head of navigation on the Brandywine to the King's Road on the south side of the Christina. A new Strauss Trunnion bascule drawbridge replaced the bridge shown here. The present bridge, built in the early 1980s, is slightly downstream from the first two. (Courtesy of the Hagley Museum and Library.)

Two

The Brandywine River

The Brandywine enters Wilmington bouncing exuberantly over rapids, boulders, and dams until it meets the head of navigation at the Market Street bridge. In its 20-mile course from where its two branches meet in Lenape, Pennsylvania, to its confluence with the Christina, the Brandywine evokes visions primarily of the beauty of urban parks and open countryside. But that is a near-sighted vision of the mercurial and sometimes irascible Brandywine. The river that is the central feature in Wilmington's most beautiful park can turn nasty and has destroyed factories, homes, and bridges with its floods. Floods of March 5, 1920; July 9, 1952; and August 20, 1955 caused extensive damage, and as late as June 23, 1972, over 100 residents had to leave their homes because of flooding in the Governor Printz, Claymont Street, and Vandever Avenue areas.

The Brandywine has worked hard for Wilmington, too. The city's 18th-century flour mills ran on Brandywine power. Sailing ships came up the river as far as the mills near the Market Street bridge and then sailed away loaded with the "superfine" product that brought fame to Wilmington. The Brandywine powered the mills outside the city that would eventually become E.I. du Pont de Nemours as well as other mills producing cotton and paper.

The parks on the Brandywine remain, and the mills are gone, but there are still many reminders of the past along the river's banks. Start upstream on the Brandywine and follow it through pictures as it curves around the city to meet its sister river, the Christina.

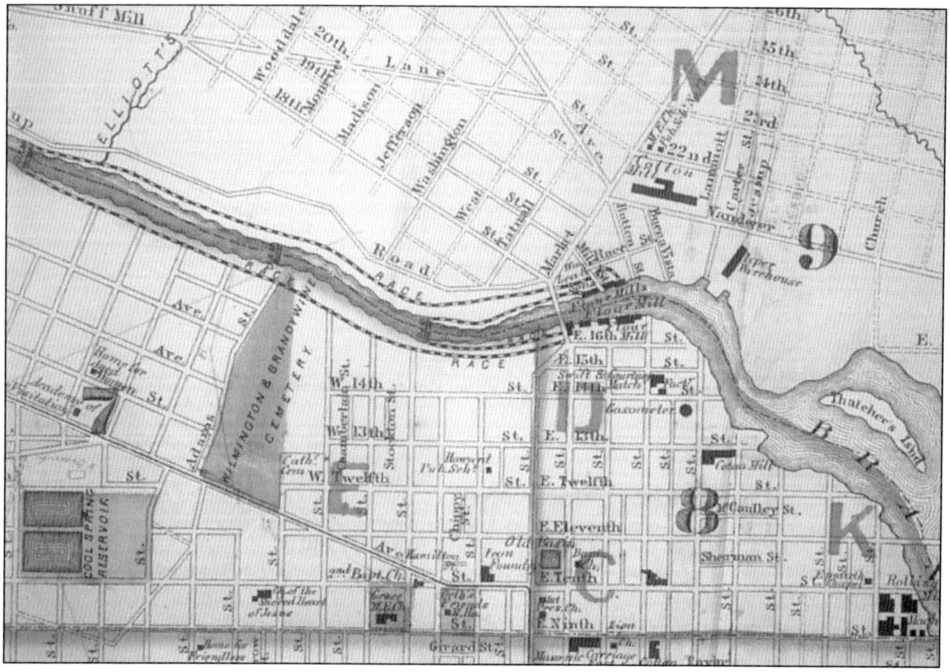

In 1876, G.M. Hopkins published an atlas of Wilmington that included this section of a map of the city. Since the western boundary of town was then at Union Street, the map shows most of the Brandywine River, which was within the city. Note the large bulge around Thatcher's Island, which no longer exists, and the water races on the map upstream from Market Street. (Courtesy of the Hagley Museum and Library.)

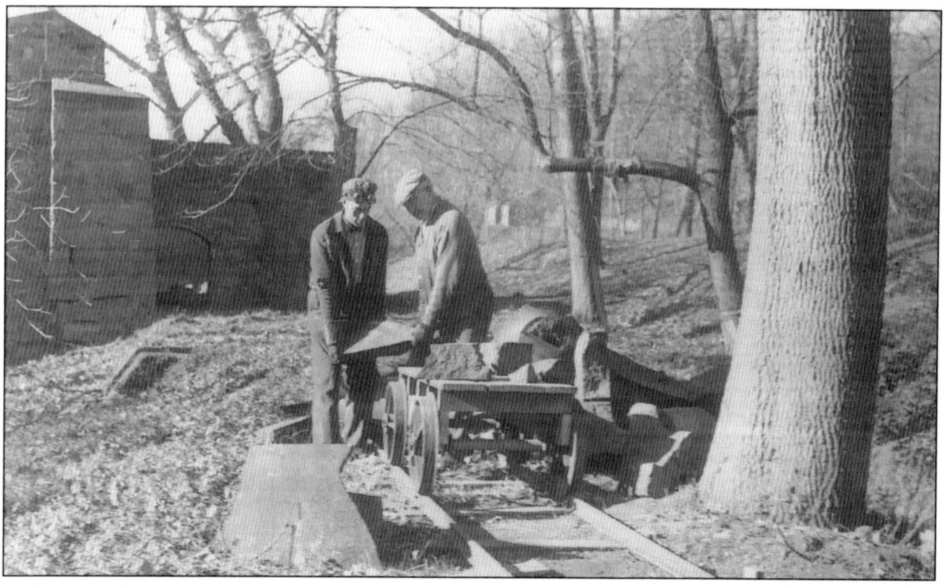

The du Pont family established powder mills on the Brandywine River outside the city limits in the early 19th century. The du Pont story appears in many books and did not really take place on rivers within the city, but this photo of men working on a railroad track at the Hagley Mill serves as a reminder of this dominant force on the upper Brandywine. (Courtesy of the Delaware State Archives.)

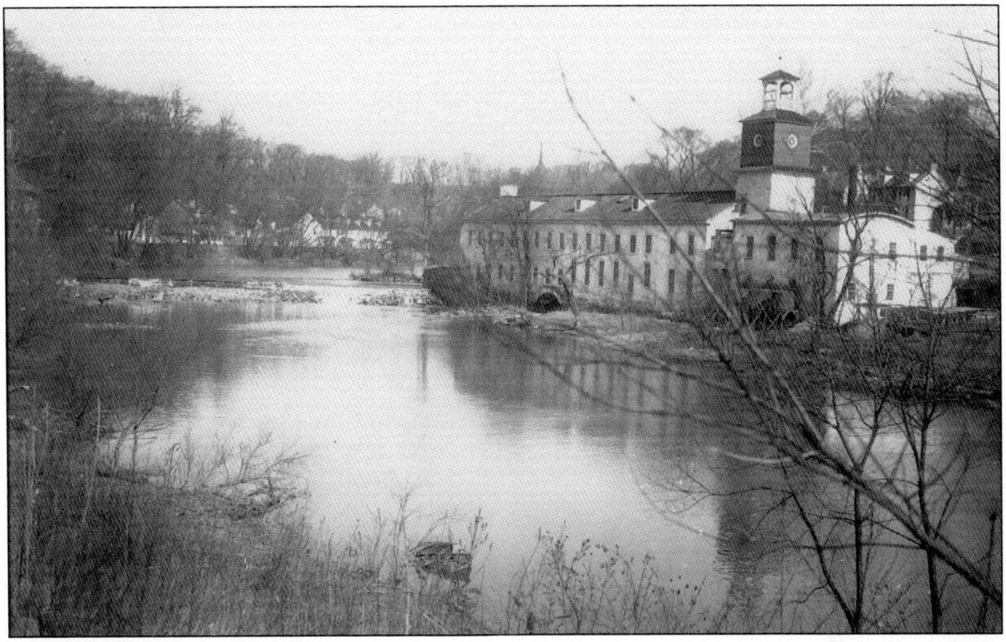

Just north of today's city boundary stands Walker's Mill, shown here in 1931. Originally a textile mill, it eventually became part of the DuPont Company holdings. Upstream, in the distance, the long white building contained tenements for some of the DuPont Company workers in Henry Clay Village. (Courtesy of the Delaware State Archives.)

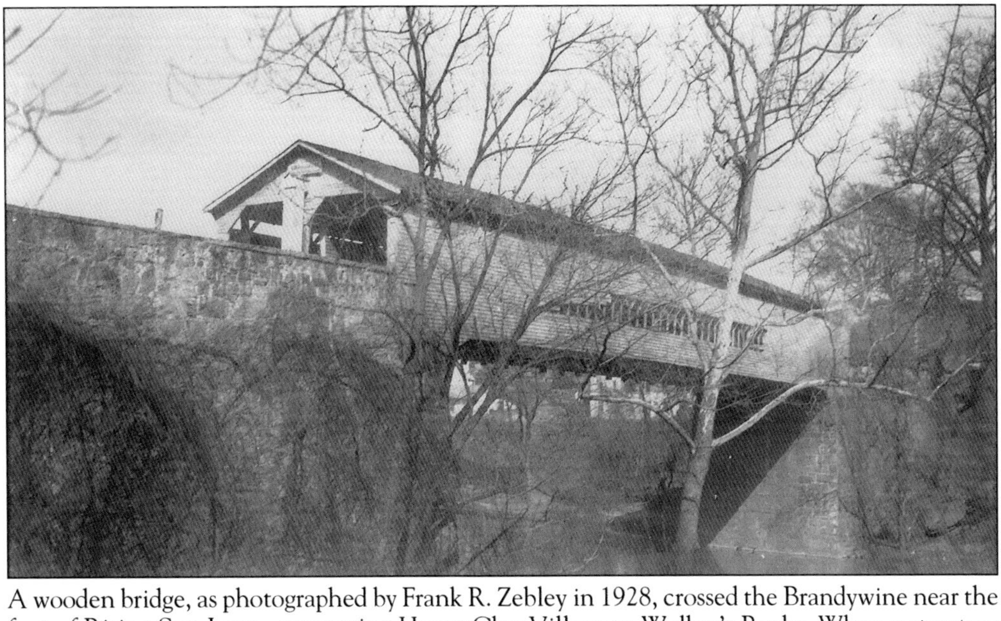

A wooden bridge, as photographed by Frank R. Zebley in 1928, crossed the Brandywine near the foot of Rising Sun Lane, connecting Henry Clay Village to Walker's Banks. When a streetcar line eventually ran from downtown Wilmington to Rising Sun Lane, the area became accessible to more people. In the meantime, the bridge was the main connection between mills on both sides of the river. (Courtesy of the Delaware State Archives.)

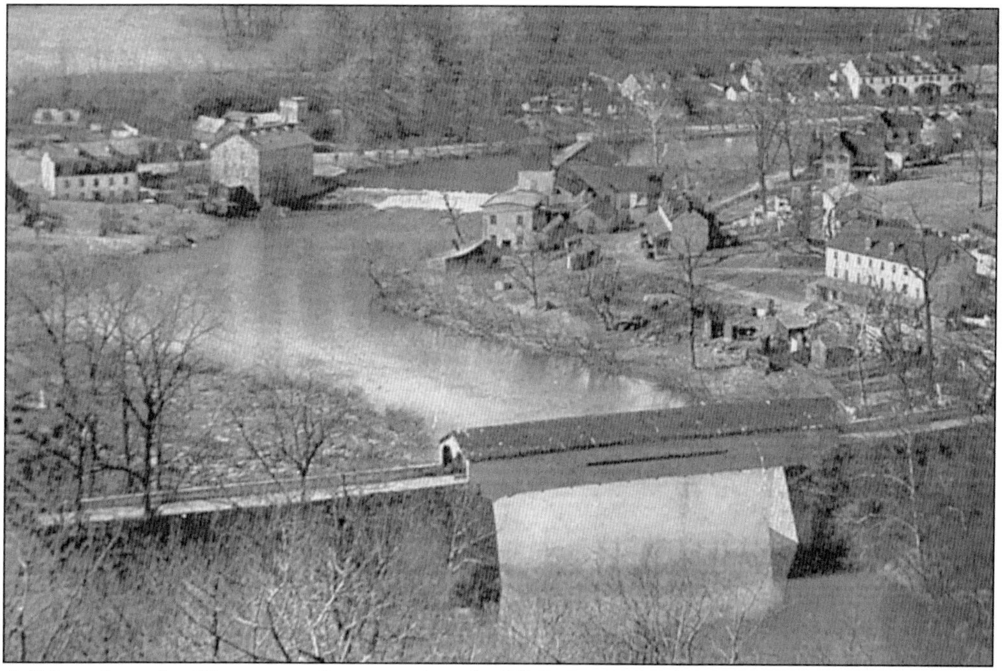

A "View from the Observatory" appeared in the Wilmington Parks Commission report of 1901. The large white building just beyond the bridge on the right is Walkers Banks, which contained worker tenements. Near the center at the curve of the river, Breck's Mill is on the left and Walker's Mill is on the right. In the distance is more housing for workers. (Courtesy of the Wilmington Parks and Recreation Department.)

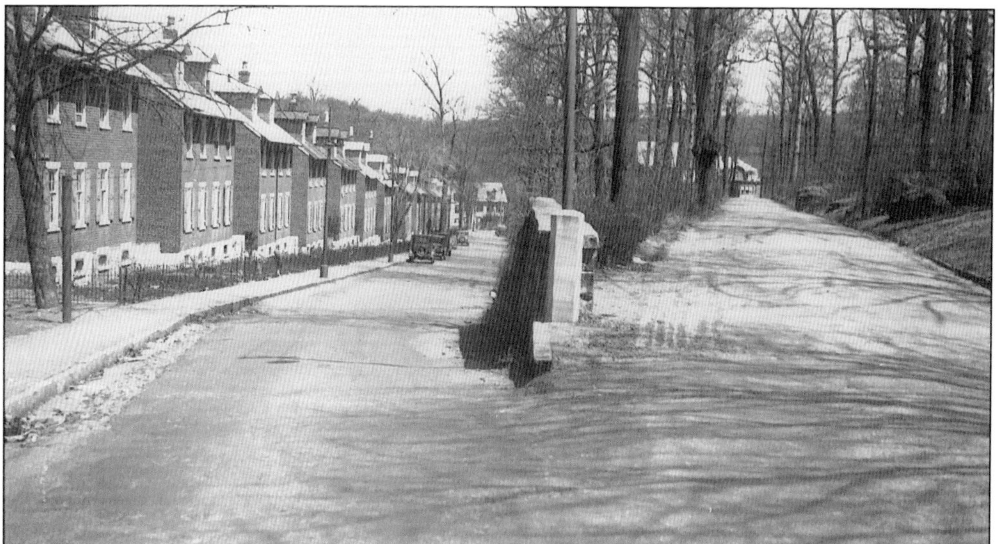

Joseph Bancroft & Sons built the houses at Rockford, shown here in a Zebley photograph of about 1930, for the workers in its cotton mill. Mill owners built several of these villages along the Brandywine, but they were not quite the fully developed company towns found elsewhere. The substantial brick Rockford houses are now within the city limits and are totally renovated for modern living. (Courtesy of the Delaware State Archives.)

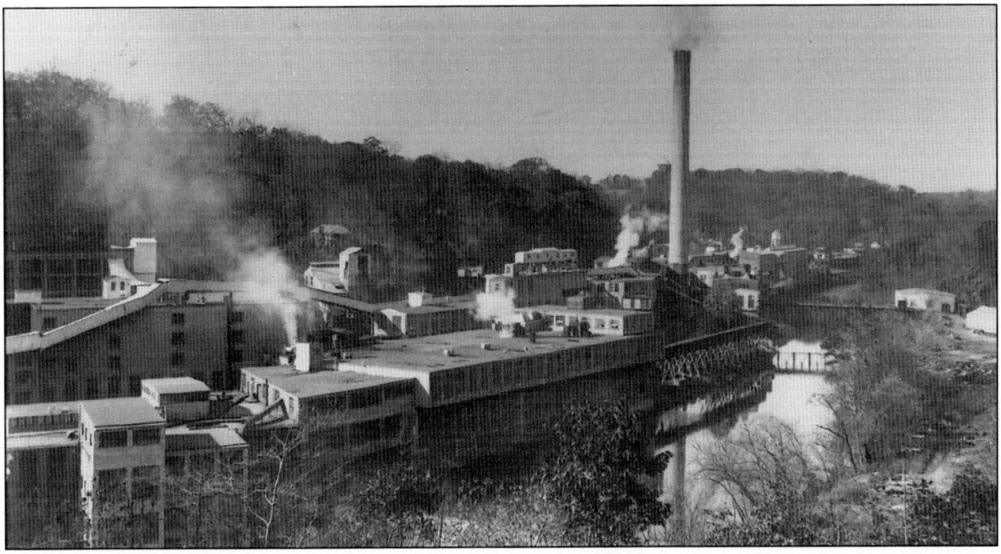

In 1831, Joseph Bancroft, a devout Quaker born in England, bought a small mill called Rockford and established his own cotton mill, which eventually covered over 100 acres along the Brandywine, as shown here. The founder's sons, William P. Bancroft and Samuel Bancroft, managed the firm after their father's death in 1874. They became two of Wilmington's greatest benefactors. (Courtesy of the Delaware State Archives.)

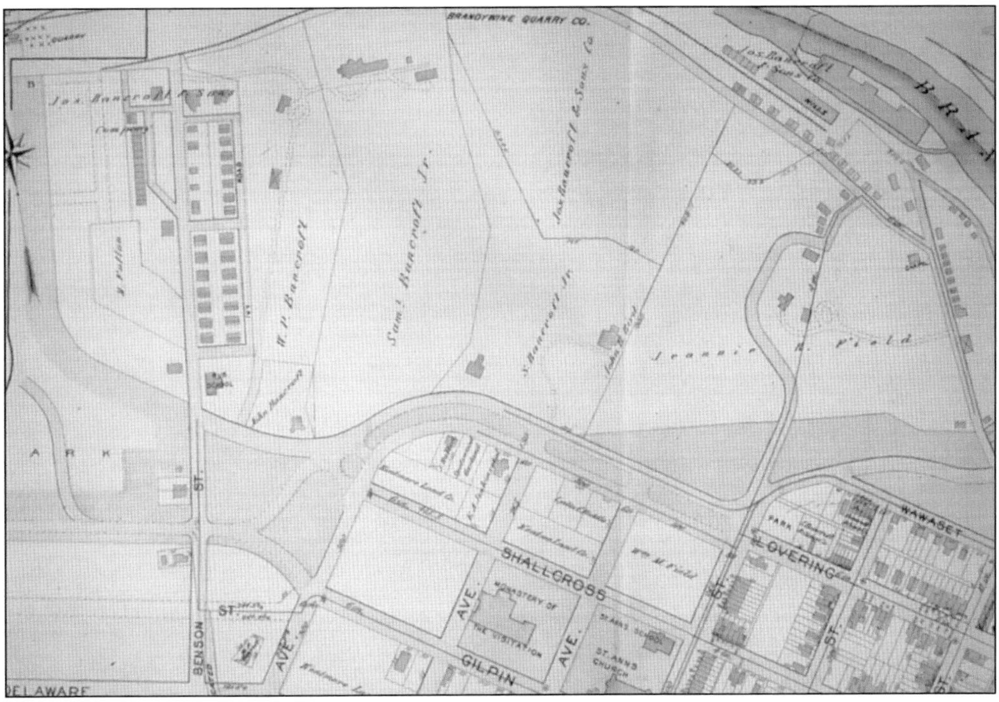

The Baist's Property Atlas of 1901 shows the Bancroft Mills at top right. The two rows of little squares on the left represent the Rockford houses, and the houses of William and Samuel Bancroft are next to the mill and the workers. The Bancroft brothers were born as Quakers, and although their lifestyles and tastes were quite different from each other, both were fully involved in the business of the cotton mill.

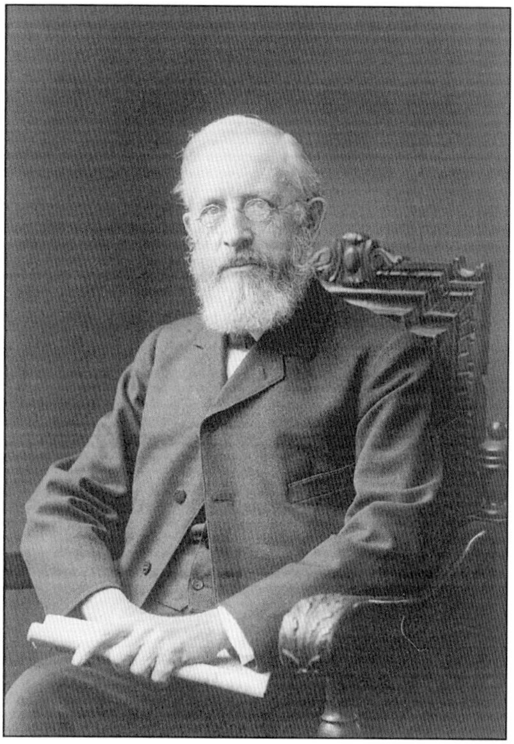

William P. Bancroft, the elder of the two brothers, became known as the "Father of the Wilmington Park System." He was the driving force behind the formation of the Park Commission and donated at least 200 acres of land for park use. William P. Bancroft is the philanthropist most responsible for the city's outstanding system of parks and parkways. (Courtesy of the Historical Society of Delaware.)

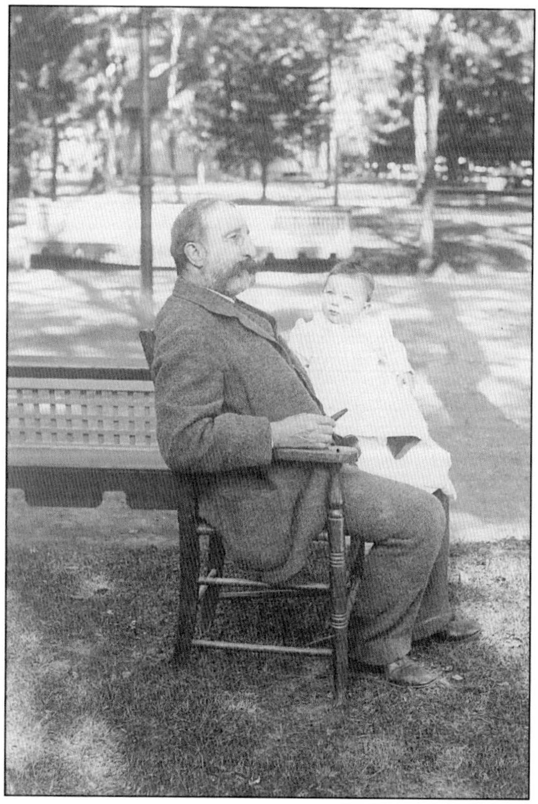

Samuel Bancroft, shown here with his grandson, Samuel Bancroft Bird, concentrated on sales and new processes for the mill. In England, Bancroft fell in love with the paintings of the Pre-Raphaelites and began amassing a large collection. After his death, Bancroft's wife and children gave the paintings and a plot of land that became a key part of the eventual development of the Delaware Art Museum. (Courtesy of the Historical Society of Delaware.)

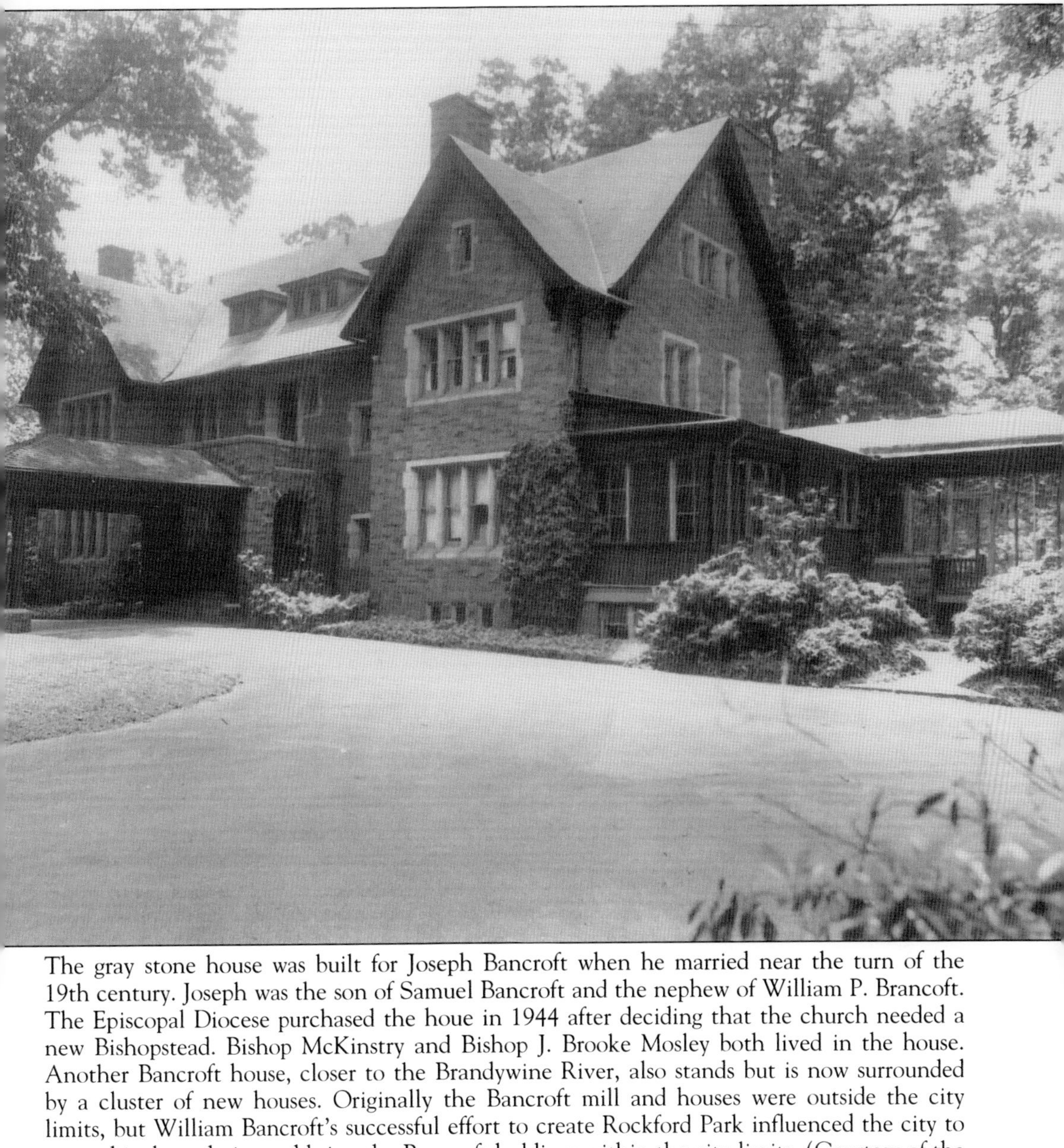

The gray stone house was built for Joseph Bancroft when he married near the turn of the 19th century. Joseph was the son of Samuel Bancroft and the nephew of William P. Brancoft. The Episcopal Diocese purchased the houe in 1944 after deciding that the church needed a new Bishopstead. Bishop McKinstry and Bishop J. Brooke Mosley both lived in the house. Another Bancroft house, closer to the Brandywine River, also stands but is now surrounded by a cluster of new houses. Originally the Bancroft mill and houses were outside the city limits, but William Bancroft's successful effort to create Rockford Park influenced the city to expand its boundaries and bring the Bancroft holdings within the city limits. (Courtesy of the Delaware State Archives.)

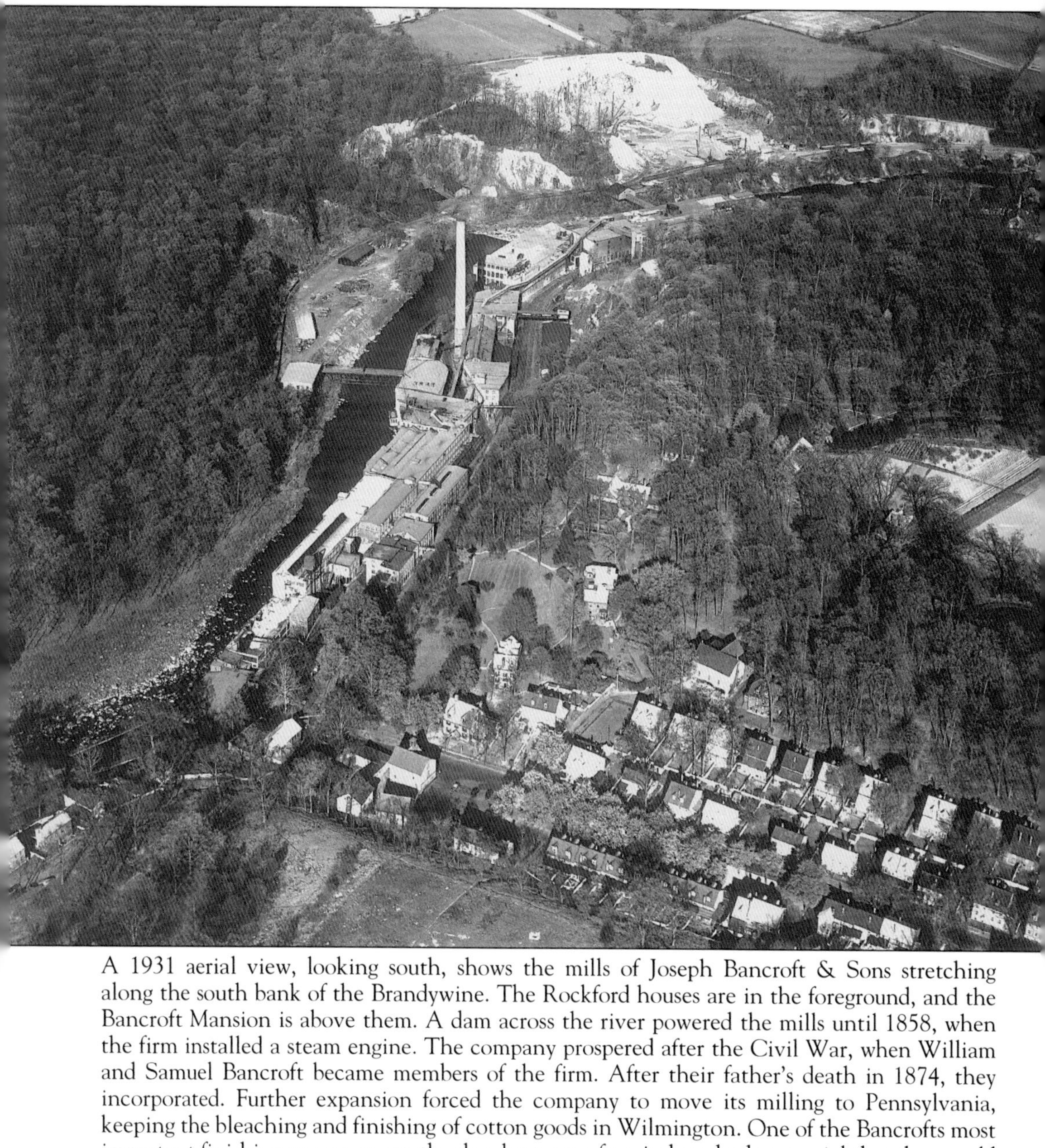

A 1931 aerial view, looking south, shows the mills of Joseph Bancroft & Sons stretching along the south bank of the Brandywine. The Rockford houses are in the foreground, and the Bancroft Mansion is above them. A dam across the river powered the mills until 1858, when the firm installed a steam engine. The company prospered after the Civil War, when William and Samuel Bancroft became members of the firm. After their father's death in 1874, they incorporated. Further expansion forced the company to move its milling to Pennsylvania, keeping the bleaching and finishing of cotton goods in Wilmington. One of the Bancrofts most important finishing processes was the development of a window shade material that they could guarantee would not fade. As president of the company, Samuel worked especially hard on this product. A black dye was another of their important developments. (Courtesy of the Hagley Museum and Library.)

A small covered footbridge connected the Bancroft Mills to the other side of the Brandywine. This photograph, by Tim Bayard, is a tranquil scene with no visible evidence of the clamor of bygone milling days. The renovated bridge is now an entrance to Alapocus Woods, where an old mill building is now a new pavilion. (Courtesy of Tim Bayard.)

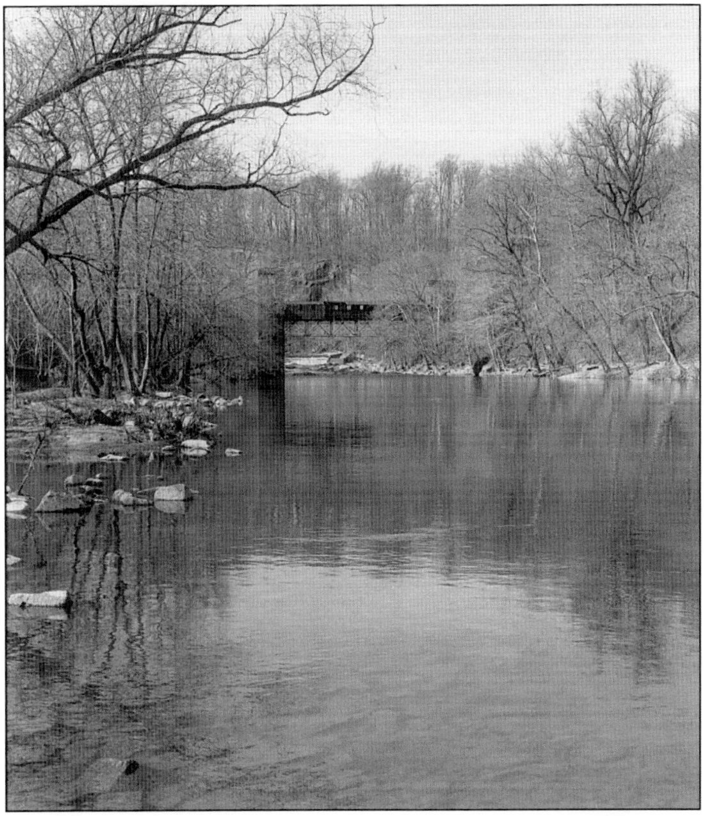

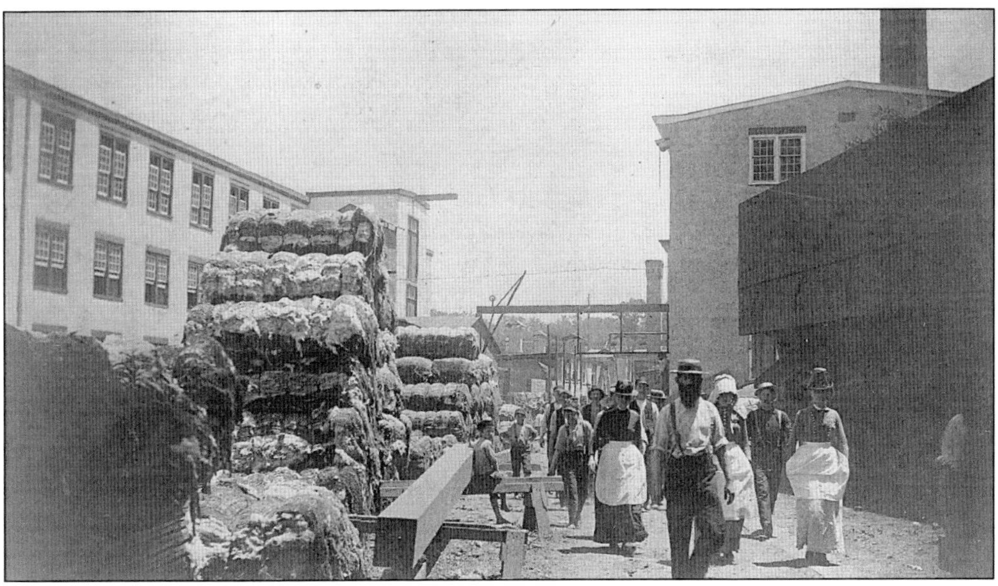

Here, workers are leaving the Bancroft Mills in the late 19th century, passing large bales of cotton that they will spin inside the mills. Wilmington's industrial workers came from American farms and small towns and from other countries to provide the labor that ran the plants that created the economic strength of the city. (Courtesy of the Hagley Museum and Library.)

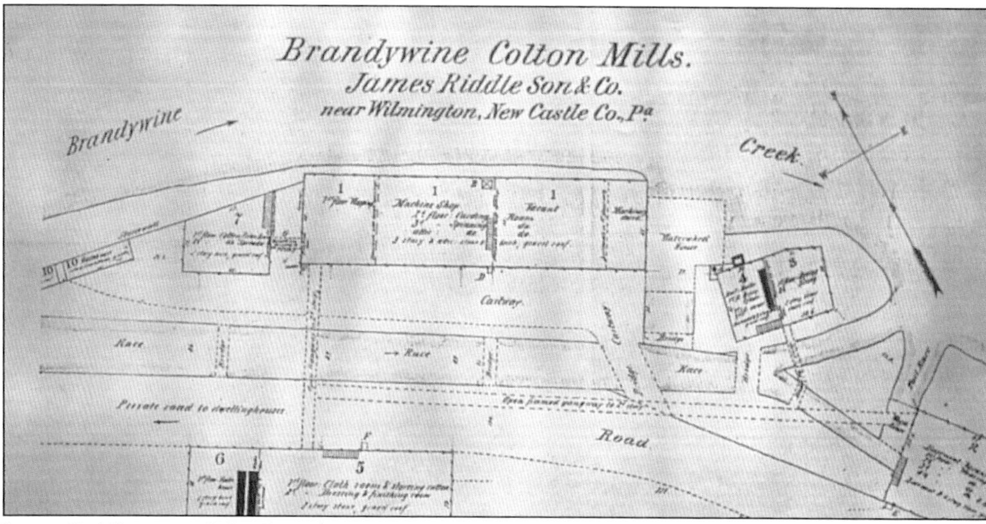

James Riddle started the Brandywine Cotton Mills in 1845. Riddle's son-in-law, William Field, later managed the mill and sold it to the Bancrofts. Field became interested in the park system, selling some land for park use and also donating some land to the city. (Courtesy of the Historical Society of Delaware.)

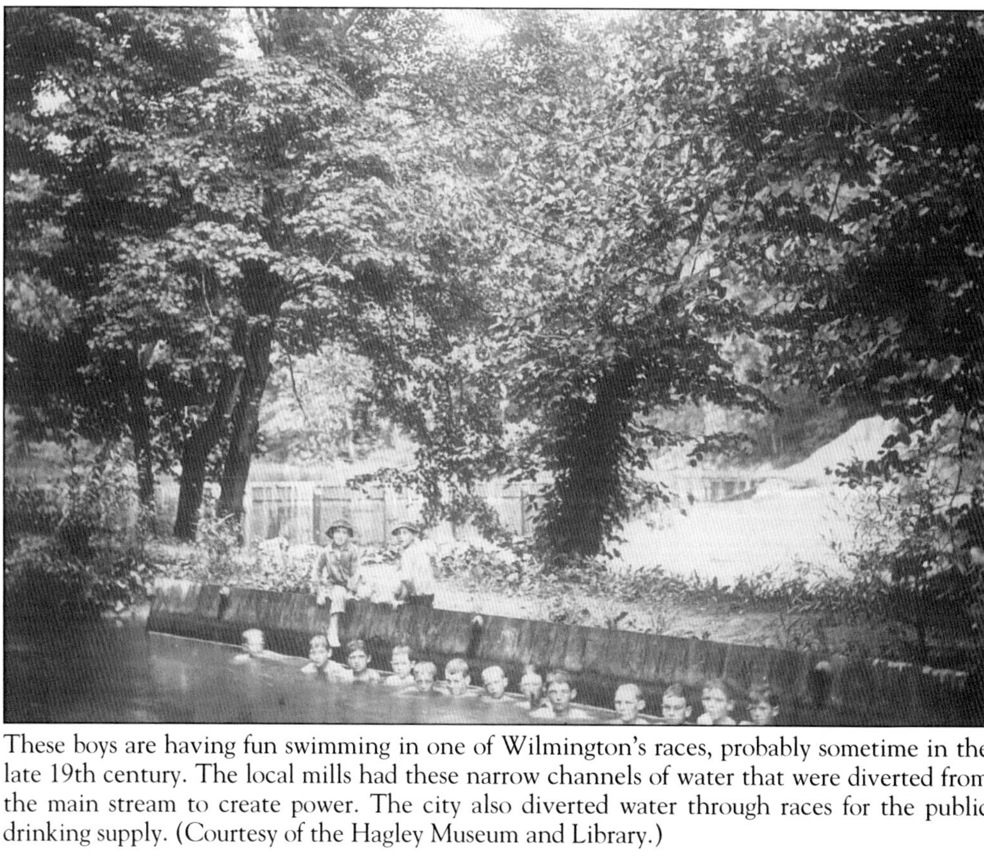

These boys are having fun swimming in one of Wilmington's races, probably sometime in the late 19th century. The local mills had these narrow channels of water that were diverted from the main stream to create power. The city also diverted water through races for the public drinking supply. (Courtesy of the Hagley Museum and Library.)

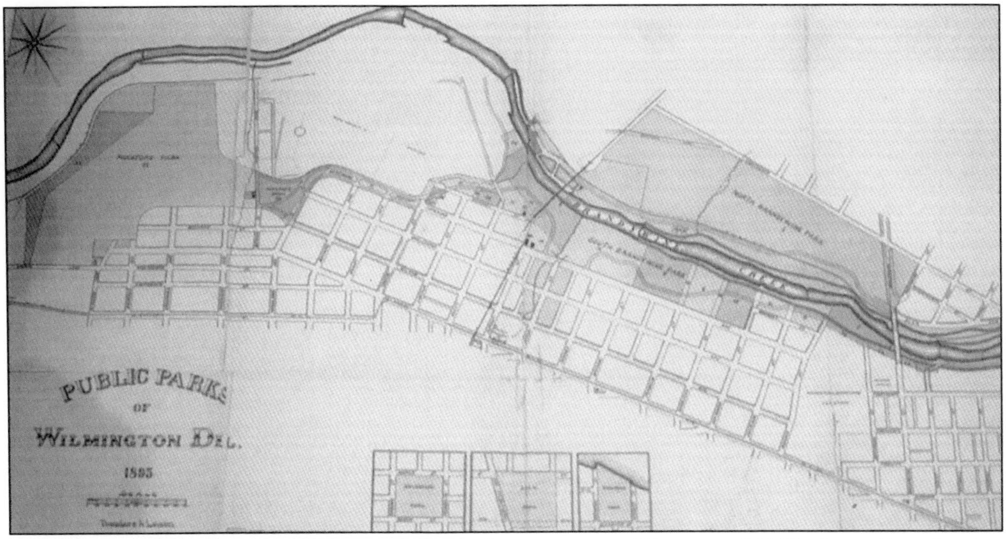

This map, published in the Wilmington Park Commissioners' Report of 1895, shows Brandywine and Rockford Parks with their connector, Kentmere Parkway. The parkway was essentially a design of the famous landscape architect, Frederic Law Olmsted, who William Bancroft personally contacted for assistance with park design. (Courtesy of the Wilmington Parks and Recreation Department.)

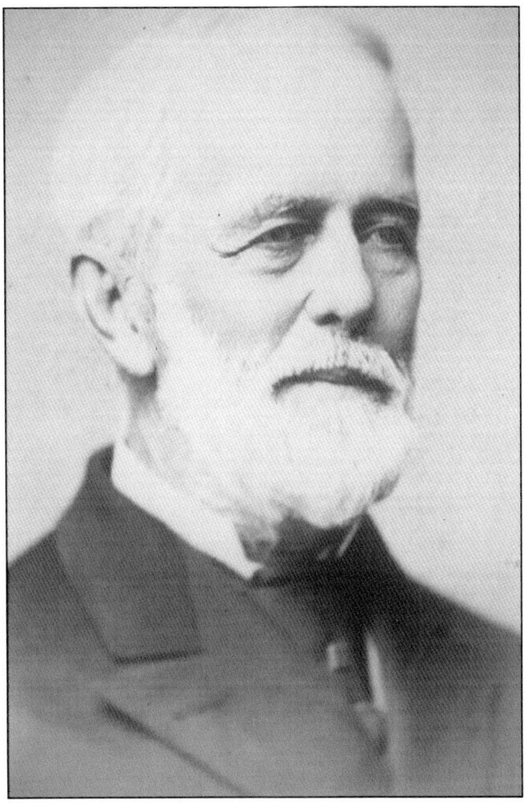

William M. Canby was president of the first Park Commission. Although his business was banking, Canby was a skilled botanist who traveled with John Muir, supervised a botanical survey for the Northern Pacific Railway, and founded the Delaware Society of Natural History. As a cousin and friend of William P. Bancroft, the two men worked together in planning Wilmington's parks. (Courtesy of the Historical Society of Delaware.)

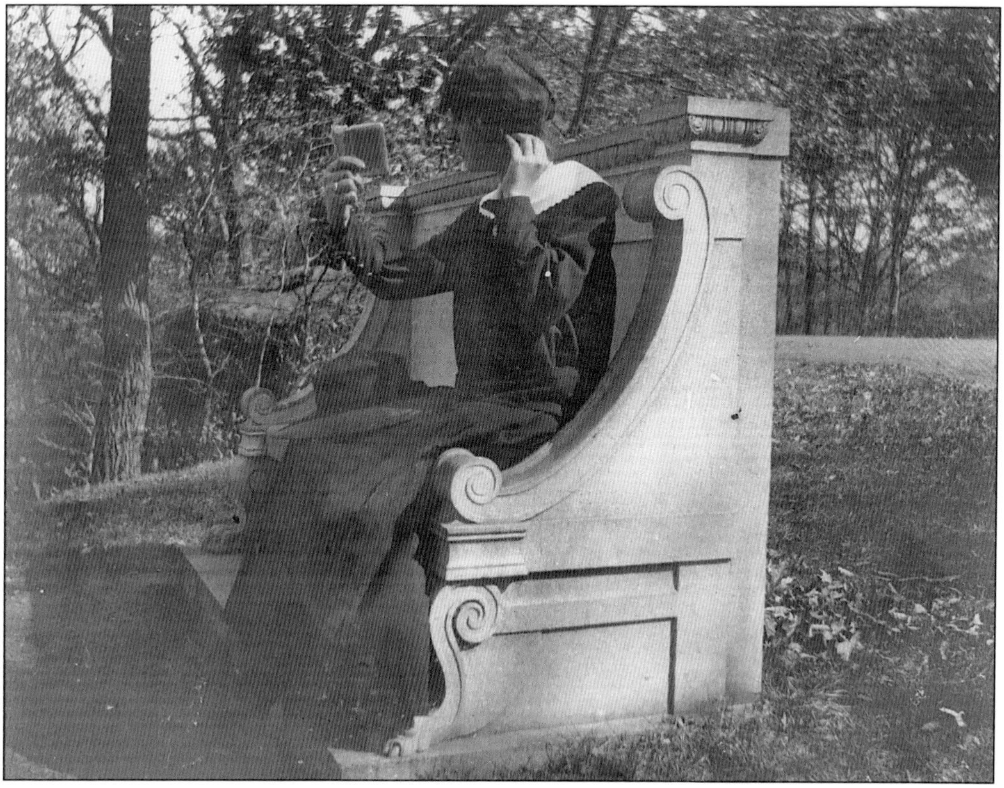

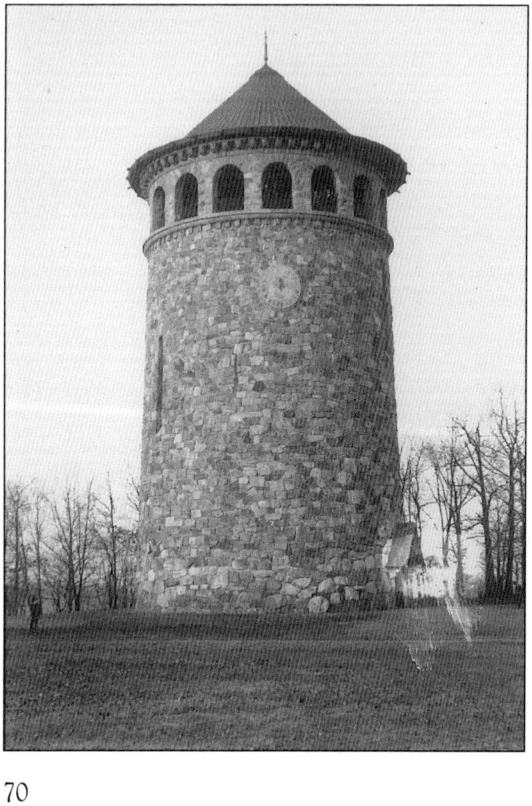

Frank R. Zebley's model posed here on the "Canby Seat," named because it overlooks William M. Canby's favorite view. Today, the view includes the DuPont Experimental Station. It took many years for William Bancroft to convince E.I. du Pont de Nemours & Co. to contribute this land; the company feared that the steep rocky hillside below might be more of a danger than an asset to the park. (Courtesy of the Delaware State Archives.)

Rockford Tower, built in 1900, is a Wilmington landmark. Its observation area was a popular destination with early park visitors. Many people are surprised to learn that the tower is also a part of the Wilmington water supply. It contains a 40-foot-wide by 60-foot-high steel standpipe with a capacity of 500,000 gallons that supplies the western section of the city and nearby suburbs. (Courtesy of the Delaware State Archives.)

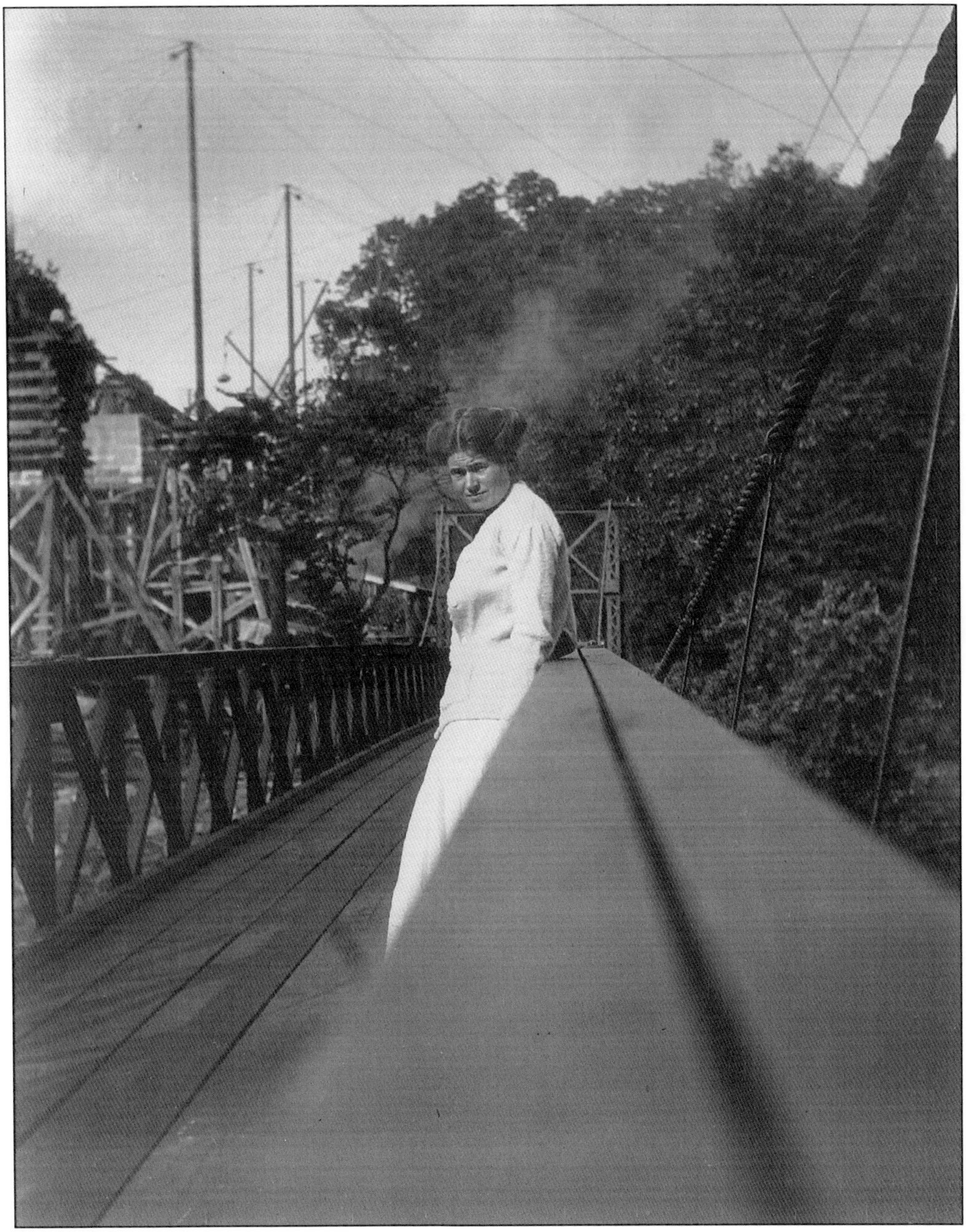

The swinging bridge, a pedestrian crossing on the upper Brandywine, provided an idyllic background for this 1910 photograph of Dorothy V. Lee (Mrs. Cosgrove G. Lee Jr.). The bridge is still a popular attraction in Brandywine Park and gets it name because it often moves slightly when people walk on it. Originally, the bridge made a convenient crossing to the paper mills on the north side of the river. The parks and parkways along the Brandywine have been one of Wilmington's most attractive assets for over 100 years. They have been a favorite spot for photographers, whether they were amateurs snapping their friends and family, early professionals posing models for stereopticon cards, or modern professionals looking for scenes of beauty. (Courtesy of the Hagley Museum and Library.)

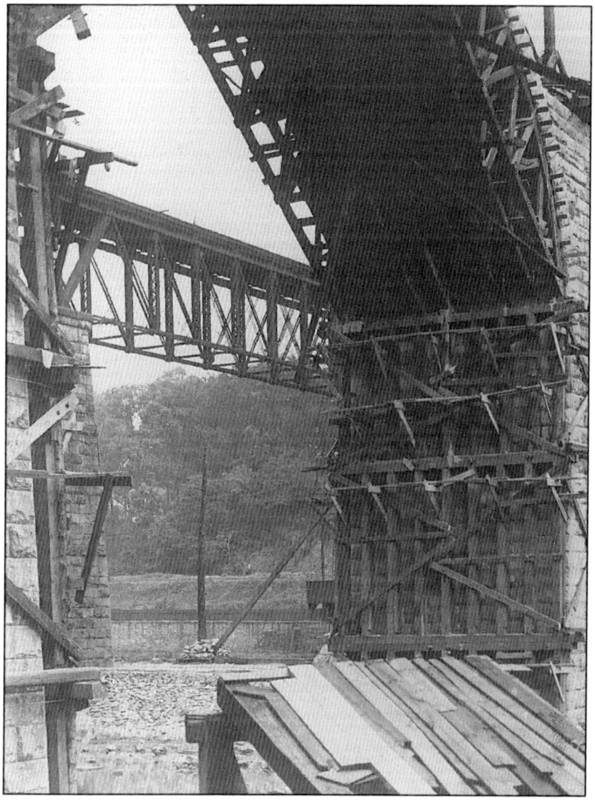

In the background is the original Baltimore & Ohio (B&O) Railroad bridge that later became an automobile bridge at the Augustine cut-off. The large stone arches are part of the construction of the new railroad bridge that the company began in 1909 to carry its faster trains. (Courtesy of the Hagley Museum and Library.)

In this photograph, a train is crossing the new B&O Railroad bridge, while a portion of the old bridge is still visible in the background. The photo dates from about the 1930s, but Zebley has dressed his model in clothes to evoke an earlier time. (Courtesy of the Delaware State Archives.)

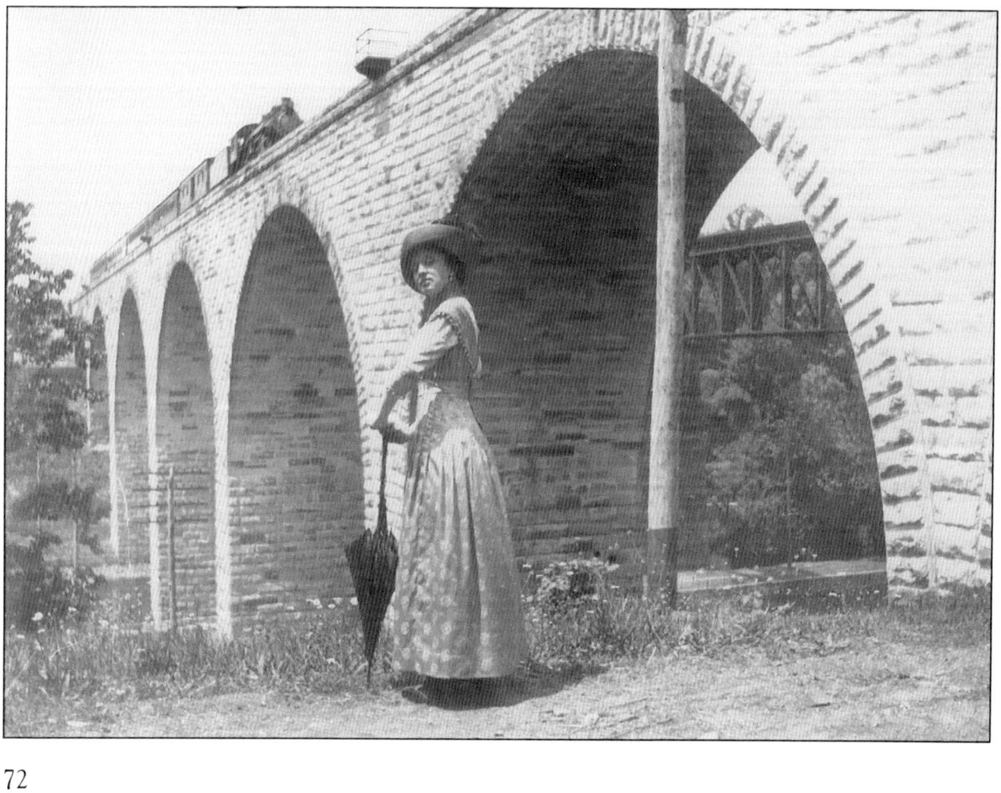

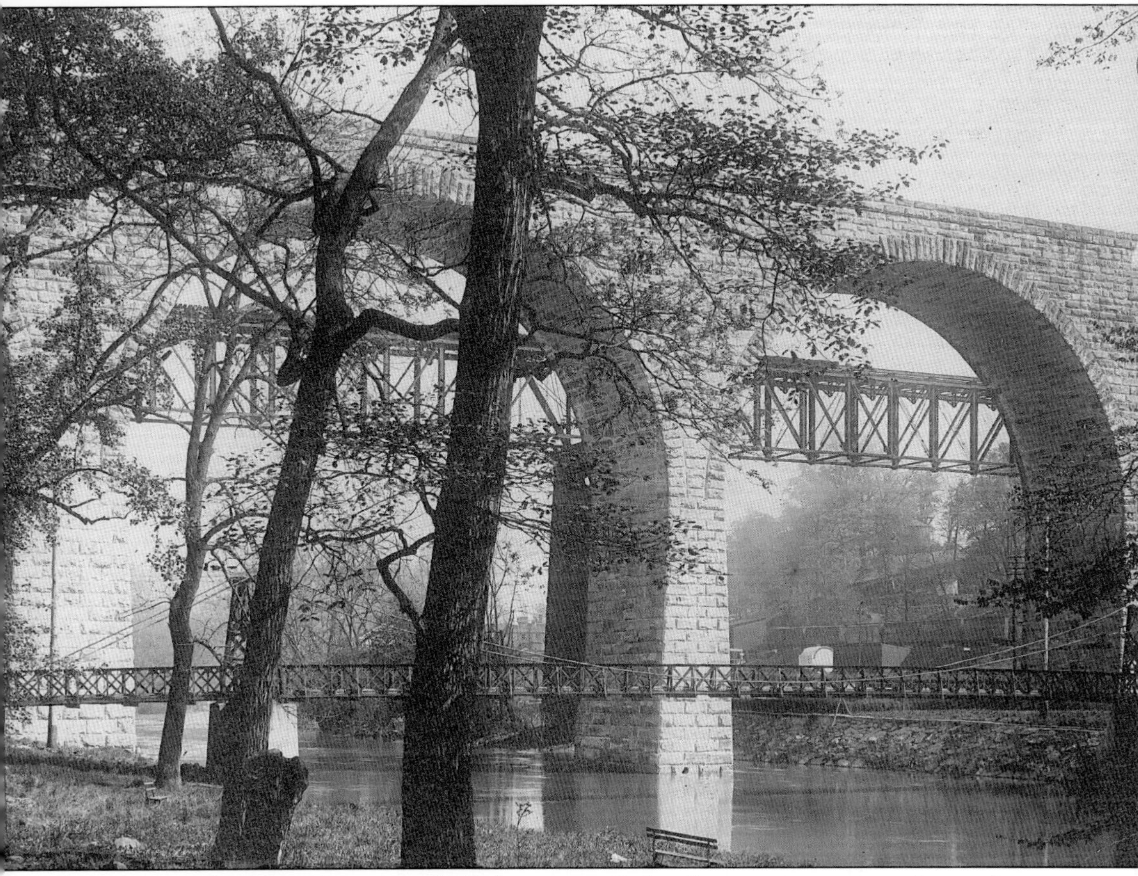

This photograph, taken for an early-20th-century Parks Commission report, shows three Brandywine River bridges clustered together. In the foreground is the swinging bridge, behind it is the completed B&O Railroad bridge, and in the background is the old B&O bridge. This view is taken from the south side of the river looking upstream. In the background, beneath the far arch of the bridge, boxcars and sheds are evidence of industrial activity. In the foreground is a park bench because this bank had become a part of South Brandywine Park, while the north side was still privately owned industrial property. (Courtesy of the Wilmington Parks and Recreation Department.)

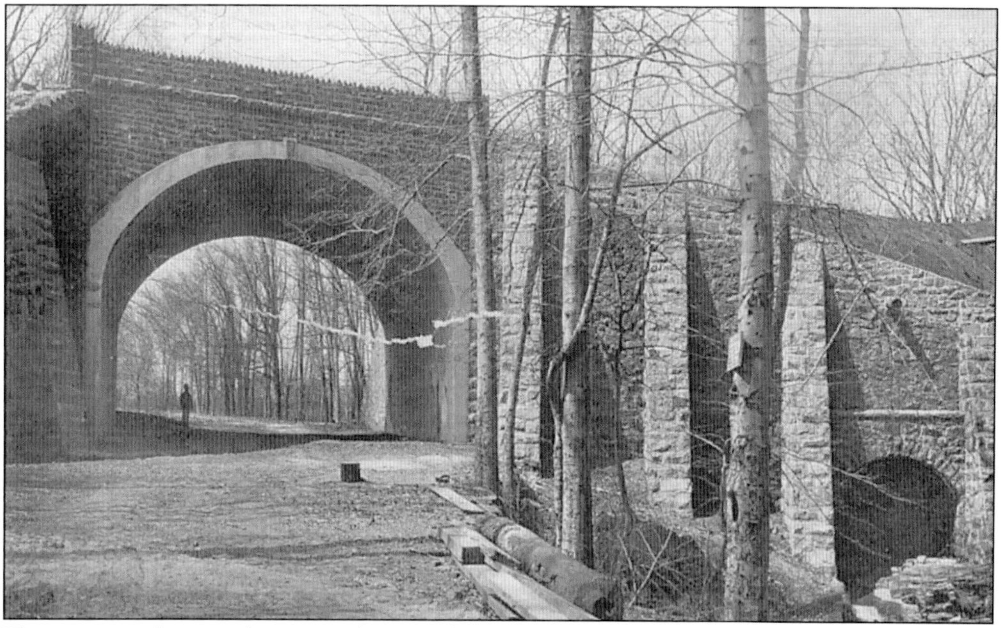

The stone roadway in this 1901 photograph carries Lovering Avenue across Rattlesnake Run, once a tributary of the Brandywine. A map of 1876 shows this as a stream running from Delaware Avenue to the river. Today, this part of Rattlesnake Run near the river is usually dry, and the small tunnel is filled in. Many of the trees are now gone, but the county has landscaping plans. (Courtesy of the Wilmington Parks and Recreation Department.)

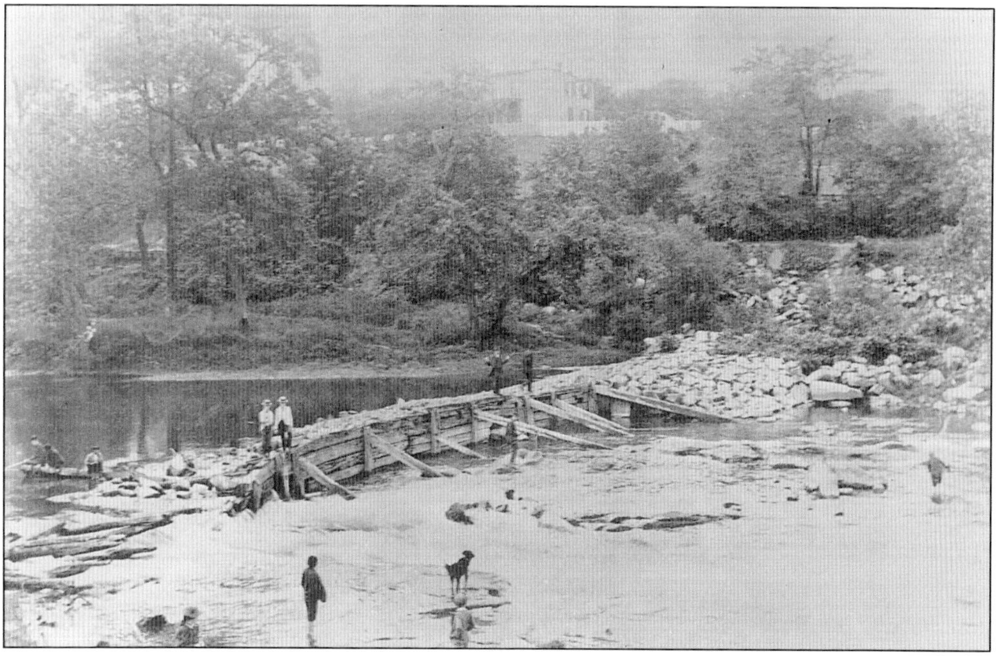

The photographer, Joseph Maybin, took this picture of the old Third Dam in about 1870. Just downstream from Rattlesnake Run, this dam diverted water into the races that ran alongside the river from here to about Market Street. The race has provided water to the Water Department since 1827. (Courtesy of the Hagley Museum and Library.)

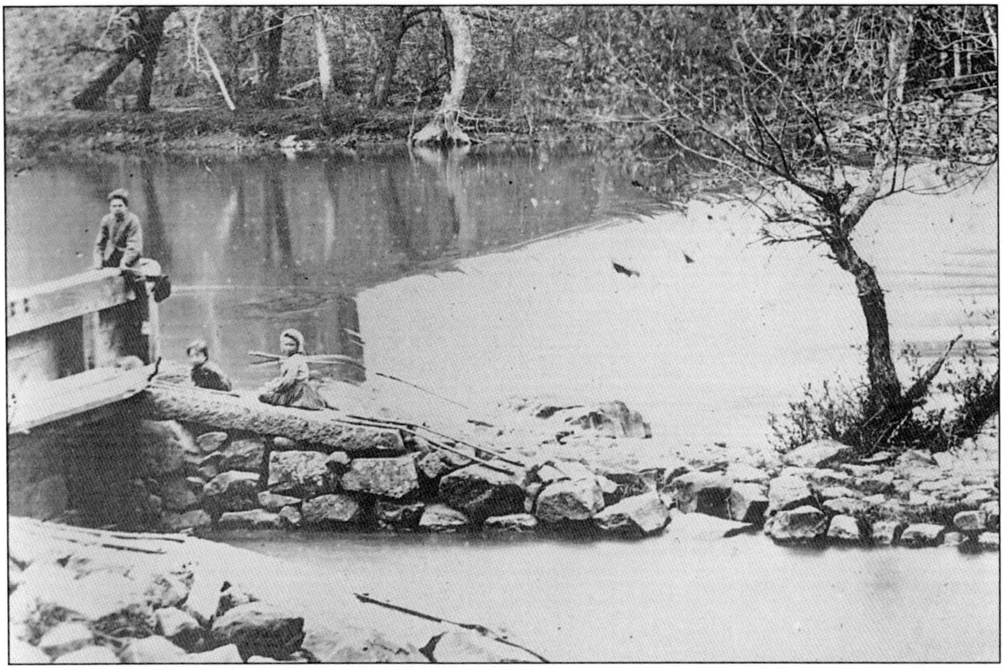

Here is another group relaxing and playing near the riverbank at the old Third Dam in about 1870. Long before the creation of Brandywine Park, the river was a magnet for Wilmington residents seeking respite from the clamor of the industrial city. (Courtesy of the Hagley Museum and Library.)

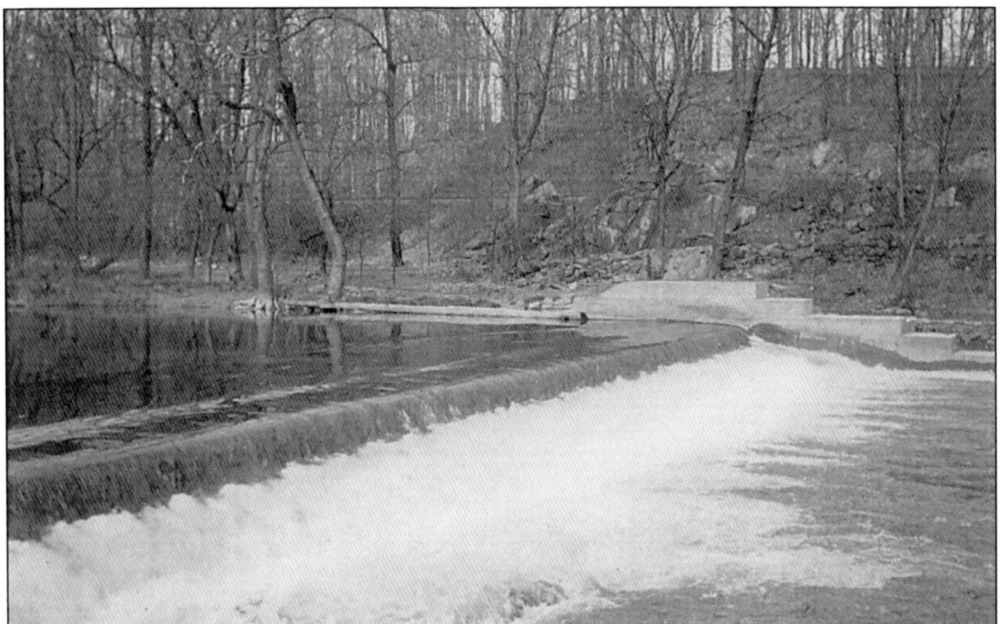

The new Third Dam, as shown in a 1902 Parks Commission photograph, replaced the old dam and served the same general purpose. The Department of Public Works rebuilt the dam in 1999, but it still looks much like this with concrete structures at the sides. (Courtesy of the Wilmington Parks and Recreation Department.)

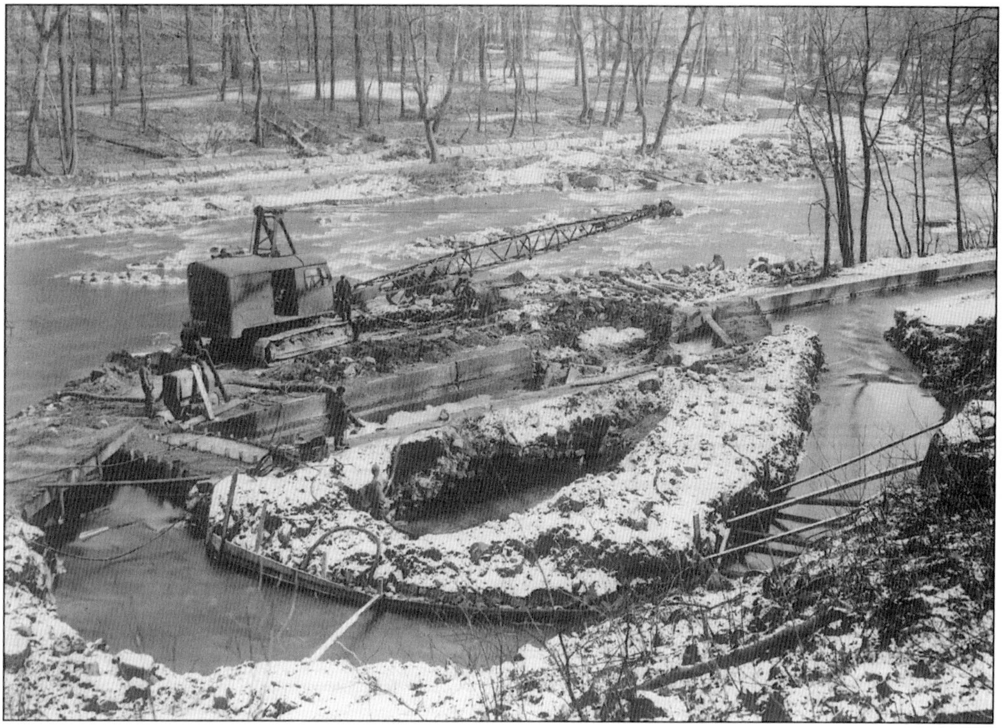

In this photo of January 16, 1948, men and machinery are at work rebuilding the head gates of the water department race. This view is from the south bank of the river looking downstream. In the foreground, the water is running from the river into the race. (Courtesy of the Delaware State Archives)

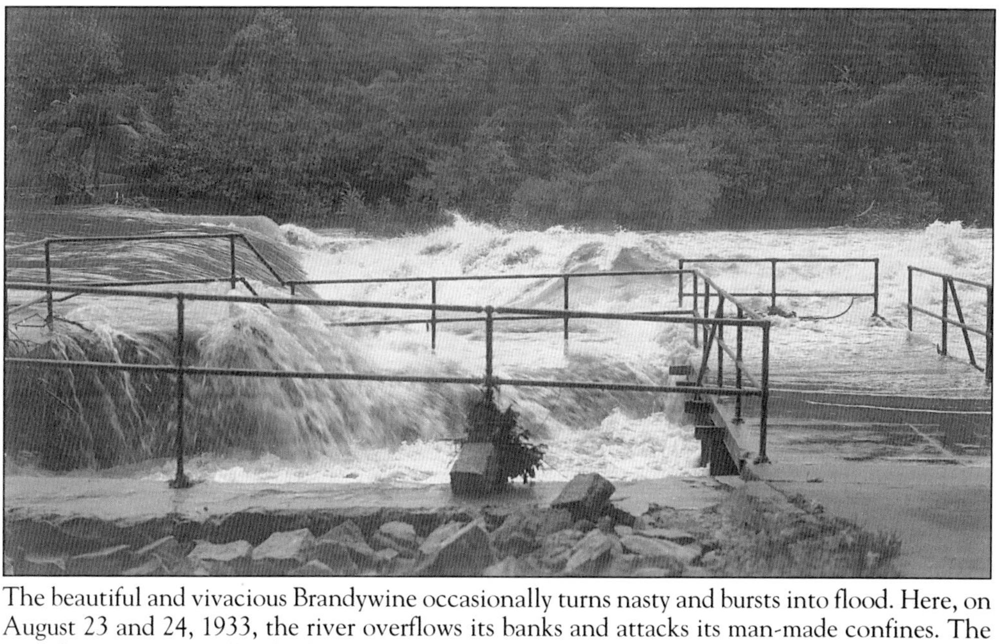

The beautiful and vivacious Brandywine occasionally turns nasty and bursts into flood. Here, on August 23 and 24, 1933, the river overflows its banks and attacks its man-made confines. The Brandywine continually challenges park managers with its flooding and erosion that destroys vegetation along its banks.(Courtesy of the Wilmington Parks and Recreation Department.)

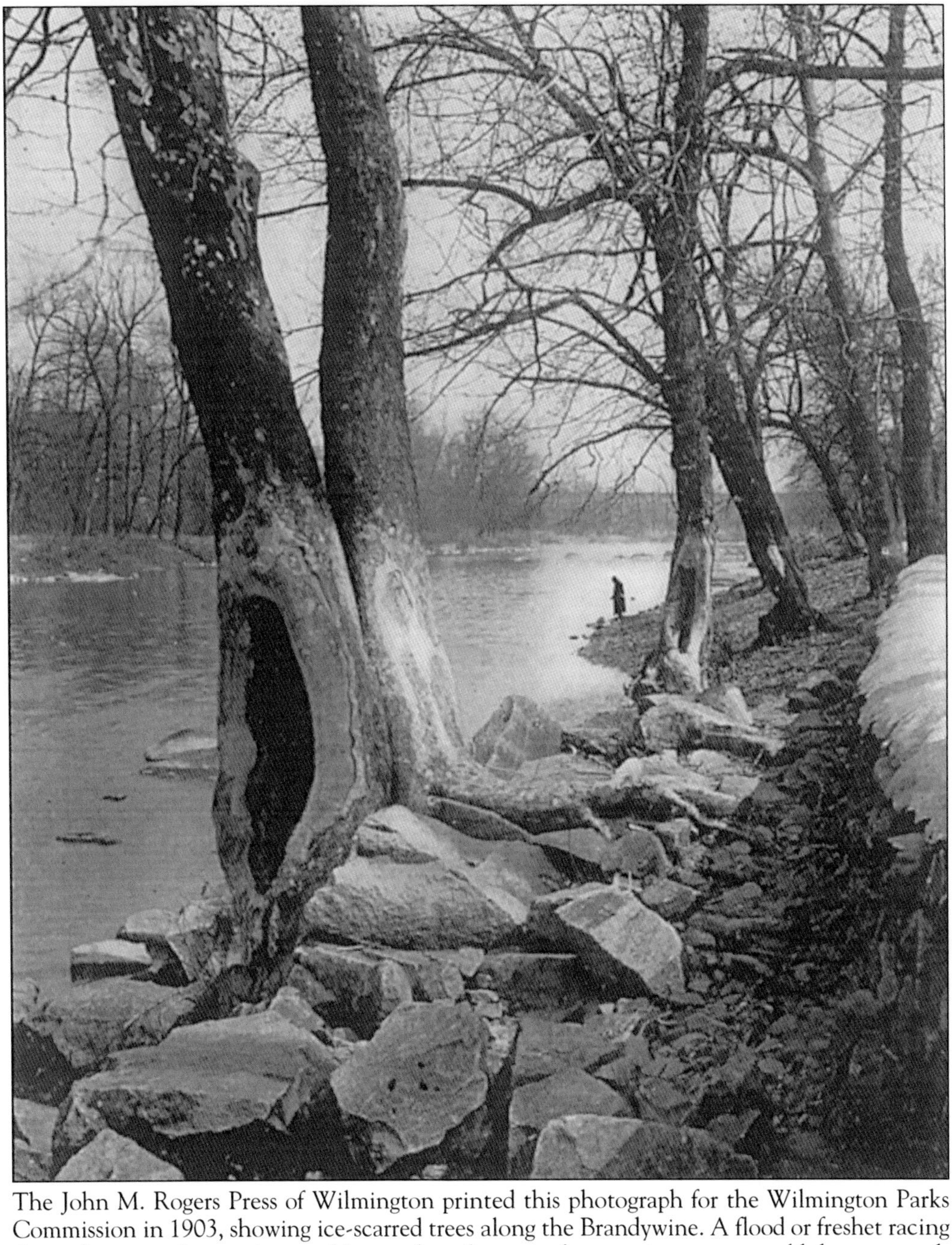

The John M. Rogers Press of Wilmington printed this photograph for the Wilmington Parks Commission in 1903, showing ice-scarred trees along the Brandywine. A flood or freshet racing down the river after a winter cold enough to freeze its fast-moving waters could damage much more than trees. A flood of February 1822 swept away a large part of the famous Gilpin Mills that produced paper. Three years later, the Brandywine tore off another section of the mills. Although Joseph and Thomas Gilpin had patented the process of making paper in continuous rolls, a great advance over the previous method of making single sheets, the damage to the buildings persuaded the owners to sell the property, which eventually became a cotton mill. Another flood nearly destroyed the early Bancroft Mills, but the young owner persevered and the business prospered. (Courtesy of the Wilmington Parks and Recreation Department.)

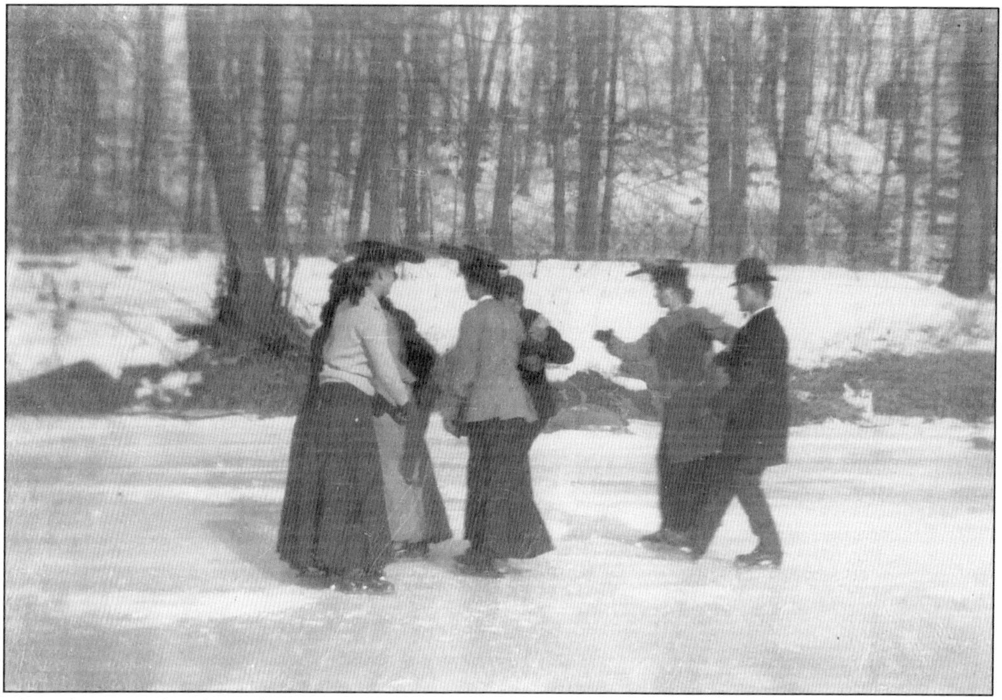

This photograph of ice skating on the Brandywine appears to date from the late 19th century. However, Zebley probably took it in the 1930s, another of his scenes of people in costume representing an earlier time. (Courtesy of the Delaware State Archives.)

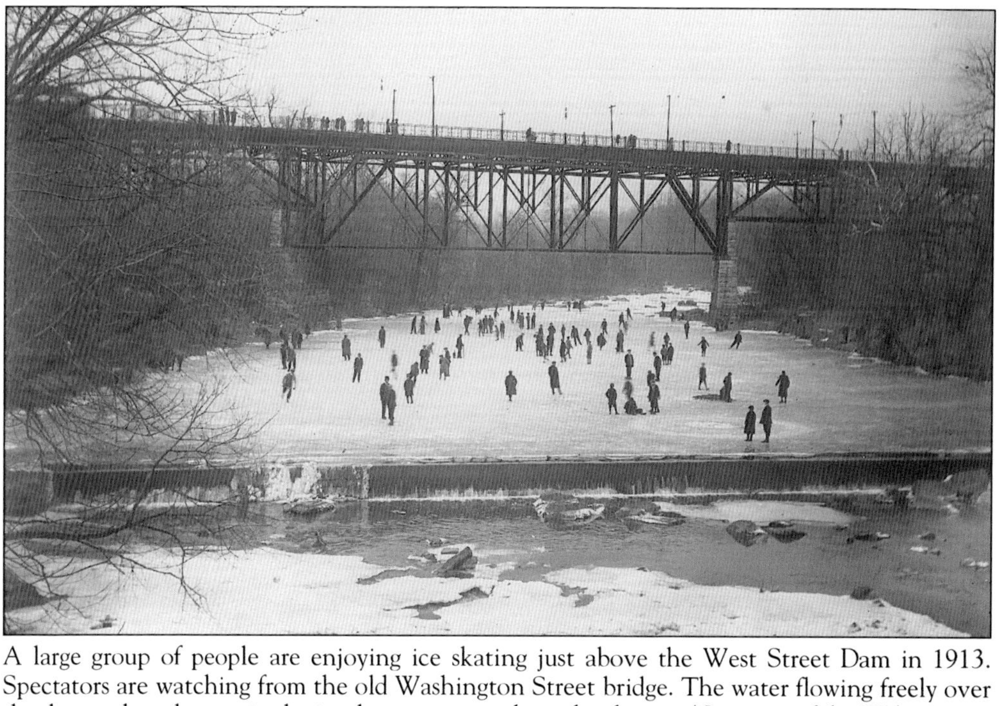

A large group of people are enjoying ice skating just above the West Street Dam in 1913. Spectators are watching from the old Washington Street bridge. The water flowing freely over the dam and weak spots in the ice do not seem to deter the skaters. (Courtesy of the Wilmington Parks and Recreation Department.)

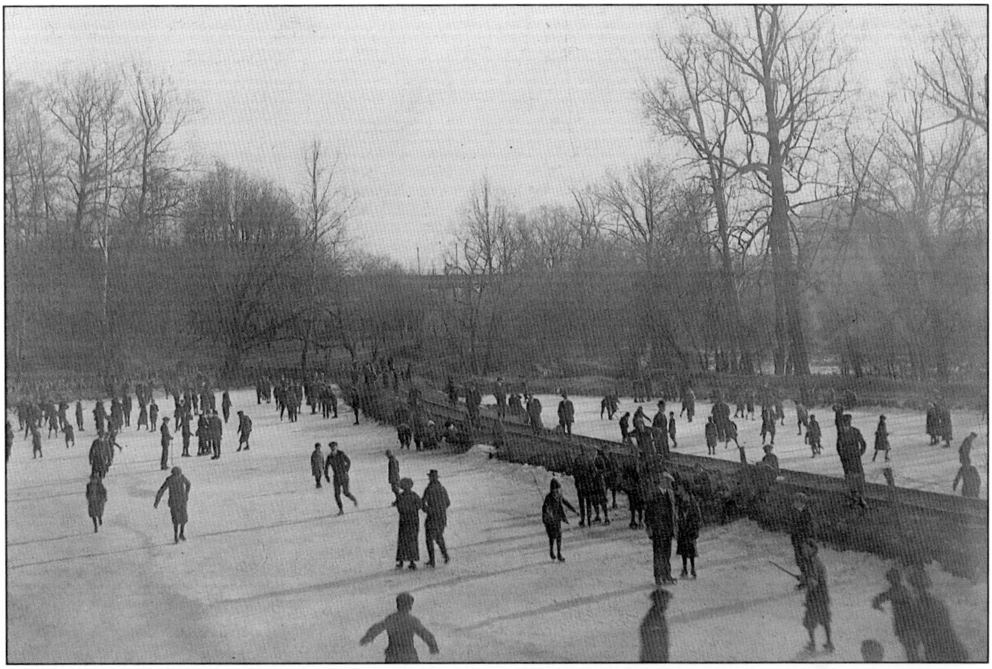

Ice skaters of all ages are enjoying skating on ponds beside the Brandywine and near the zoo in this photograph of 1914. The outline of the park bandstand shows faintly through the trees to the left of the old Washington Street bridge in the background. (Courtesy of the Wilmington Parks and Recreation Department.)

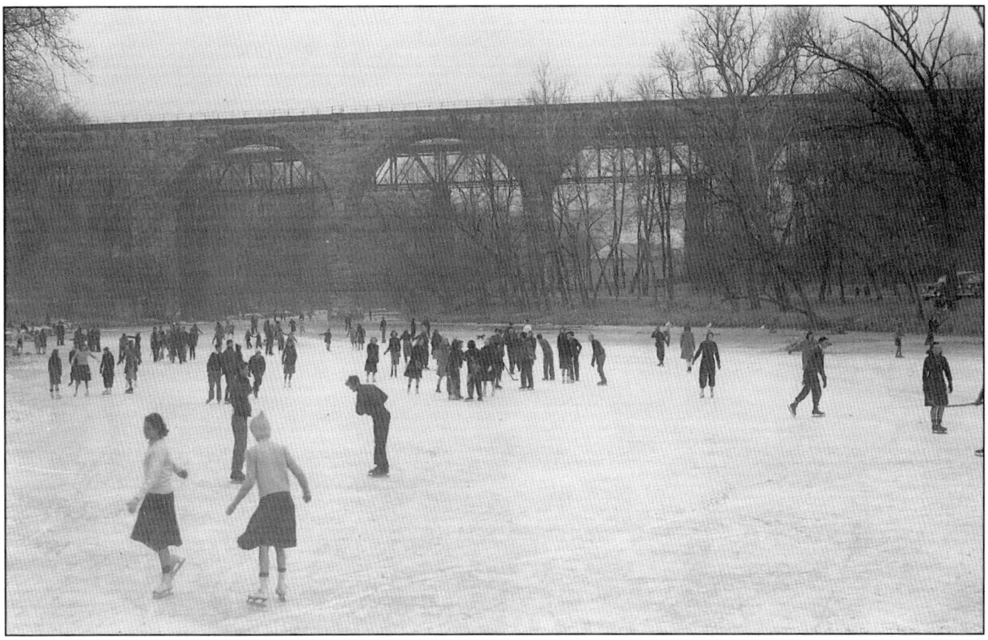

Ice skaters are wearing shorter skirts as they enjoy their sport on the Brandywine in the 1940s. They are above the Third Dam, and the new Baltimore and Ohio Railroad bridge is in the background as the photographer faces upstream. (Courtesy of the Wilmington Parks and Recreation Department.)

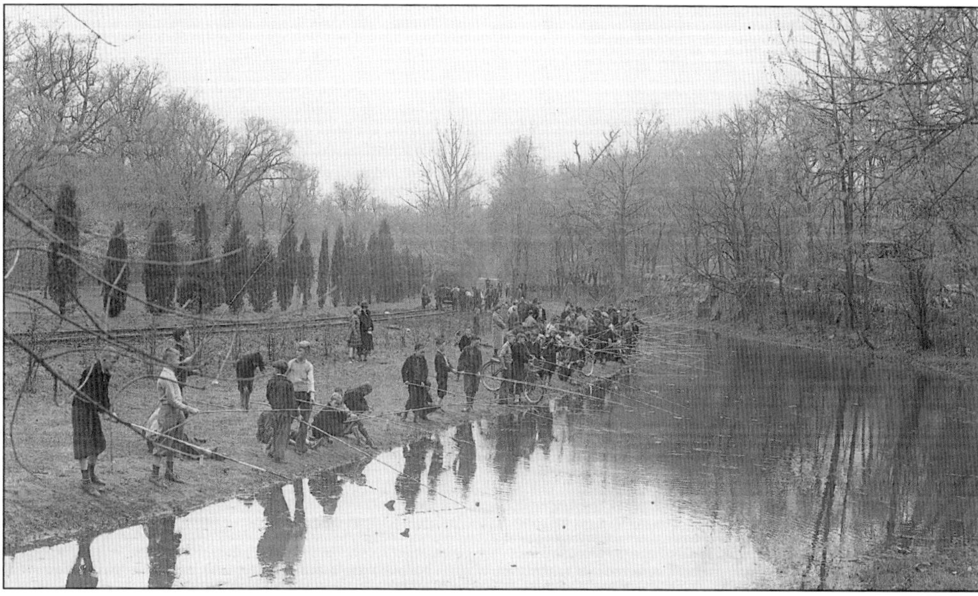

Workers push a small car along the railroad spur to the mills as a crowd of young people gather to fish in the same ponds beside the Brandywine where they could have been skating in the winter. Fishing has always been popular on the Brandywine, but this is a pretty large group for such a small pond. (Courtesy of the Wilmington Parks and Recreation Department.)

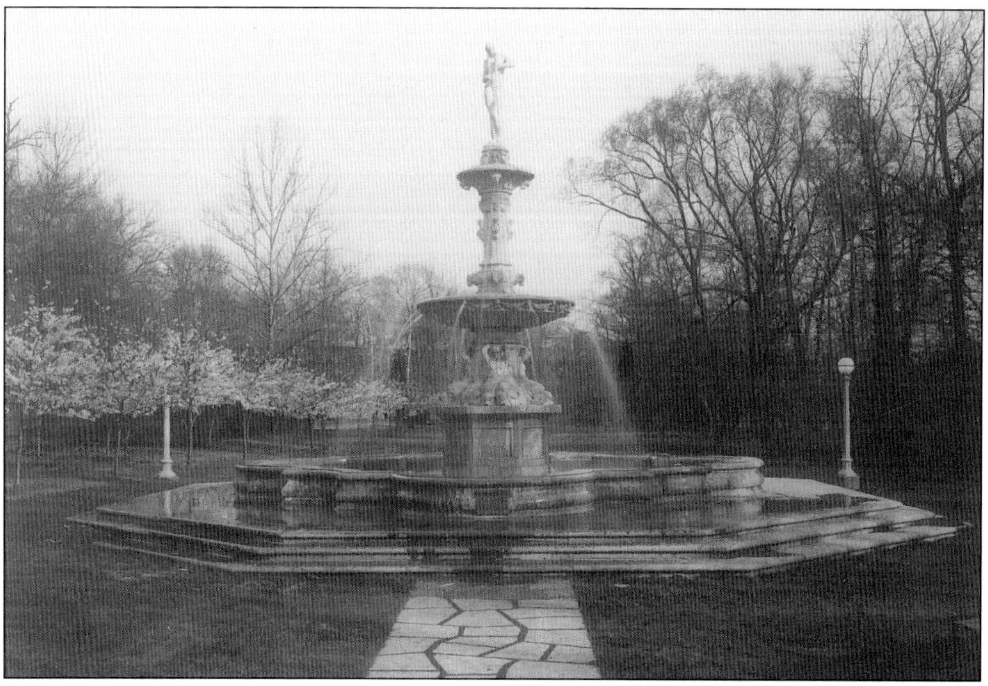

In 1930, Gen. J. Ernest Smith gave money to fill in the pond shown in the above picture and to plant Japanese cherry trees. The following year, his wife, Josephine, died, and Smith provided funds to build an ornamental fountain in her memory, creating a trust fund to maintain it. The Josephine Gardens, shown here in 1933, are where the Brandywine Arts Festival has been held since 1961. (Courtesy of the Historical Society of Delaware.)

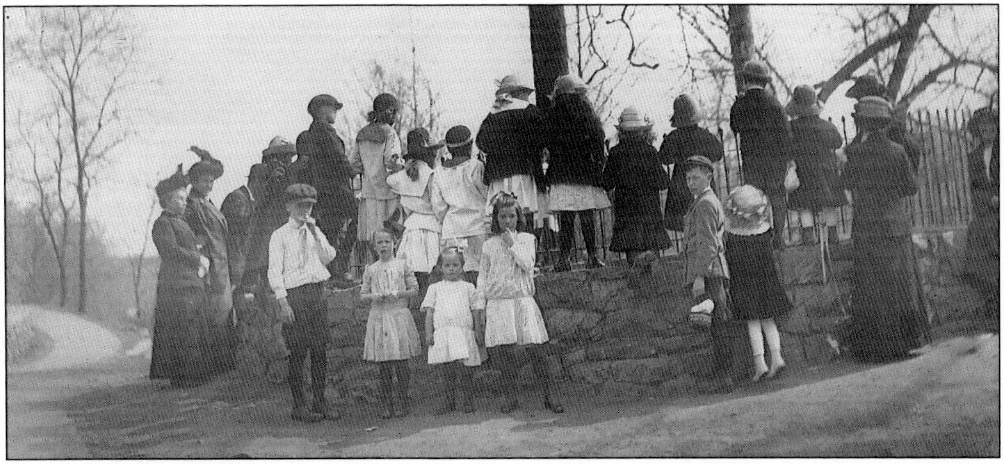

A group of children accompanied by a few adults crowd around the bear pit at the zoo in North Brandywine Park. Unfortunately, we cannot see the bears, but in this 1915 photo, some of the children seem to be just as interested in the photographer. (Courtesy of the Wilmington Parks and Recreation Department.)

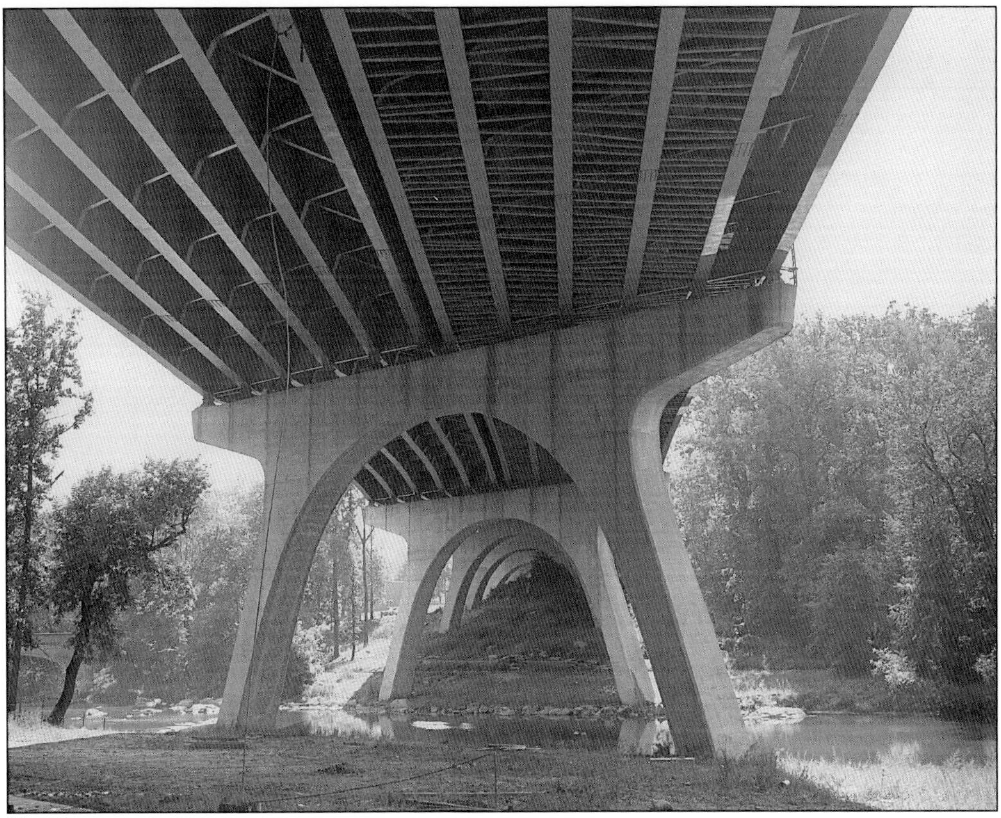

The location of Interstate Highway 95 was the subject of heated debate in Wilmington. The final decision was to cut a swath through the Adams-Jackson Street area and cross the Brandywine west of Washington Street. Demolition of residential areas began in 1959, and construction of the I-95 bridge, shown here, began soon after. (Courtesy of the Wilmington Parks and Recreation Department.)

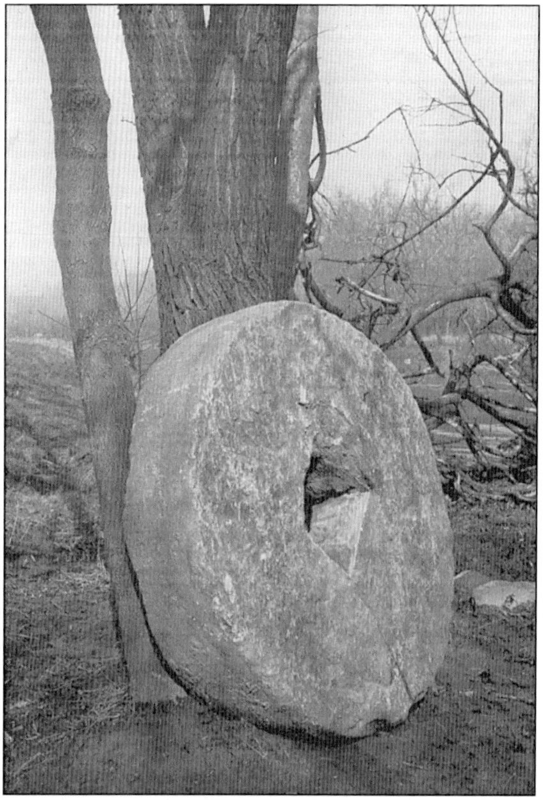

The Park Commissioners' Report of 1905 included this photograph of the millstone from the old Barley Mill. The mill, which was on the river in the general vicinity of Adams Street, has been the subject of many romantic reminiscences and paintings of Wilmington. (Courtesy of the Wilmington Parks and Recreation Department.)

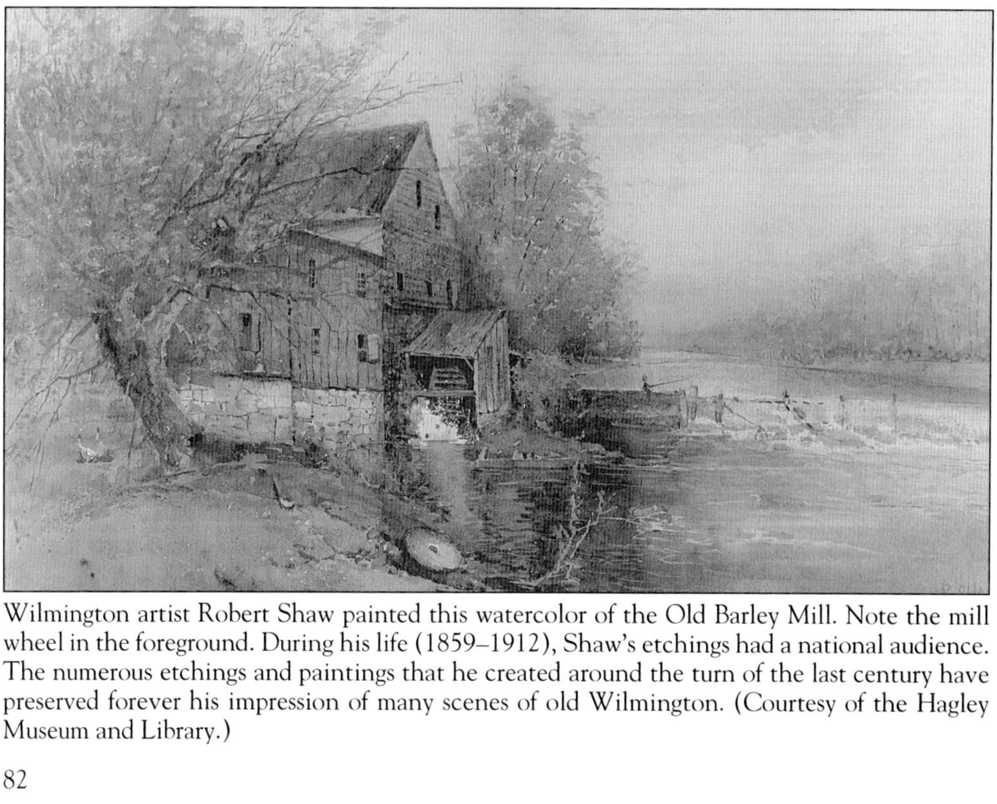

Wilmington artist Robert Shaw painted this watercolor of the Old Barley Mill. Note the mill wheel in the foreground. During his life (1859–1912), Shaw's etchings had a national audience. The numerous etchings and paintings that he created around the turn of the last century have preserved forever his impression of many scenes of old Wilmington. (Courtesy of the Hagley Museum and Library.)

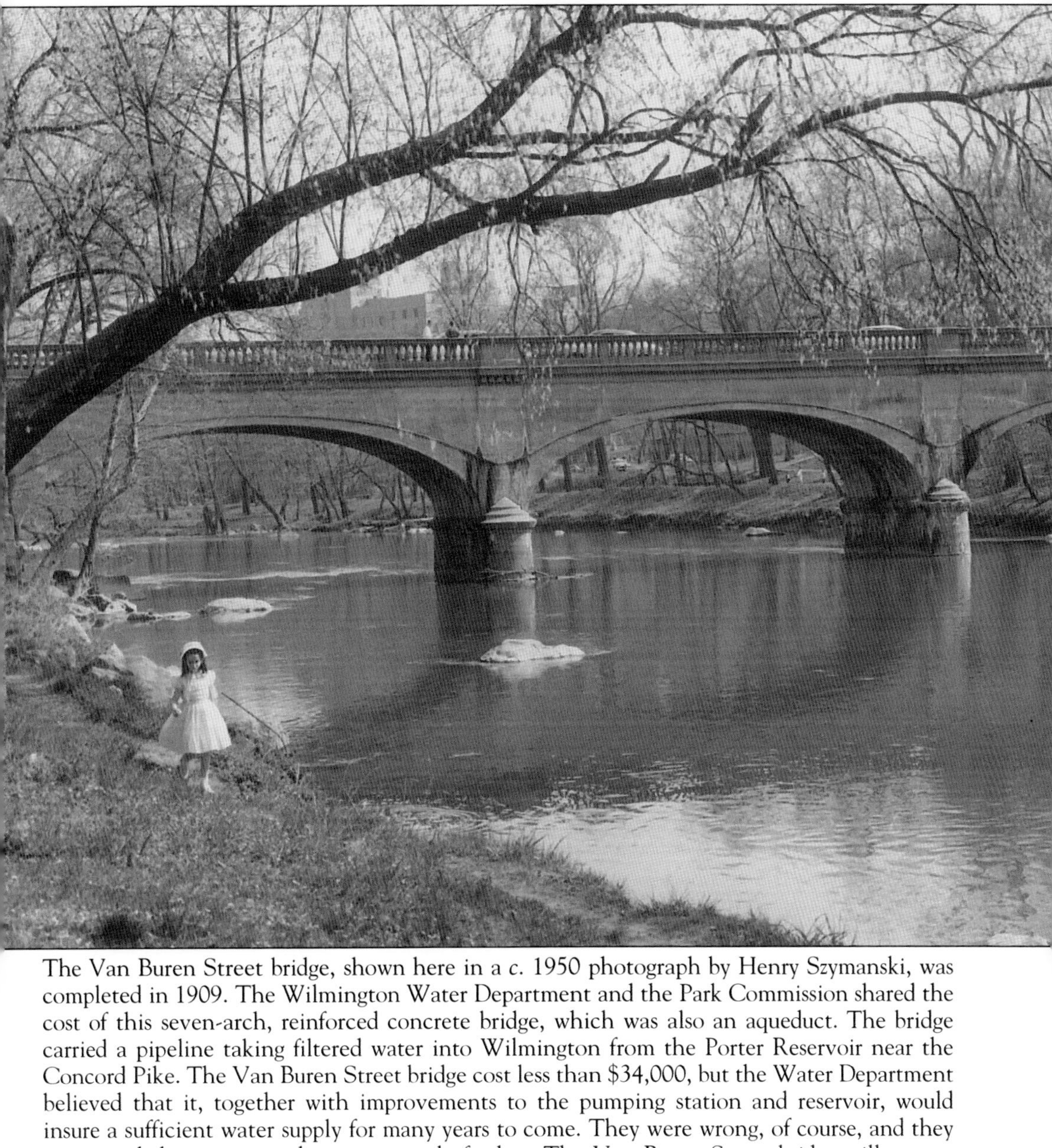

The Van Buren Street bridge, shown here in a *c.* 1950 photograph by Henry Szymanski, was completed in 1909. The Wilmington Water Department and the Park Commission shared the cost of this seven-arch, reinforced concrete bridge, which was also an aqueduct. The bridge carried a pipeline taking filtered water into Wilmington from the Porter Reservoir near the Concord Pike. The Van Buren Street bridge cost less than $34,000, but the Water Department believed that it, together with improvements to the pumping station and reservoir, would insure a sufficient water supply for many years to come. They were wrong, of course, and they soon needed to increase the water supply further. The Van Buren Street bridge still crosses the Brandywine but is no longer an aqueduct. Rebuilding of the bridge in the 1990s moved the water into a pipe that goes beneath the Brandywine. (Courtesy of the Wilmington Parks and Recreation Department.)

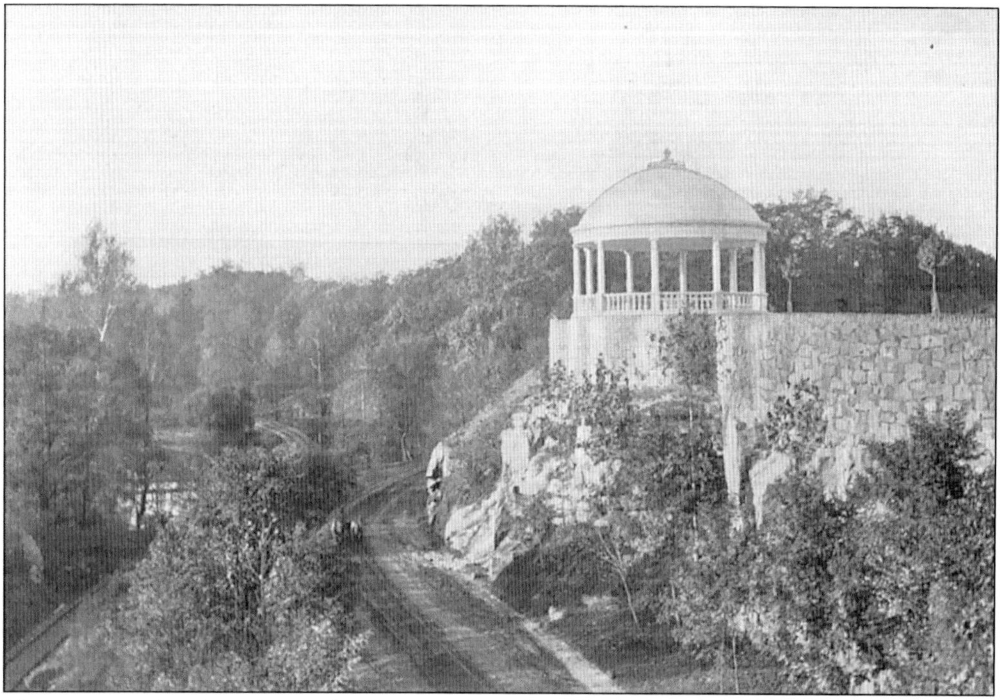

The gazebo or bandstand with the dome roof stood in Washington Heights near the north end of the Washington Street bridge. The stone wall that supports it shows up well in this picture, which appeared in the 1902 report of the Wilmington Park Commission. (Courtesy of the Wilmington Parks and Recreation Department.)

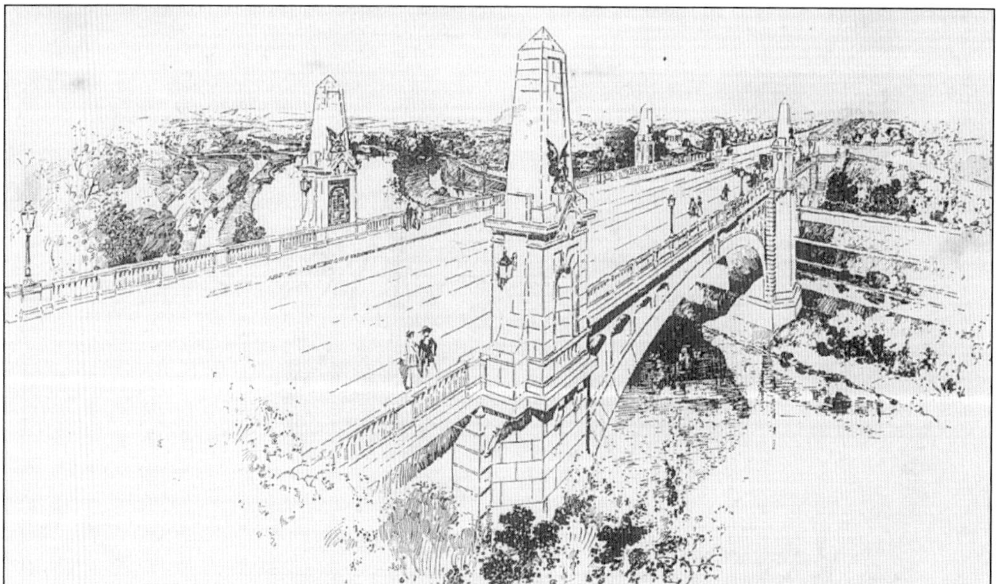

A 1919 sketch shows the proposed new Washington Street Memorial Bridge. It replaced an older bridge at this spot and is a memorial to Delawareans who died in World War I. Their names are inscribed on tablets on the bridge. (Courtesy of the Wilmington Parks and Recreation Department.)

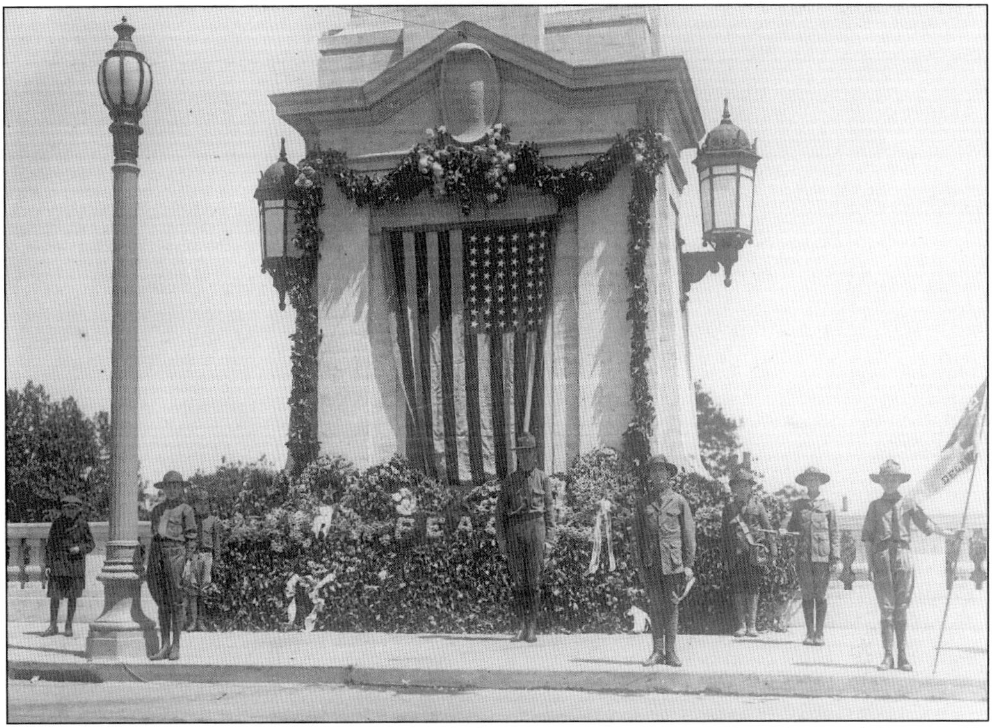

The Washington Street Memorial Bridge dedication service on May 30, Memorial Day, 1922, appropriately included veterans of World War I. Although this photograph from the Sanborn Collection does not specify the precise location, it is probably at the pylon where the names of the World War I dead are listed. (Courtesy of the Historical Society of Delaware.)

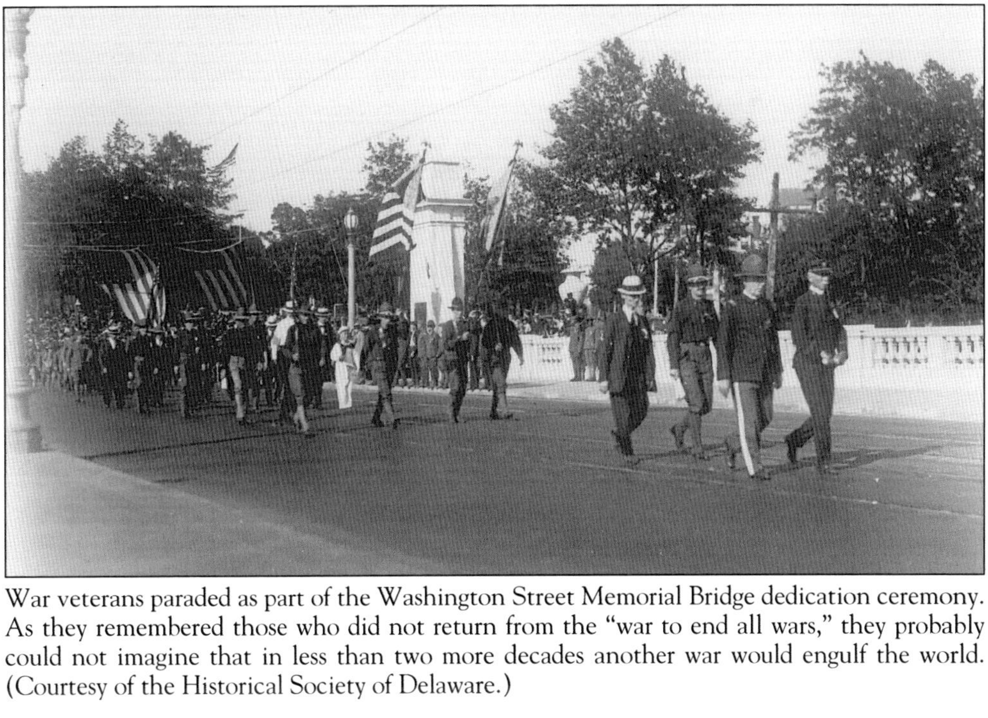

War veterans paraded as part of the Washington Street Memorial Bridge dedication ceremony. As they remembered those who did not return from the "war to end all wars," they probably could not imagine that in less than two more decades another war would engulf the world. (Courtesy of the Historical Society of Delaware.)

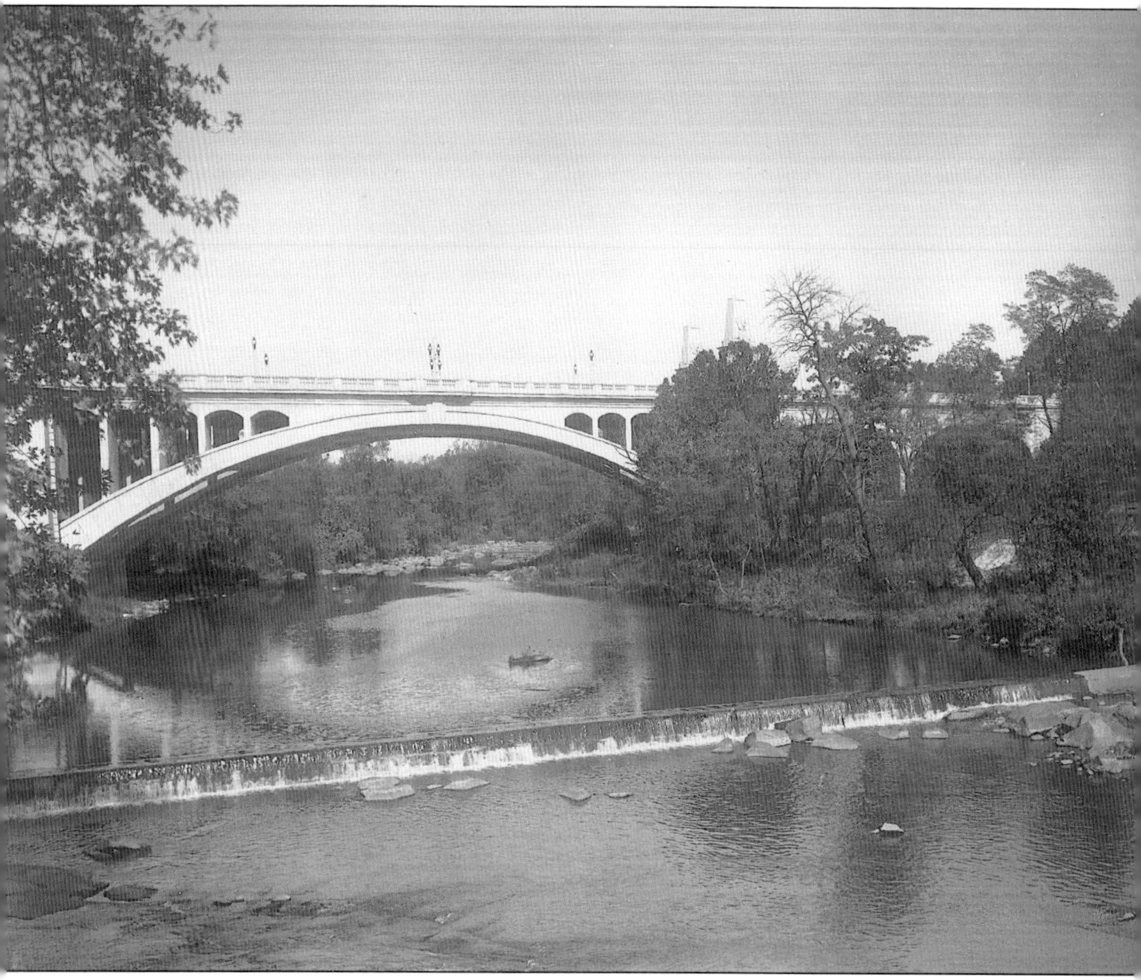

A peaceful scene of October 21, 1925, shows the Washington Street Memorial Bridge just a few years after it was built. Alfred I. du Pont chaired the commission that oversaw the construction of the bridge. Other commission members were Benjamin F. Shaw, John S. Rossell, Isaac C. Elliott, and Albert Stetser. Vance W. Torbert was the architect responsible for the design, and Benjamin H. Davis was the engineer. While the names of the World War I dead are on one pylon, the other pylons list the names of those involved in the planning and construction of the bridge. The width of the bridge, its architectural style, its pedestrian walkways, and the pleasant areas at both ends make it the city's grandest bridge. (Courtesy of the Delaware State Archives.)

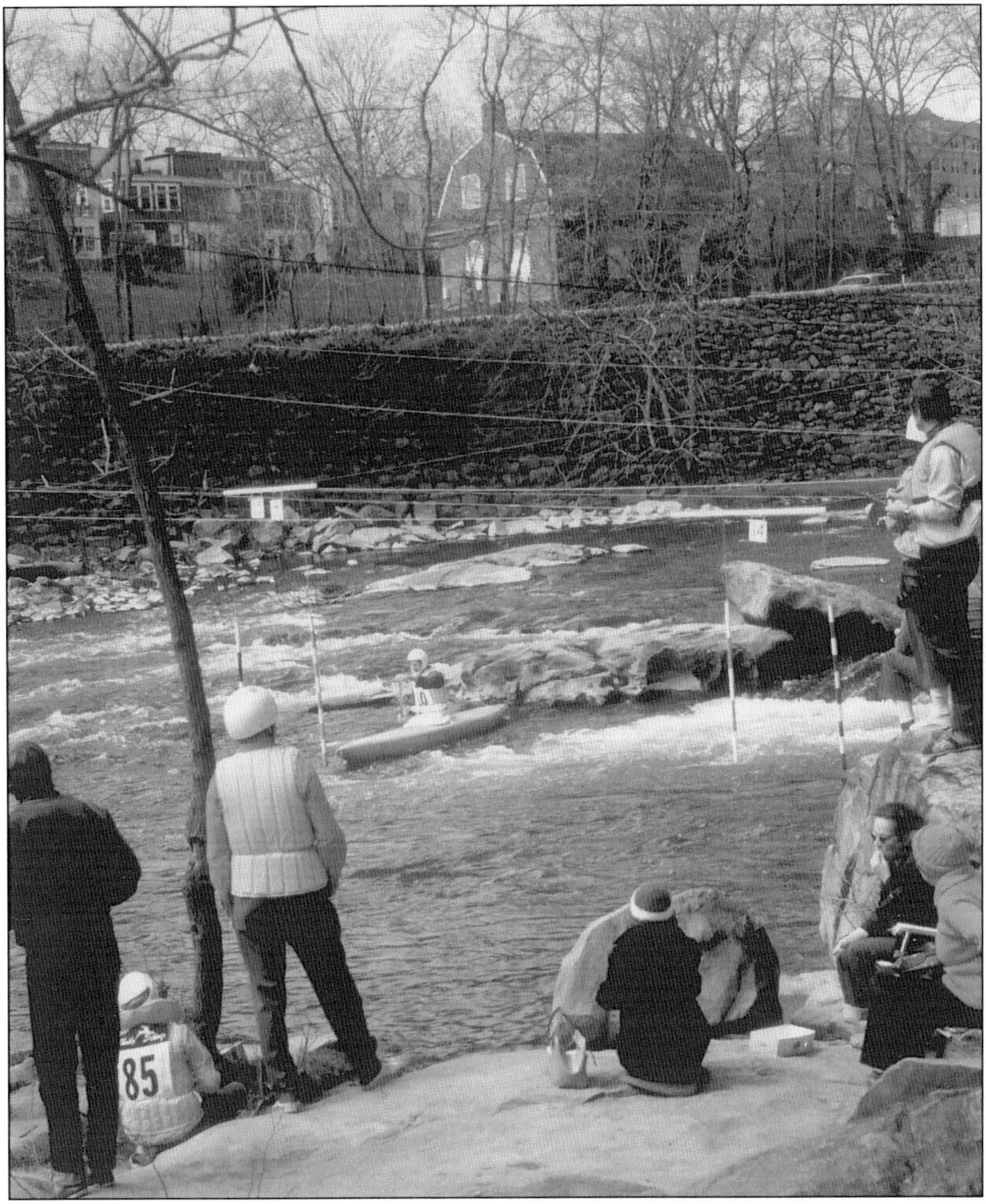

This photograph of the 1970s shows a kayak slalom race. While one participant works his way through the gates set up in the river, others watch from the north bank. The Philadelphia Canoe Club sponsored annual kayak races, which were a popular event for many years. Competitors came from a wide area, and the races attracted hundreds of spectators. This photo, taken from the north bank of the river, shows the old First Presbyterian Church that originally stood on Market Street between Ninth and Tenth Streets and was built in 1740. The congregation eventually expanded to a larger church, and by 1879, the historical society occupied the building. When the construction of the new library meant the demolition of the old church, Pierre S. du Pont gave funds for restoration if the city would move it to another location. The city agreed to move the old church to this spot on public park land, and it became the home of the Colonial Dames.

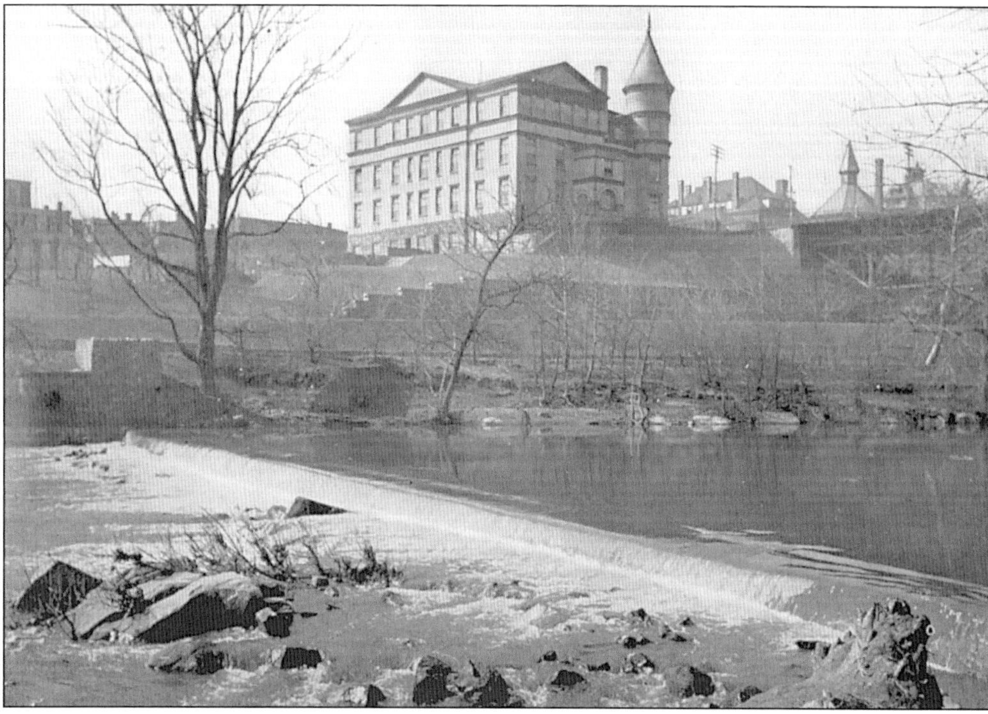

The Park Commissioners' Report of 1905 included this picture taken the previous year of the new first dam on the Brandywine. In the background is the Washington Street School with its round tower. To the right of the school, the old Washington Street bridge is visible. (Courtesy of the Wilmington Parks and Recreation Department.)

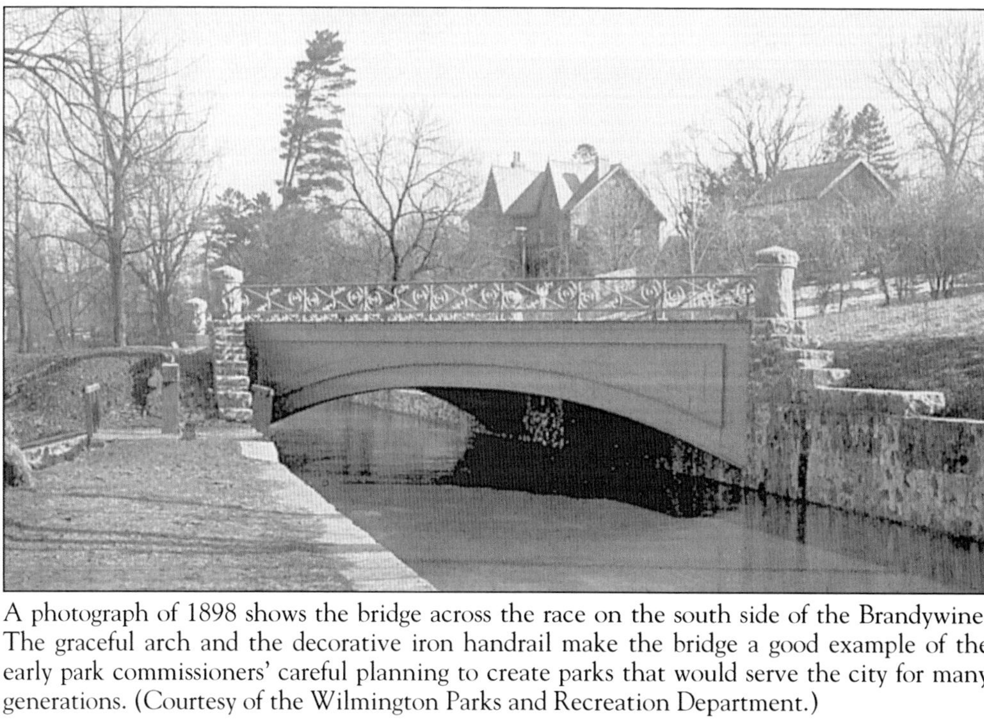

A photograph of 1898 shows the bridge across the race on the south side of the Brandywine. The graceful arch and the decorative iron handrail make the bridge a good example of the early park commissioners' careful planning to create parks that would serve the city for many generations. (Courtesy of the Wilmington Parks and Recreation Department.)

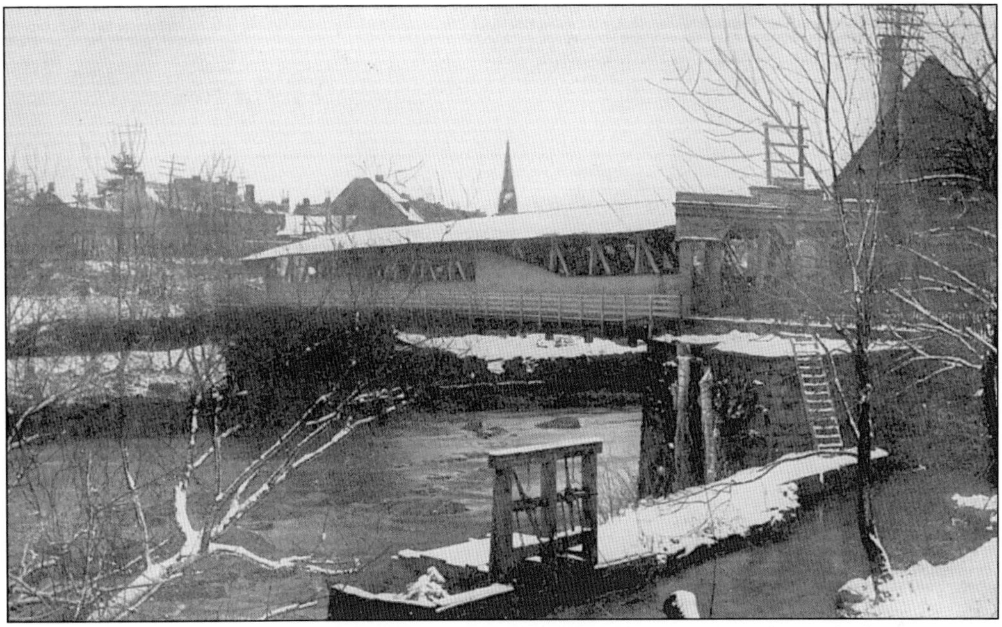

The photographer was standing on the south bank of the Brandywine as he took this picture in 1883. This wooden bridge was the fourth to cross the river at Market Street and was built in 1839. The river was once navigable up to this point. Small ships could sail up as far as this bridge where the rapids meet tidal waters. (Courtesy of the Wilmington Parks and Recreation Department.)

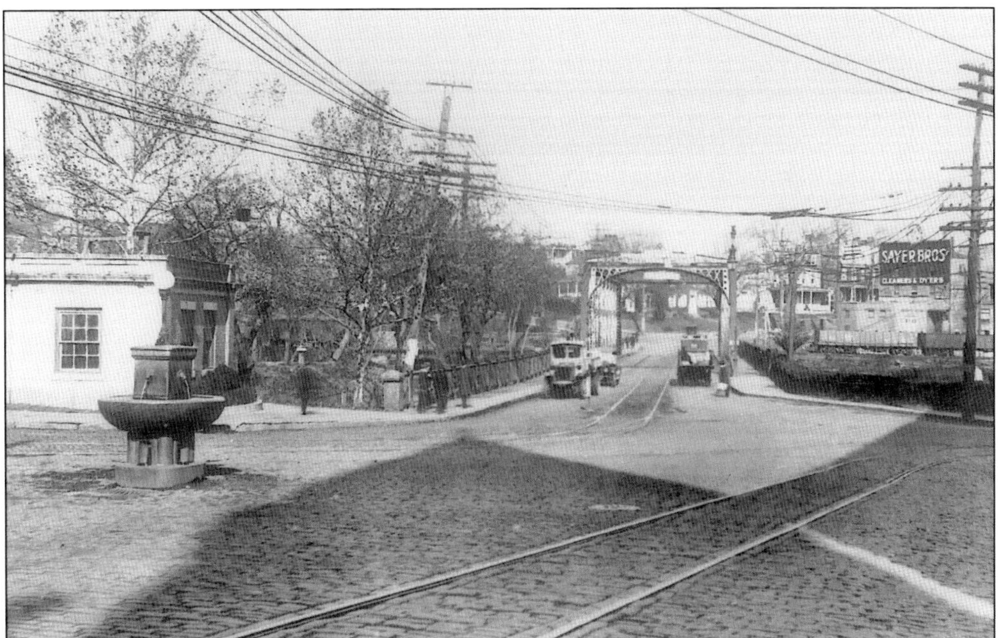

The fifth bridge across the Brandywine at Market Street was a steel bridge that replaced the previous wooden bridge. Here, we are looking north across the bridge in 1925. Note the trolley tracks crossing the bridge and the fountain and watering trough in the foreground. (Courtesy of the Delaware State Archives.)

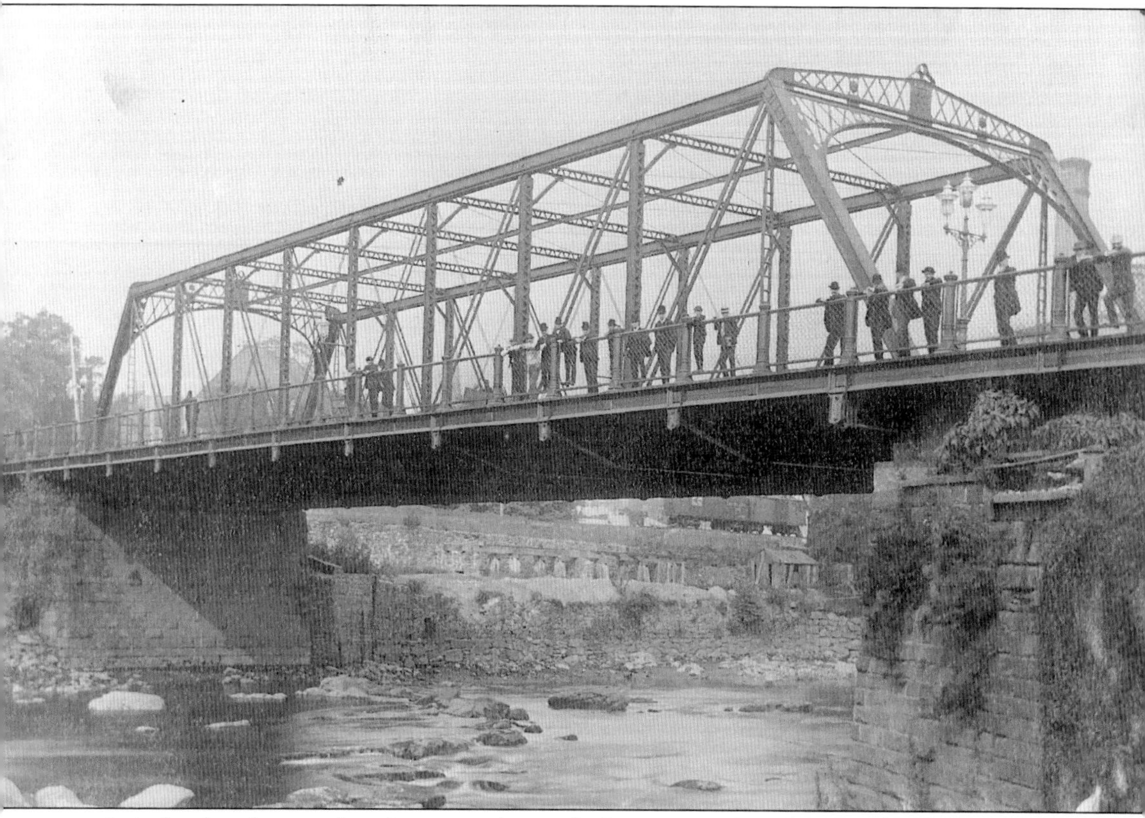

It is hard to know what these people are looking at in this photograph of about 1900 by Joseph Maybin. Market Street was once part of a toll road to Philadelphia, and the first bridge crossed the Brandywine near here in about 1770. Floods, freshets, and heavy use destroyed the earlier bridges, including two wooden ones. The Levy Court constructed this iron bridge in 1886, and it served until 1928. An ornate gas light provided illumination, an improvement over the darkness of the earlier covered bridges. In the mid-1800s, Wilmington began installing gas street lamps, for which it paid $10 each per year. At the same time, individual houses could also receive gas service. Construction along the river has changed its appearance, but one can still see the tide rising and falling below the Market Street bridge and imagine sailing vessels coming up to this point. (Courtesy of the Hagley Museum and Library.)

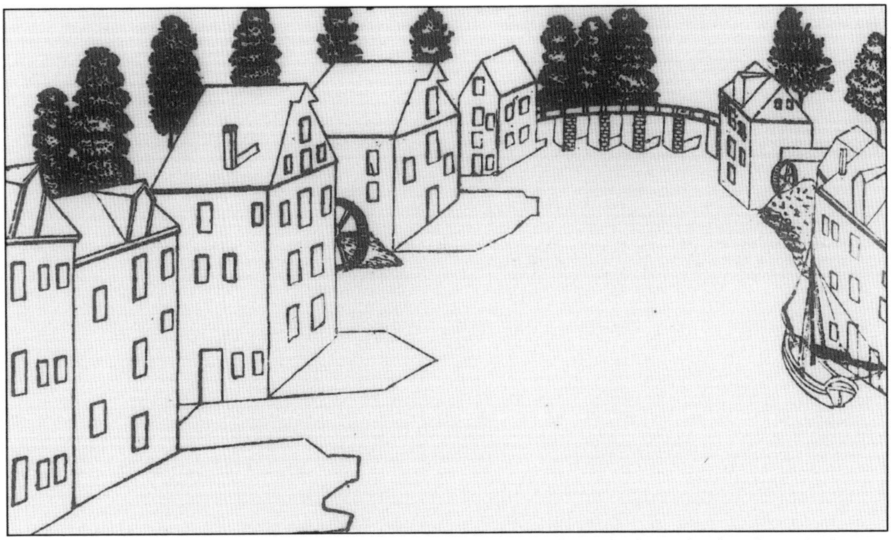

This early sketch of the Brandywine Mills looks upstream from below the bridge. A sloop is tied up at a mill on the north bank, and two mill wheels are visible. The Superfine flour produced by local millers, most of whom were Quakers, brought fame and wealth to Wilmington in the 1700s. (Courtesy of the Delaware State Archives.)

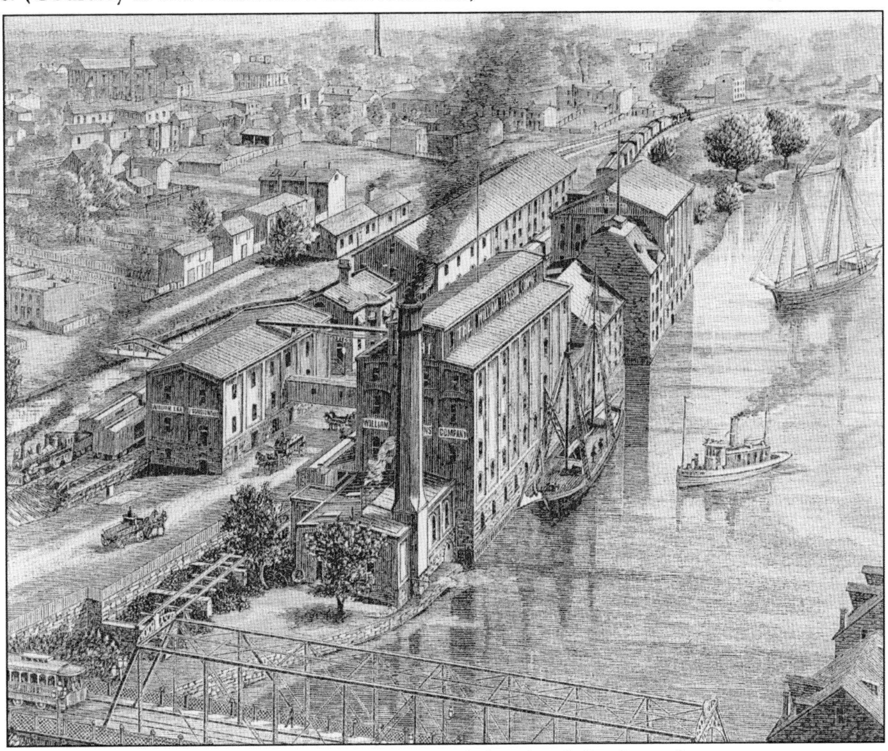

The mills of William Lea and Sons on the north bank of the Brandywine were extensive, as shown in this engraving of 1888. The company had its beginnings in the milling company owned by Joseph Tatnall about 100 years earlier. As this picture shows, both trains and ships served the mill. The fifth Market Street bridge is in the foreground. (Courtesy of the Historical Society of Delaware.)

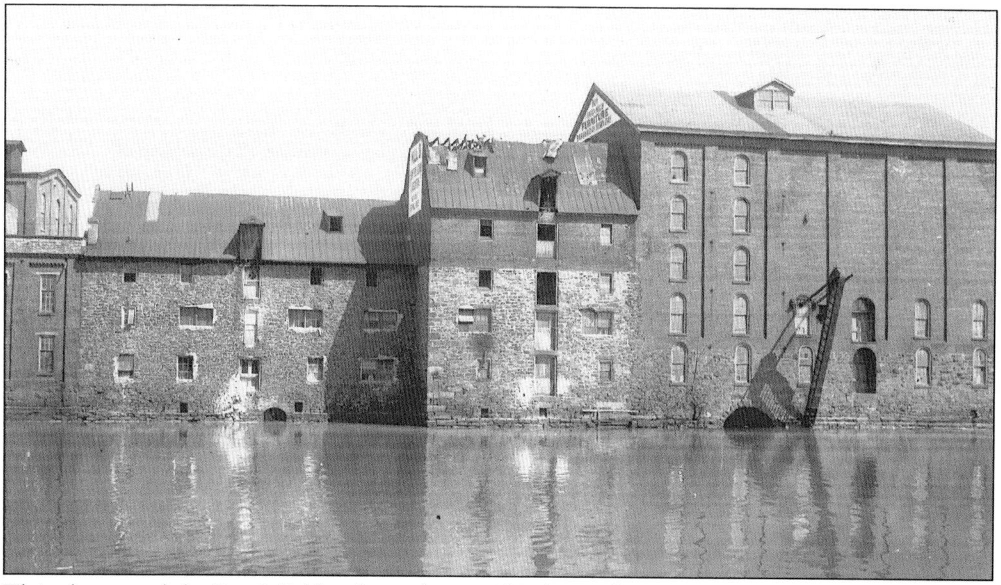

This photograph by Frank Zebley from about 1930 shows the Lea Mill buildings as they looked at that time. The rafters poke through the roof of one building. After reorganizations in the 1890s and 1920s, the Lea family sold the property and had no further connection with the business after 1926. By 1979, one of the buildings was gone and the others housed various industries. (Courtesy of the Delaware State Archives.)

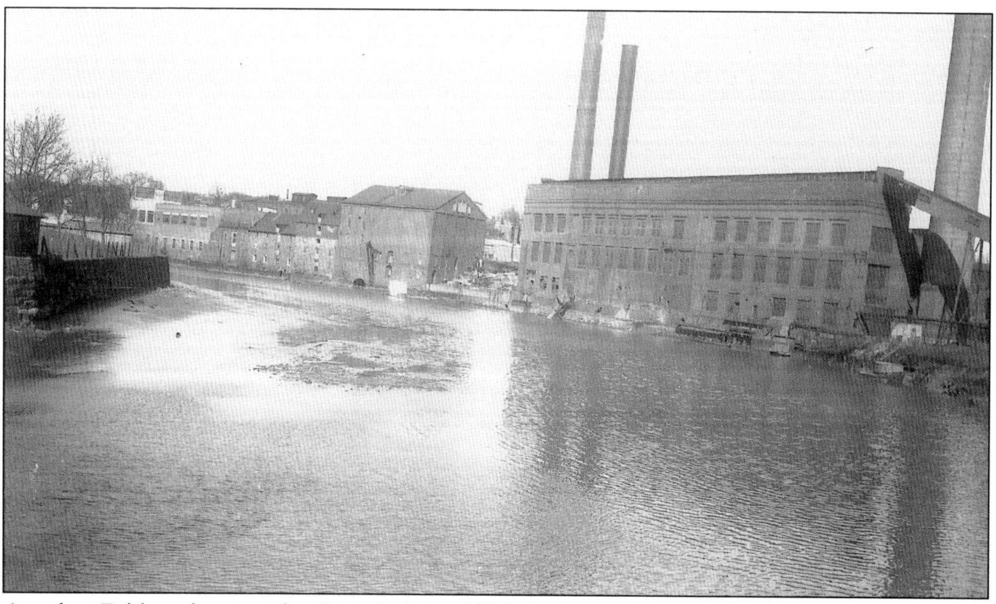

Another Zebley photograph, also of about 1930, looks up the Brandywine from downstream with the Lea Mill buildings far to the left. In 1980, the Chalfant family began renovation of the mill buildings on the left and created the condominiums called Superfine Lane. (Courtesy of the Delaware State Archives.)

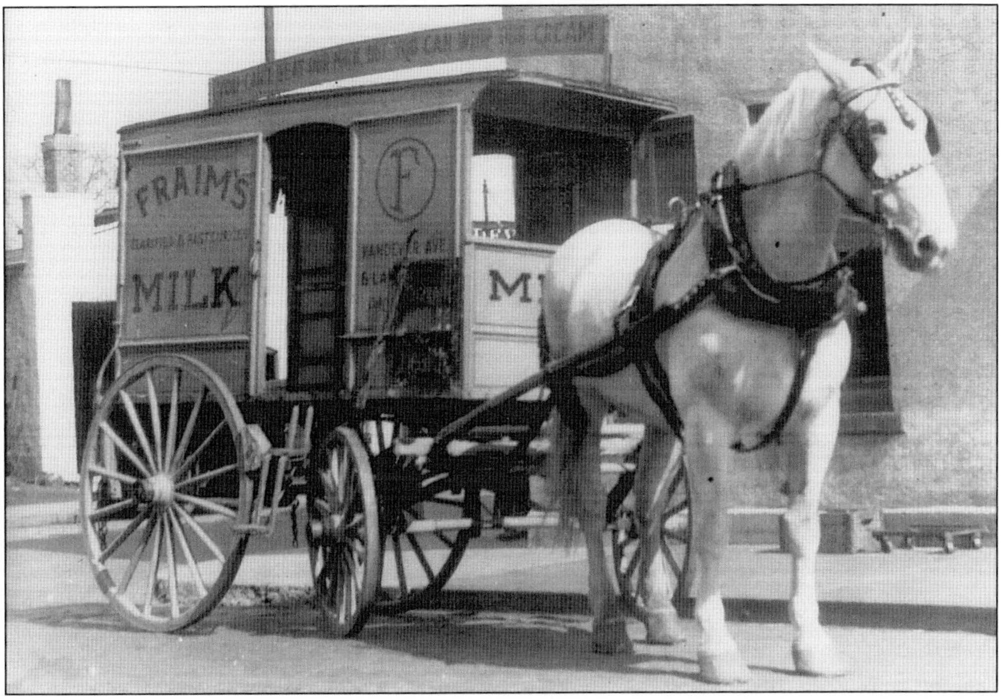

Fraim's Dairies occupied buildings near the Lea Mills complex and the Market Street bridge in the 1920s. Those were the days when horse-drawn carriages like this delivered bottled milk early every morning. Note the slogan on top of the wagon: "You can't beat our milk but you can whip our cream." (Courtesy of the Delaware State Archives.)

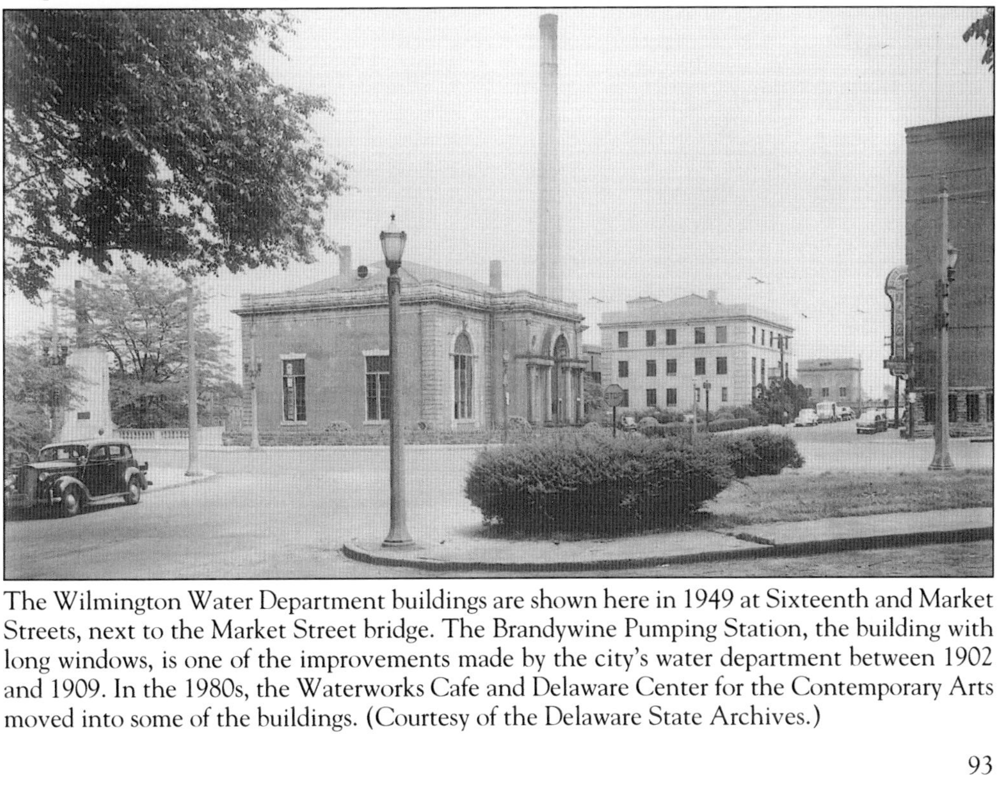

The Wilmington Water Department buildings are shown here in 1949 at Sixteenth and Market Streets, next to the Market Street bridge. The Brandywine Pumping Station, the building with long windows, is one of the improvements made by the city's water department between 1902 and 1909. In the 1980s, the Waterworks Cafe and Delaware Center for the Contemporary Arts moved into some of the buildings. (Courtesy of the Delaware State Archives.)

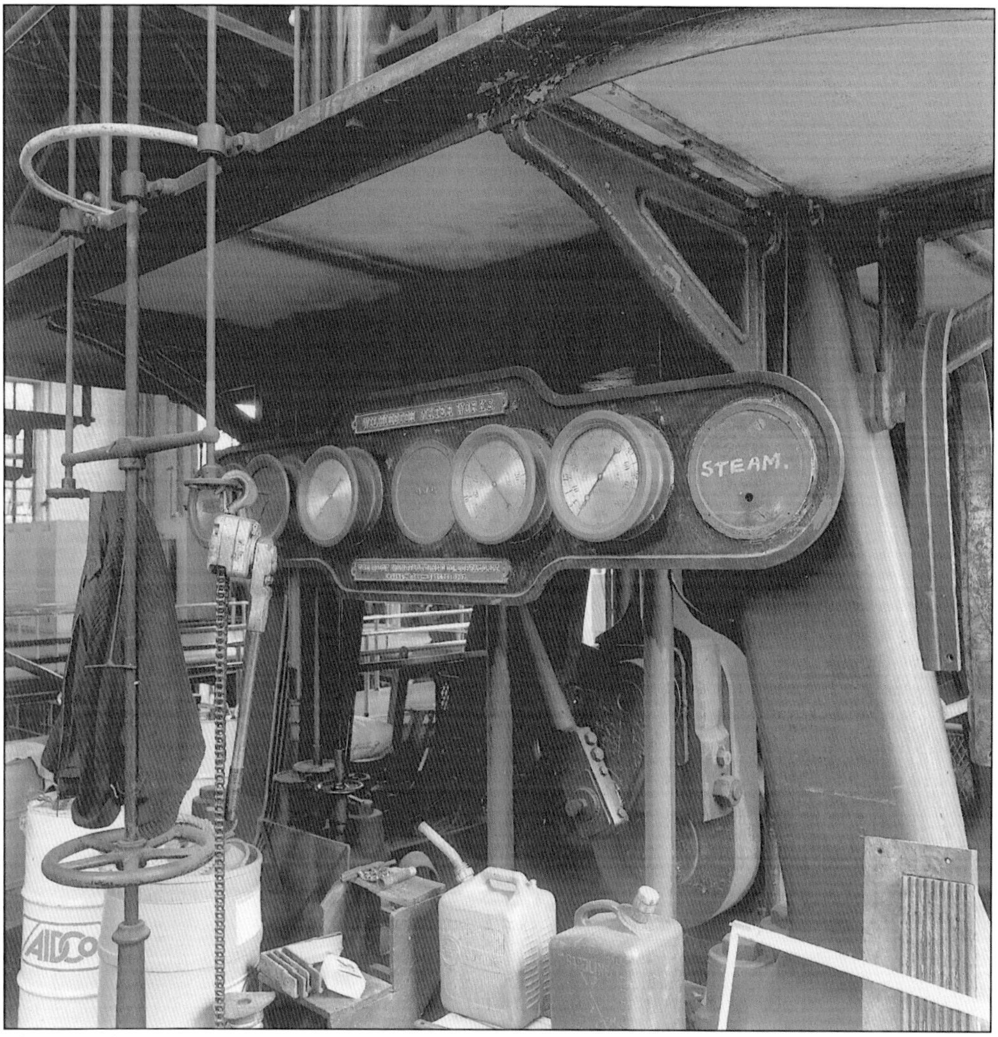

The Brandywine Pumping Station measures 110 feet by 60 feet and is built of Brandywine granite. It houses two Holly vertical, three-cylinder, triple-expansion steam pumping engines. Each engine, approximately three stories high, was rated at 12 mgd (million gallons per day). From January 1908 to 1968, these engines pumped raw water from the Brandywine raceway to the Porter Reservoir. The water department removed one Holly steam pumping engine in 1968 and installed a new electrical centrifugal pumping unit. The second Holly engine (engine number 580), shown in this photograph by Tim Bayard, remains intact, but no one has used it in recent years. It has taken engineering skill, public interest, and civic action to maintain a good water supply for the city of Wilmington. The Brandywine provided the water, and many of the structural elements of the water system are attractive additions to our river banks. (Courtesy of Tim Bayard.)

For many years, the Diamond Ice and Coal Company occupied the land along Jessup Street between the Brandywine and Vandever Avenue. This business began as the Lea Pusey Company, which started manufacturing ice in 1887. Ice for the summer and coal for the winter was a logical combination for a year-round business, so the firm expanded into coal, which it stored in the huge silos shown here.

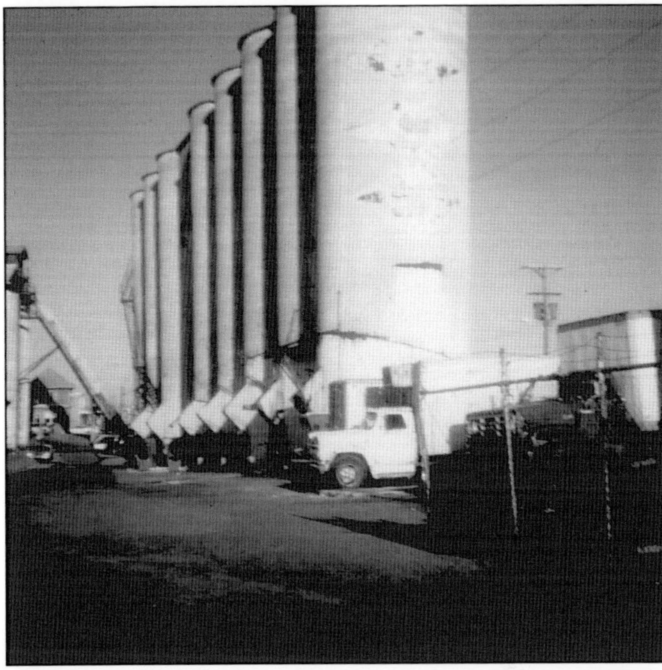

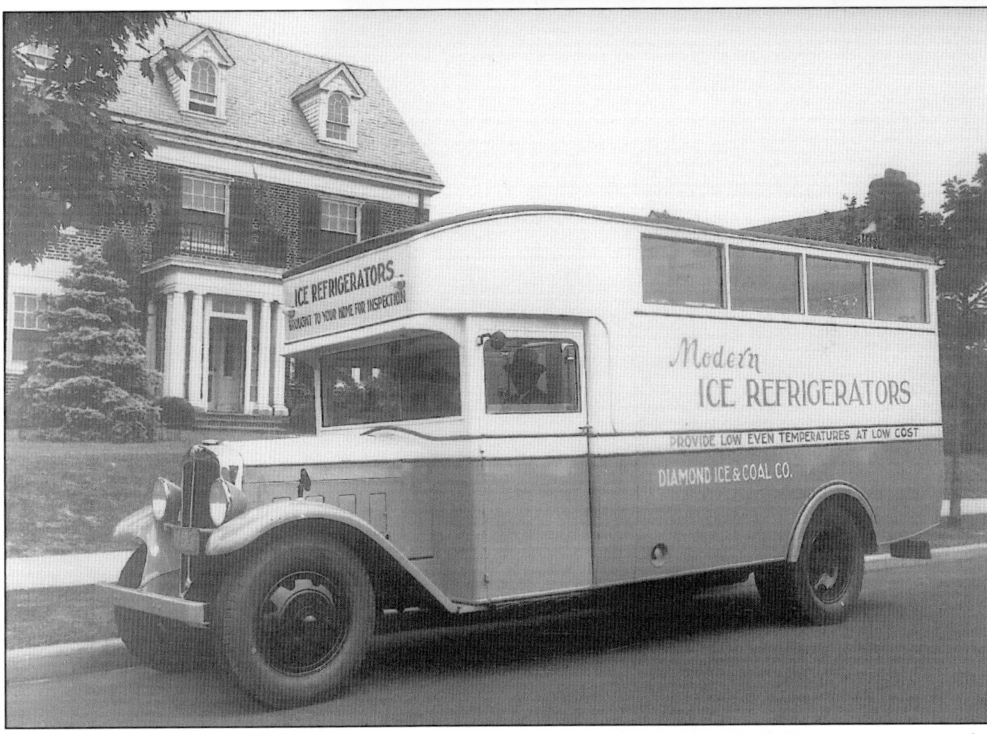

Diamond Coal and Ice evolved over nearly a century and a half with different owners and a variety of products including cold storage, "ice refrigerators," custom kitchens, and insulation. This is one of the company's trucks in 1932, and since ice was their business, they are presumably delivering ice for use in one of their "ice refrigerators." (Courtesy of the Historical Society of Delaware.)

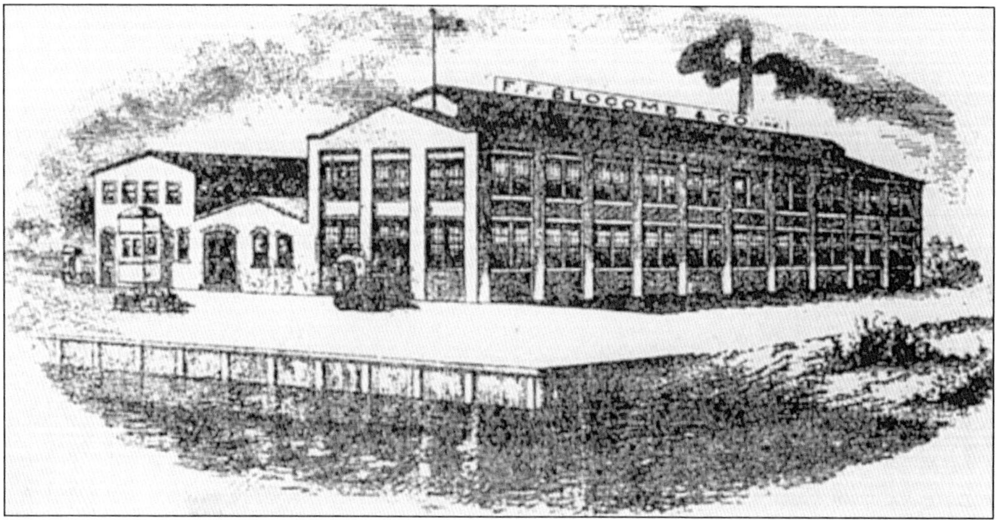

The F.F. Slocomb Company moved into its new buildings on the Brandywine at Poplar Street in 1900. The company made machinery for leather manufacturers who were numerous in Wilmington. Slocomb was probably best known for its "Brandywine Staking Machine," which represented an improvement over the earlier hand-stretching process in leather production. (Courtesy of the Historical Society of Delaware.)

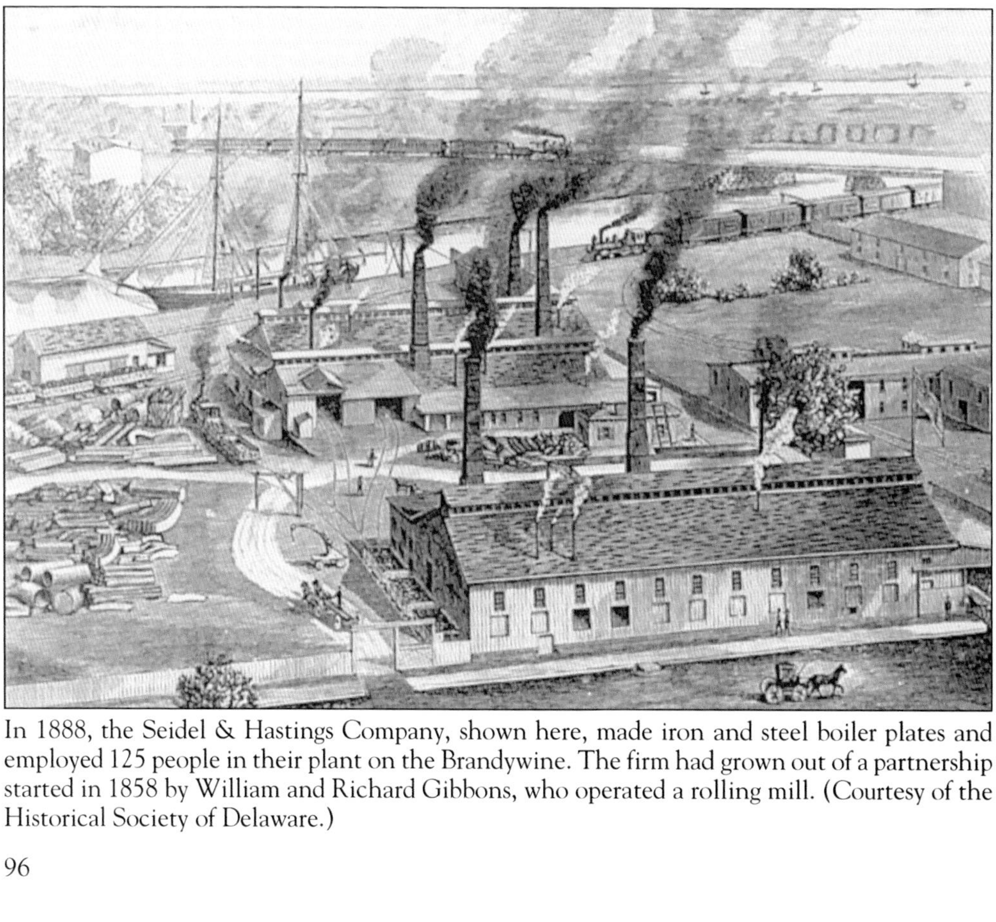

In 1888, the Seidel & Hastings Company, shown here, made iron and steel boiler plates and employed 125 people in their plant on the Brandywine. The firm had grown out of a partnership started in 1858 by William and Richard Gibbons, who operated a rolling mill. (Courtesy of the Historical Society of Delaware.)

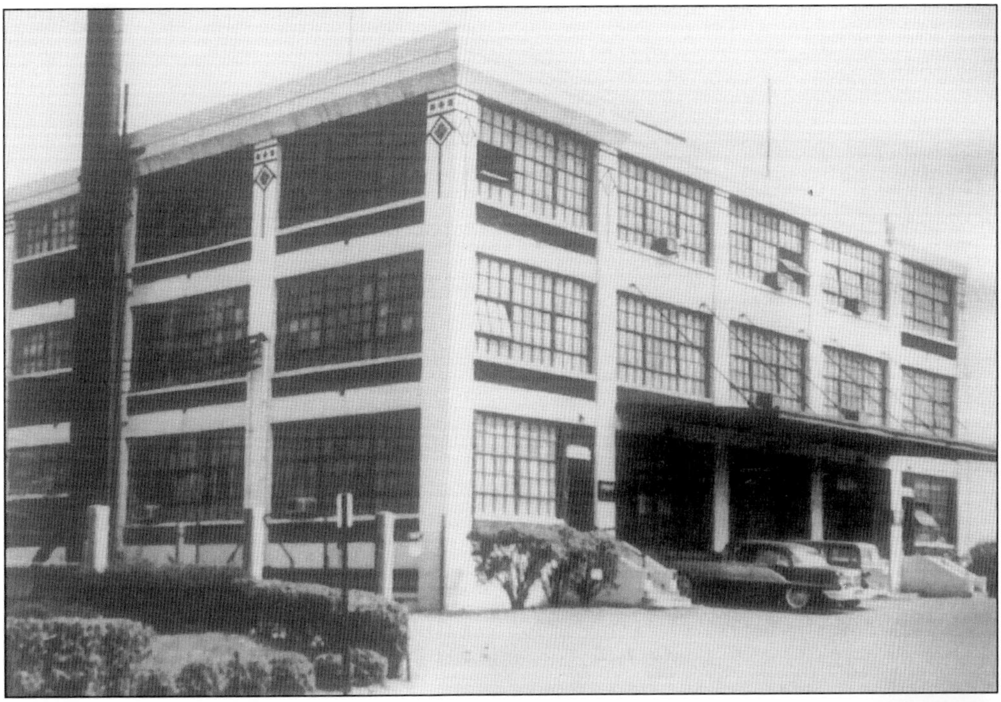

The Kaumagraph Building, as it is called in its National Register of Historic Places listing, was built in 1917 as a warehouse for the New Castle Leather Company. This fireproof building was designed to hold 2 million goat skins. Although its purpose was strictly utilitarian, the building is architecturally impressive; its commercial-style exterior originally carried tile trim. (Courtesy of the National Register of Historic Places.)

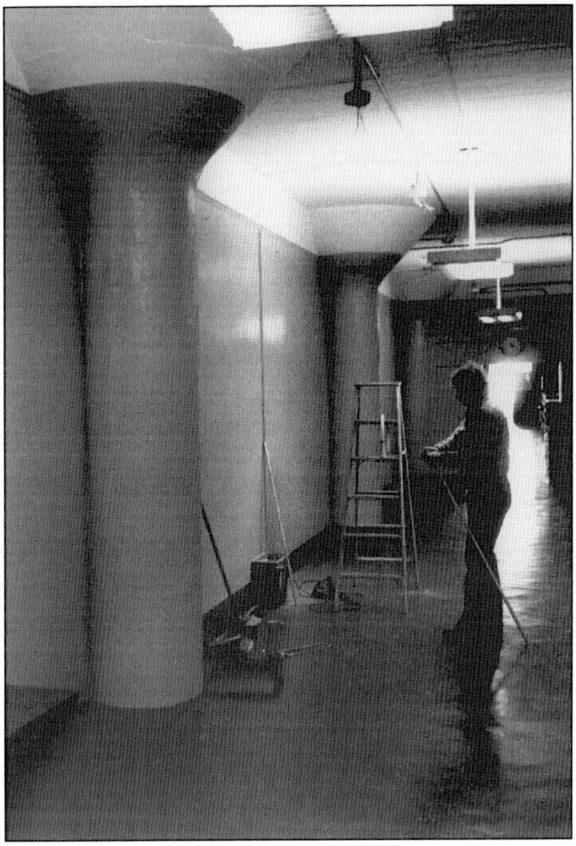

Large flared pillars support the floors of the building that originally held tons of kidskins. The Kaumagraph Company purchased the building in 1944. The company started in New York, printing trademarks on textiles. In Wilmington, Kaumagraph developed methods for printing on such diverse items as plastic plates, sporting goods, and automobile dashboards. (Photo by J.A. Thompson; courtesy of the National Register of Historic Places.)

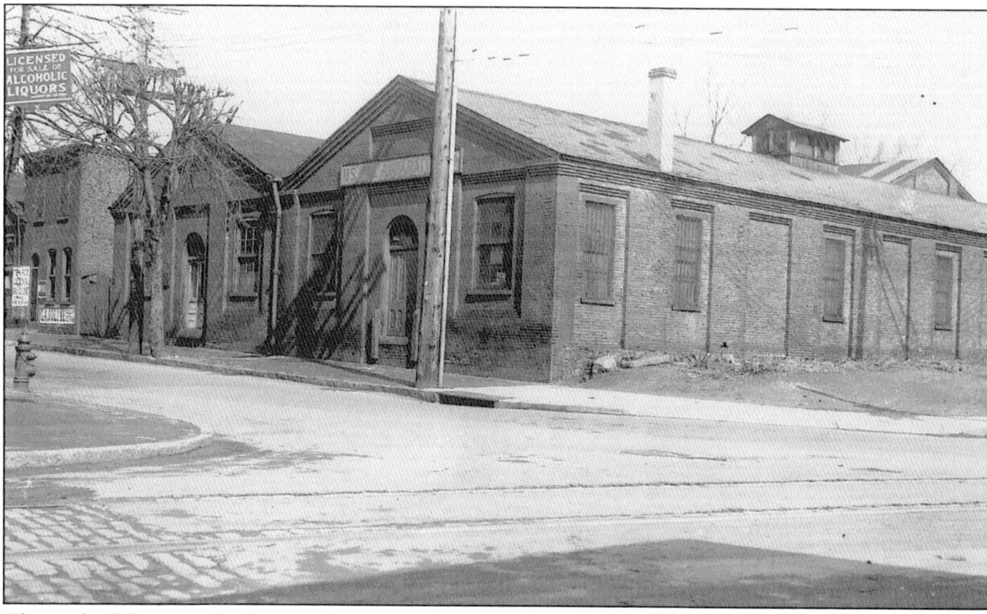

These buildings, which stood just west of the entrance to the Church Street bridge, housed the U.S. Fire Apparatus Company before their demolition in 1934. Originally, Smith & Painter, a manufacturer of fruit syrups for soda fountains, occupied the site. (Courtesy of the Delaware State Archives.)

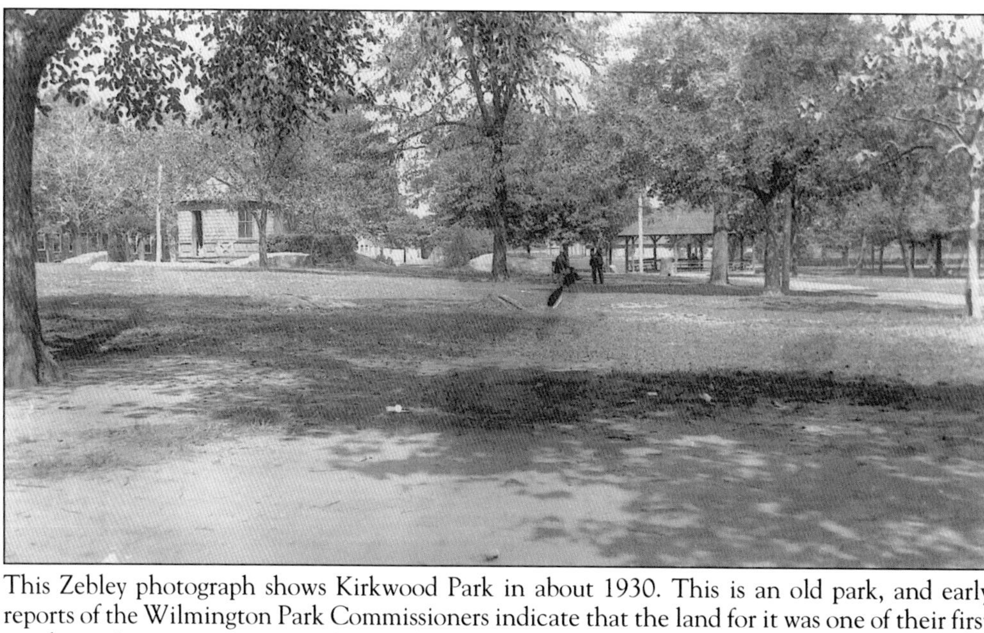

This Zebley photograph shows Kirkwood Park in about 1930. This is an old park, and early reports of the Wilmington Park Commissioners indicate that the land for it was one of their first purchases. It appears on an 1895 map of city parks. (Courtesy of the Delaware State Archives.)

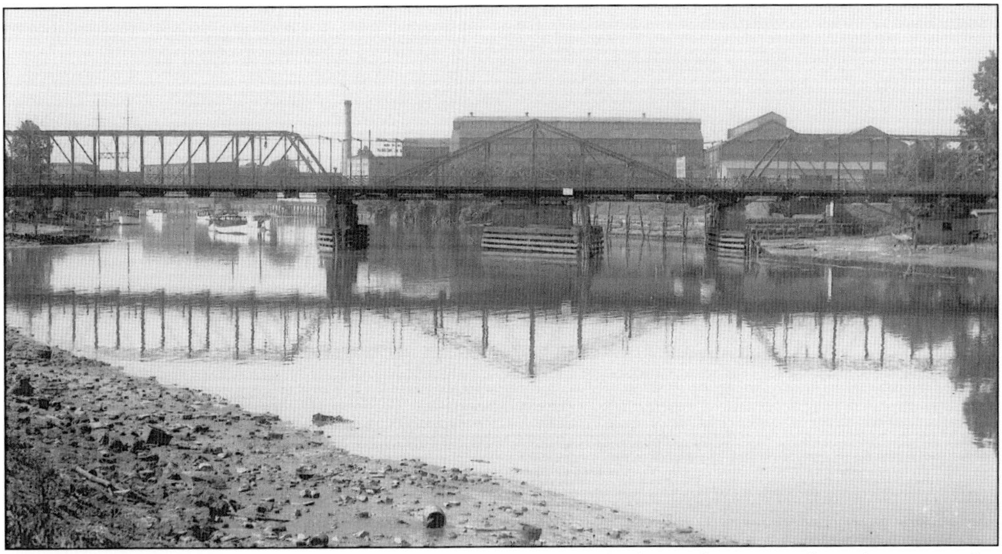

The old Eleventh Street bridge followed the course of Eleventh Street directly across the Brandywine. The bridge carried a streetcar line as well as other traffic. This Zebley photograph of about 1930 shows the Hilles & Jones plant in the right background. (Courtesy of the Delaware State Archives.)

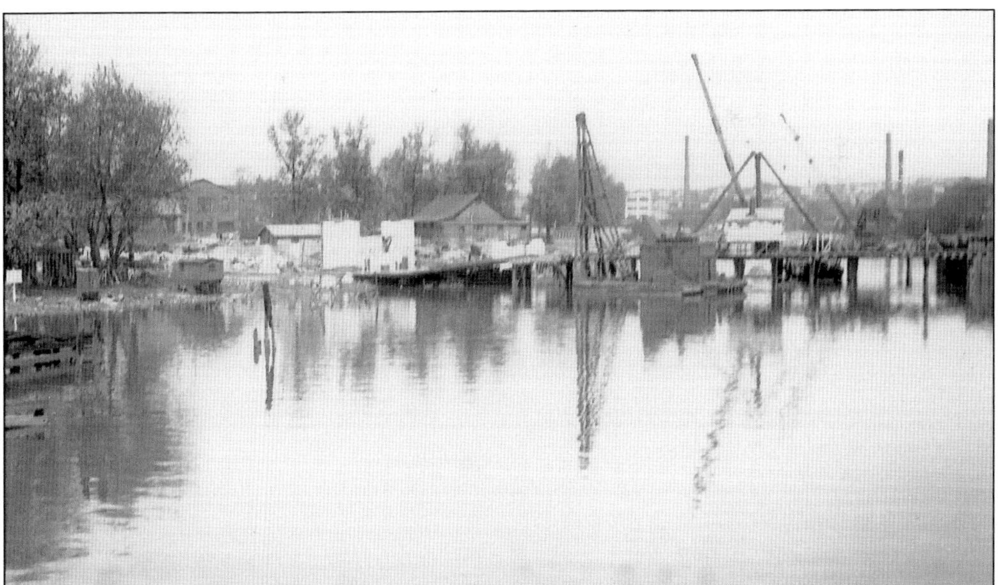

This 1932 photograph shows the new Eleventh Street bridge, more properly called the Church Street bridge, under construction. The new bridge leads to Northeast Boulevard and follows a different route than the old one, which was eventually demolished. (Courtesy of the Delaware State Archives,)

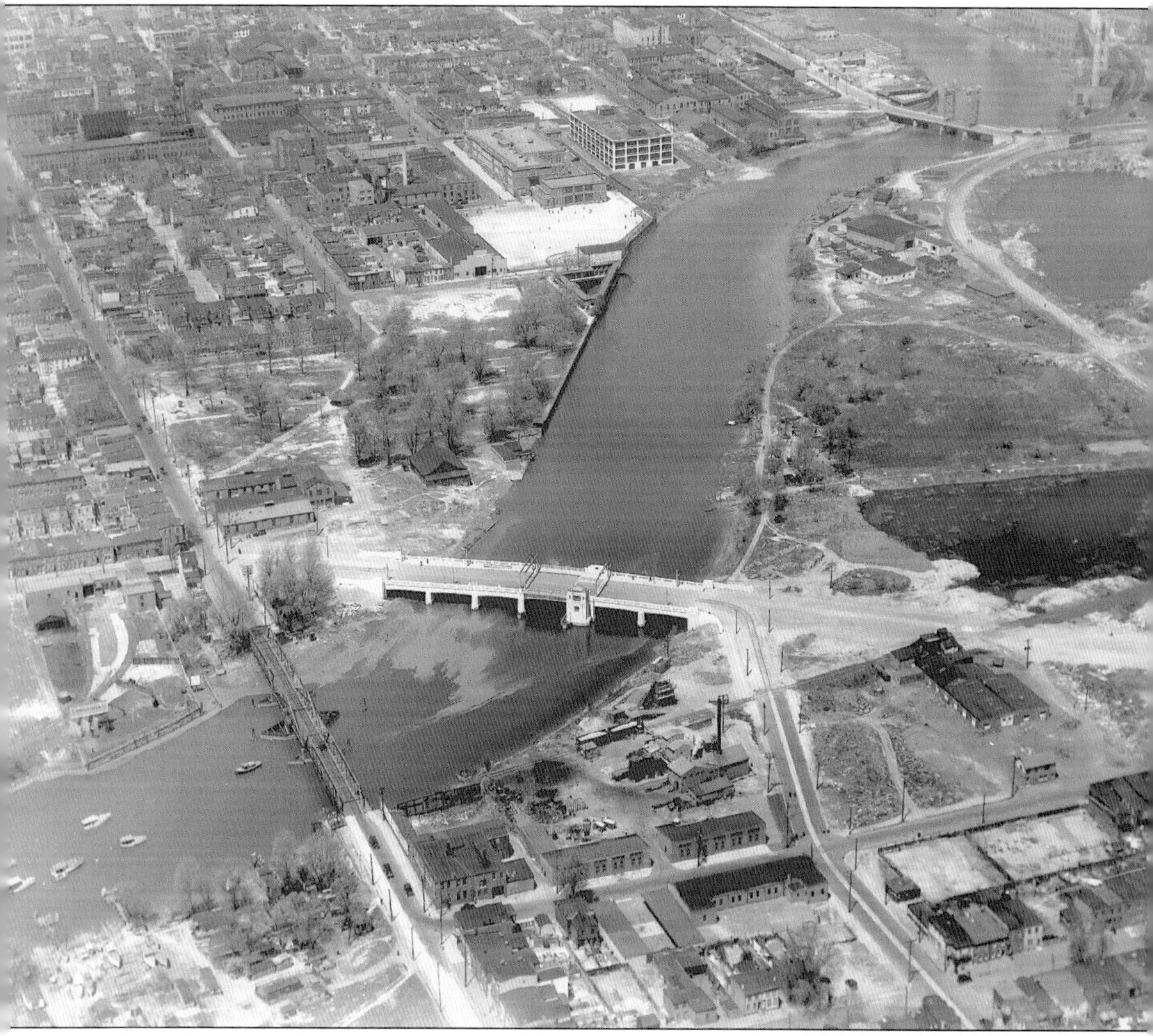

Three bridges and many prominent buildings are clearly visible in this 1933 aerial photograph of the lower Brandywine. The old Eleventh Street bridge is still in use in the lower part of the picture. Above it is the new Church Street bridge, and the Sixteenth Street bridge is near the top of the picture. In the upper right corner is a quarry. Just below the Sixteenth Street bridge on the left is the square white Kaumagraph Building. Below it is Howard High School, and the trees indicate Kirkwood Park. Thatcher Island was on the right side of the river, between the two upper bridges. There are pleasure boats on the river in the lower left. More boats are on shore in the "Orchards" area. This picture is particularly interesting because it was taken during the brief time when both the old and new Church/Eleventh Streets bridges were in place. (Courtesy of the Hagley Museum and Library.)

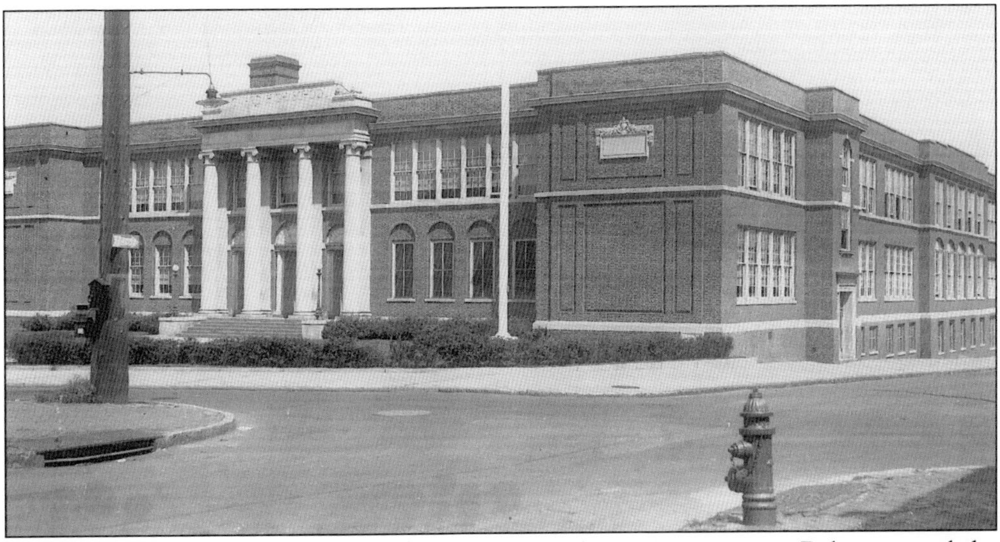

Howard High School was the only high school for African-Americans in Delaware until the mid-1930s. The second Howard High School is shown here only a few years after its construction in 1927. The first Howard High School was on Orange Street. After the enactment of the 1919 Delaware school code, it became necessary to remedy the inequities in the city's racially segregated schools. (Courtesy of the Delaware State Archives.)

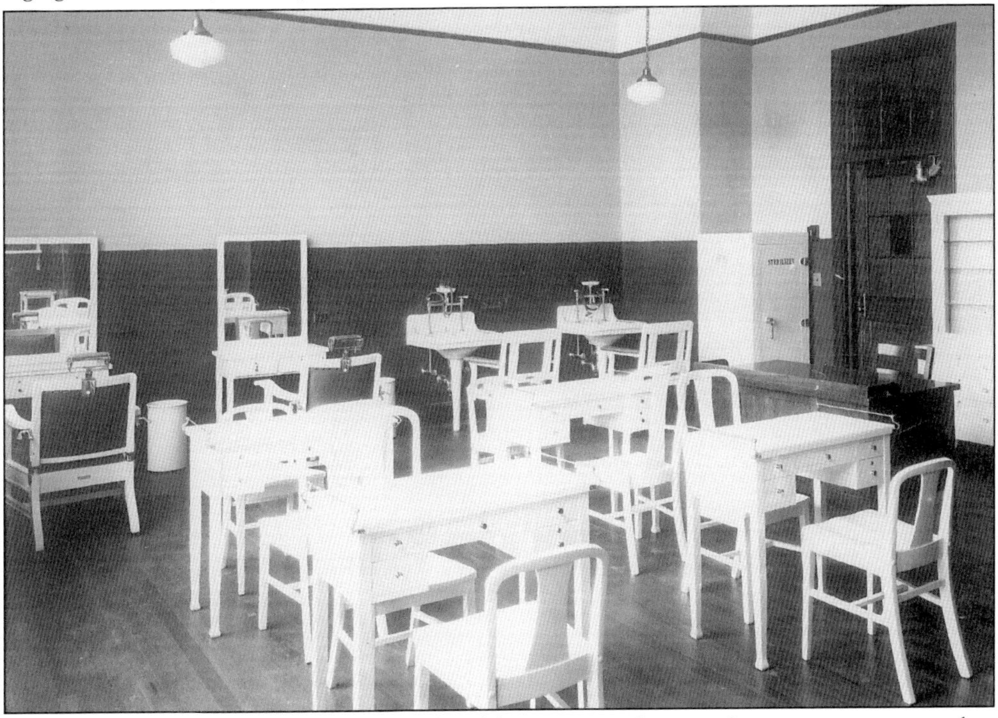

The new school code aimed to change the old separate and unequal system to a separate but equal system. At about the time the new code came into effect, Pierre S. du Pont and his cousin Alfred tried to outdo each other not only in business but also in philanthropy. Pierre offered to build Howard High School. Vocational training was part of the curriculum, and this is the beautician training room. (Courtesy of the Historical Society of Delaware.)

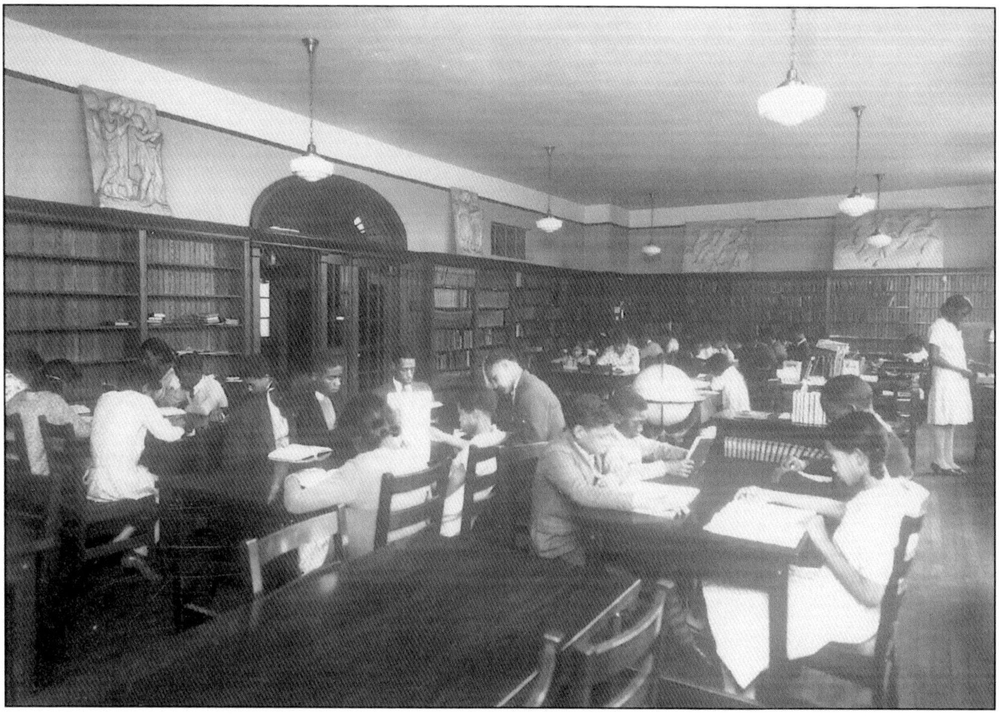

The curriculum at Howard High School went beyond vocational courses. These students are in the school's library. Music and art as well as standard academic subjects were among the courses offered. Howard High School evolved into the integrated Howard Career Center. (Courtesy of the Historical Society of Delaware.)

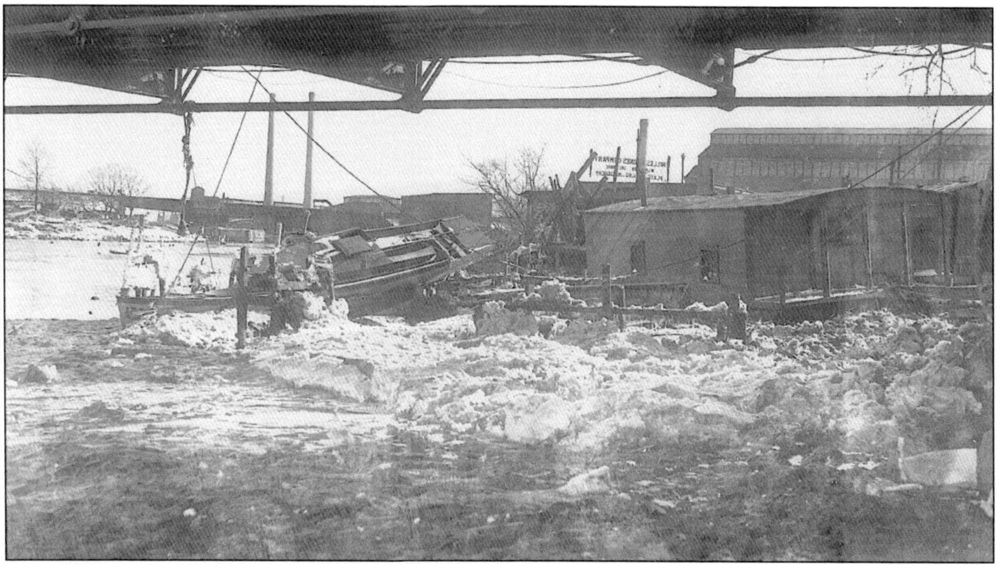

A cold winter and flood conditions could put the Brandywine into a rage. When Zebley took this photograph in about 1930 the river had scattered ice, small boats, and buildings on her banks. This scene, downstream from Howard High School, shows the top of the Hilles & Jones building in the right background. (Courtesy of the Delaware State Archives.)

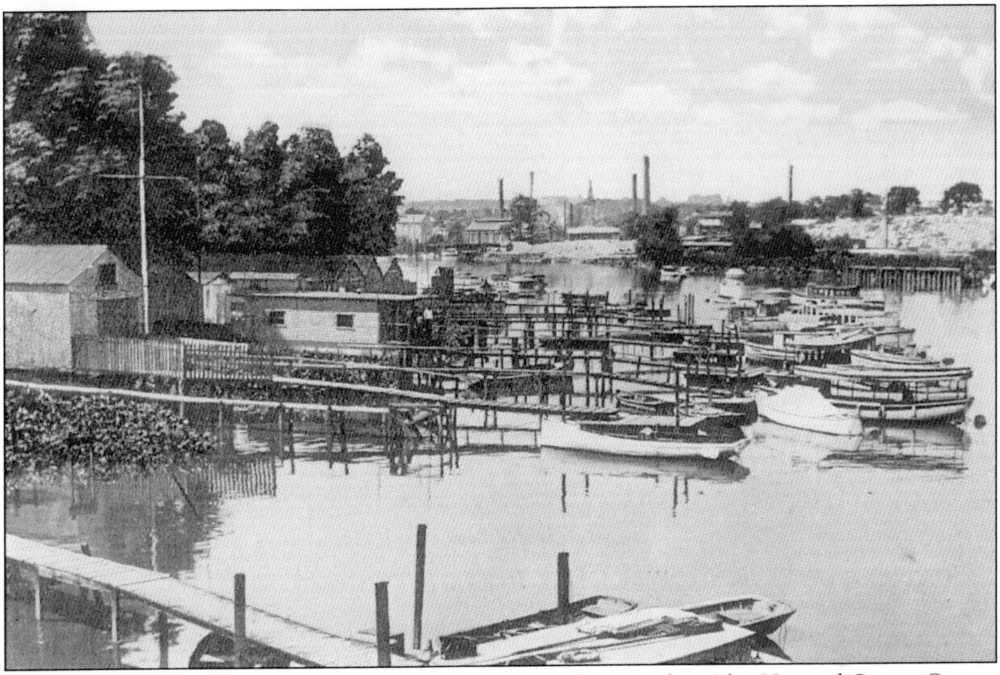

Some Wilmingtonians still remember this spot across the river from the Howard Career Center as the "Orchards." The Delaware Terra Cotta Company once had a plant here, but it became a haven for pleasure boats before 1900. The Star Boat Club and the Olive and Rose Clubs all used this area. The *Spitfire*, which belonged to the owner of the nearby Slocomb machine shop, anchored here. (Courtesy of the Hagley Museum and Library.)

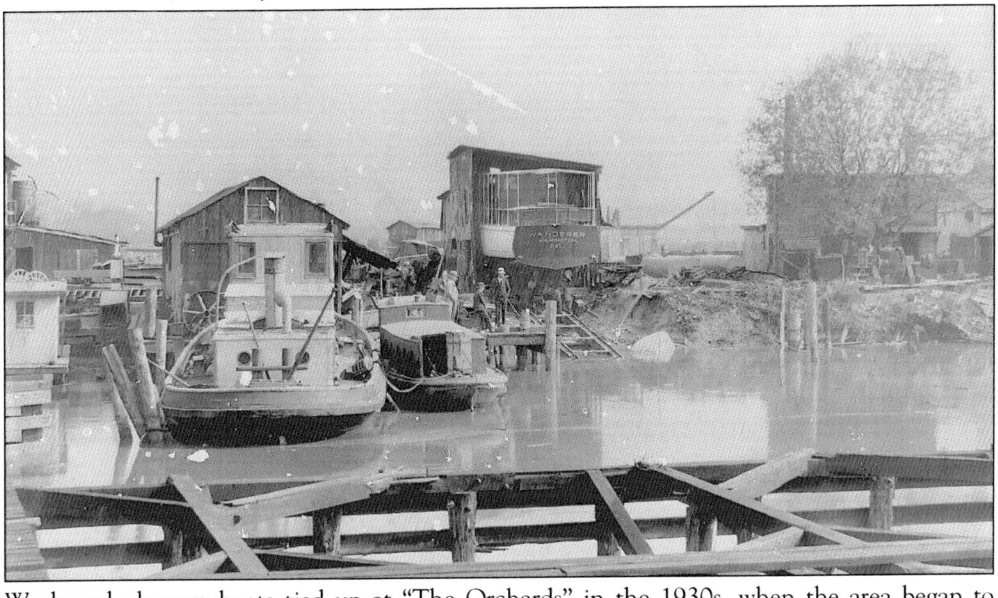

Work and pleasure boats tied up at "The Orchards" in the 1930s, when the area began to develop into a houseboat colony. After one fisherman built a houseboat so that he could stay out in the Delaware Bay all night if the fishing was good, many others followed. With the advent of fast motorboats, houseboat owners pulled their crafts ashore and lived in them. (Courtesy of the Hagley Museum and Library.)

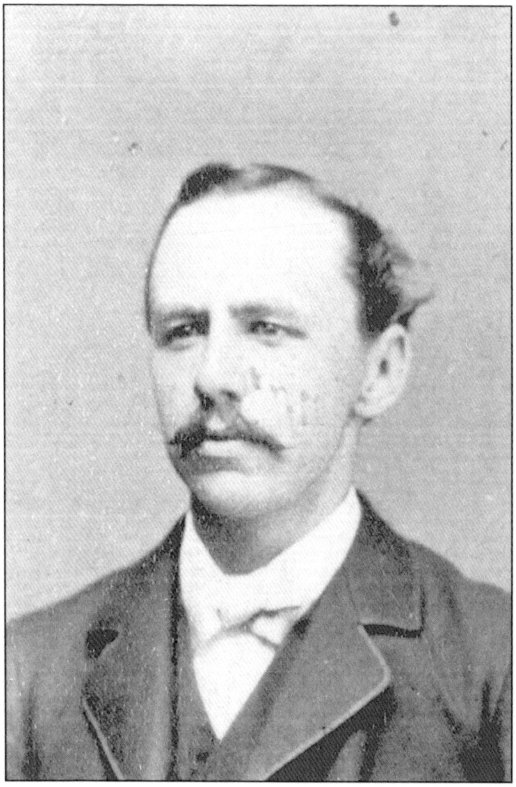

Richard Pim established the Malleable Iron Works in 1878 at the corner of Taylor and Buttonwood Streets, adjacent to the Brandywine. The firm had a fast process for making malleable iron, and one of its best sellers was a lightweight and durable horseshoe. Malleable eventually employed about 175 men who made all kinds of hardware specialties. (Courtesy of the Historical Society of Delaware.)

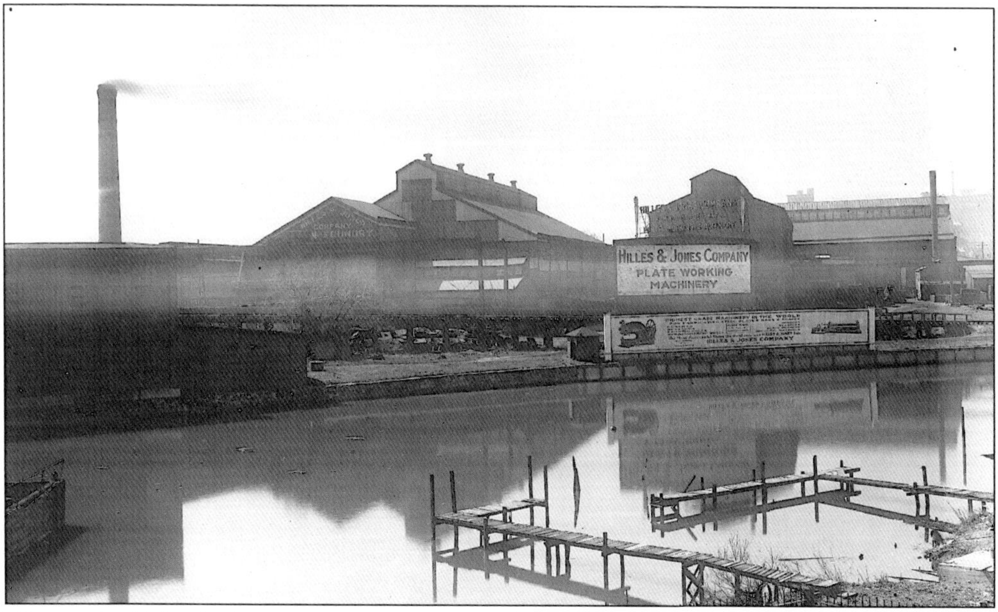

This is the Hilles & Jones Company plant on April 14, 1926. The company began in 1854 when two machinists started making engines, boilers, and a few wooden ships. The business gradually changed over to the manufacture of tools and machinery, for which it had a world-wide reputation. Note the dock for small boats in the foreground. (Courtesy of the Delaware State Archives.)

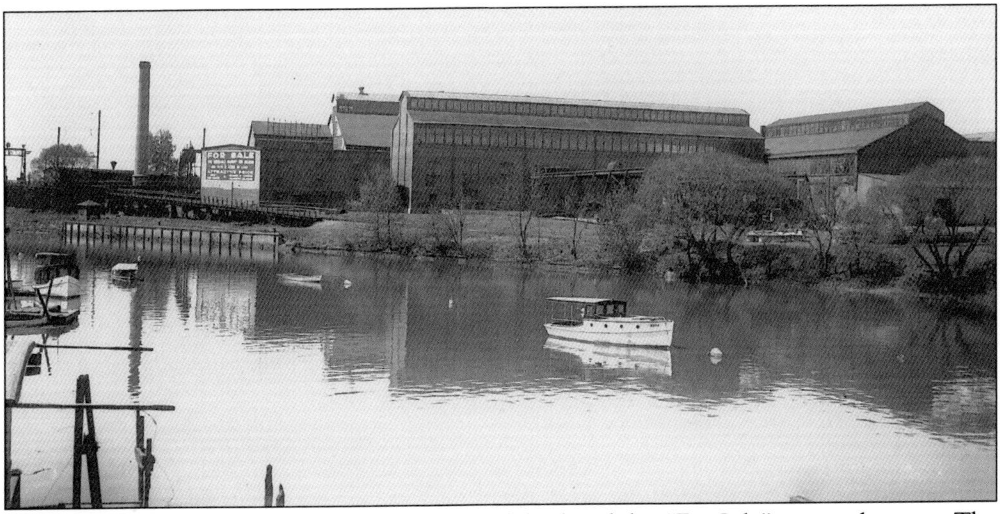

The Hilles & Jones Company closed in 1927 and displayed this "For Sale" sign in that year. The plant covered a large area and, as was typical of many Wilmington industries, made use of both water and rail transportation. There are several motor boats in the river, and the ends of docks are in the lower left. (Courtesy of the Delaware State Archives.)

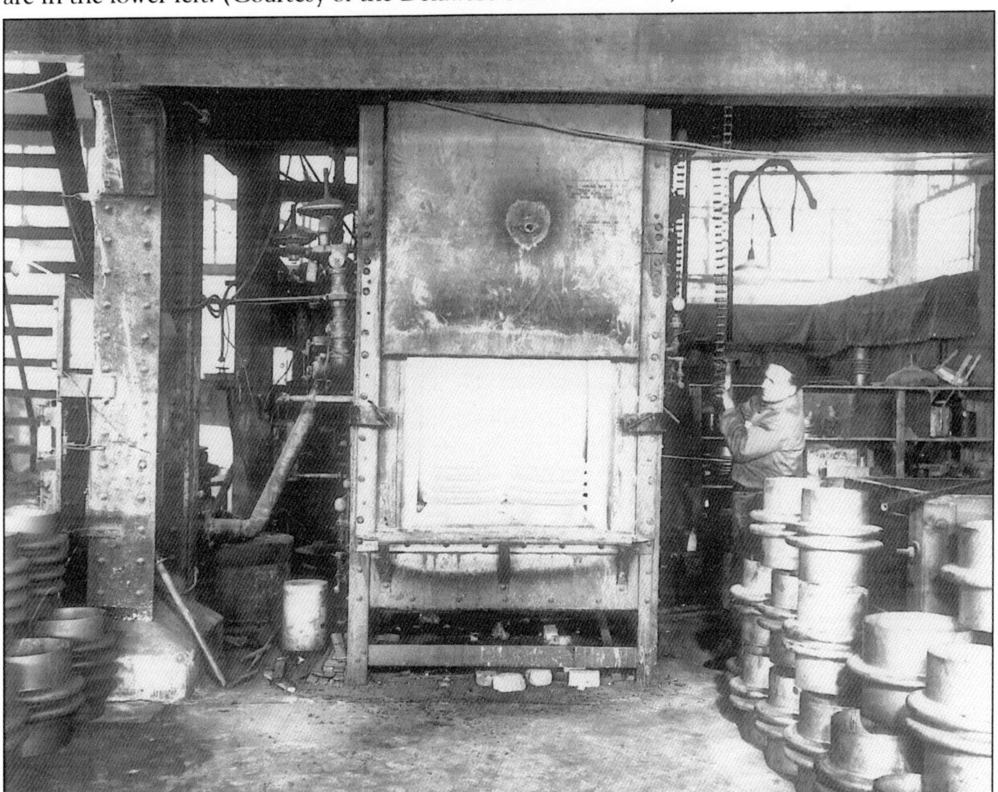

In 1939, Zallea Brothers and Johnson purchased the Hilles & Jones foundry, power house, engine room, and pattern storage building. Zallea stayed here for over 40 years and, in the 1970s, employed 150 people making connectors for railroad cars. This photograph shows a Zallea worker. (Courtesy of the Delaware State Archives.)

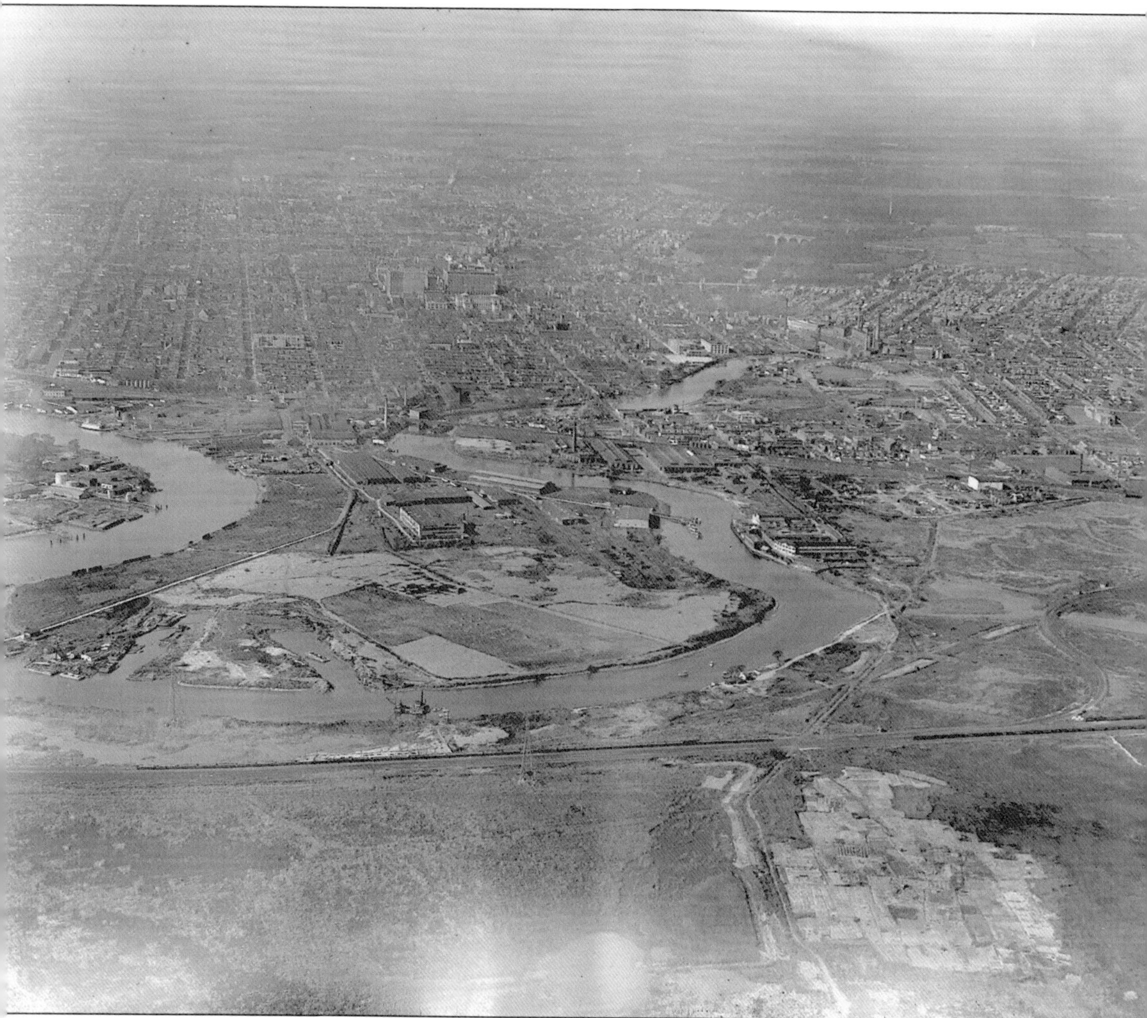

On October 28, 1929, the Wilmington peninsula looked like this from an airplane headed west. Part of the Christina River shows on the left. On the right, the Brandywine runs downstream through the city and nearly meets the Christina, creating a slender bridge of land. The Brandywine then loops around to lose itself in the wider river. Downtown Wilmington clusters near the center of the picture with residential areas spreading out in all directions. Let your eyes follow the Brandywine back upstream past industrial areas, Howard High School, and the many bridges across the river to Brandywine Park on the upper right. The shape of the peninsula is not too different than is shown on the 1772 drawing at the beginning of the book. The narrow neck of land provided an ideal spot for a defensible settlement in the early 1600s. With two navigable rivers having the potential to provide power for mills and an endless supply of fish and timber, this land was an ideal place to start a colony. (Courtesy of the Hagley Museum and Library.)

Three

The Peninsula and Port

The Brandywine and Christina Rivers nearly surround the peninsula before they join and flow to the Port of Wilmington. The two maps at the beginning of this book help tell the story of the peninsula. In 1772, nearly a century and a half after Swedish settlers established the first permanent settlement on the Delaware, the peninsula carried the label "Brandywine Marsh." Black Cat Creek was a small stream running from the center of the peninsula into the Brandywine. Similar conditions probably existed at the time the Swedes landed, compelling them to establish their colony at the neck of land connecting the peninsula to what is now the east side of Wilmington.

The map of 1895, showing roads and the Jackson & Sharp Car Works on the peninsula, makes it evident that filling and construction had radically altered the peninsula before the 20th century. Today, much of the area is old dredge fill. Despite the debris that man has put here over the years, nature can heal itself, and there is now both a new woodland and a "Superfund" clean up site on the peninsula. A few remnants of Jackson & Sharp remain, and some businesses, including a restaurant, still operate there.

The Fort Christina Monument commemorating the landing of the Swedes, the Seventh Street Park, and the Kalmar Nyckel Foundation, with its replica of the Swedish ship, are helping to recreate the atmosphere of an earlier time. Rowers, young and old, have returned to the rivers as well as jet-skiers and power boaters. Perhaps there will be additional recreational uses in the future.

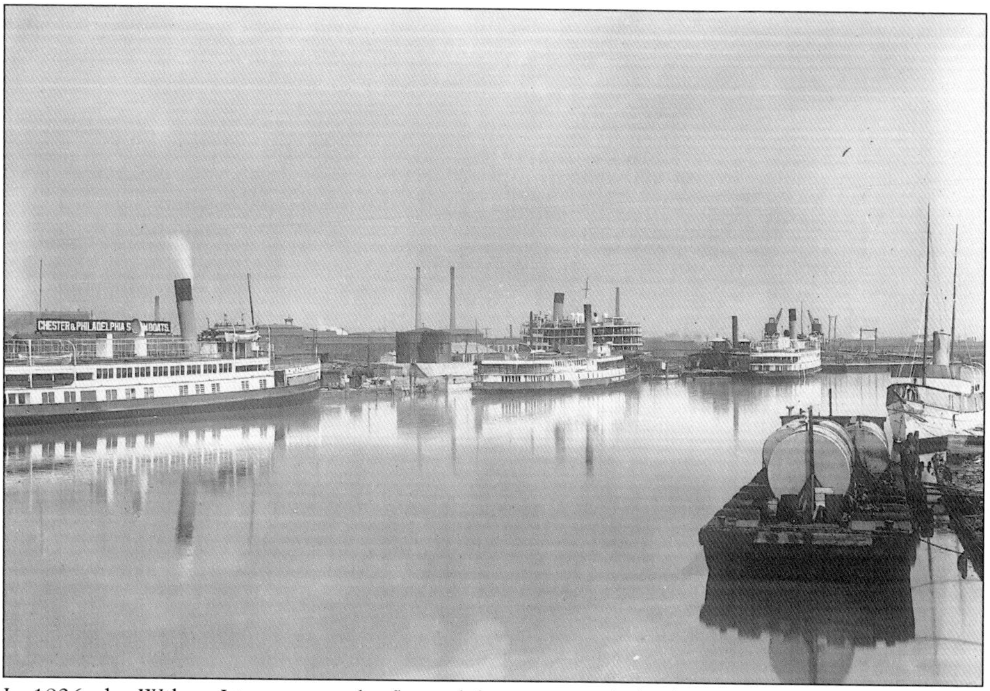

In 1926, the Wilson Line operated a fleet of ships, some of which are lined up at their landing here. As the sign indicates, Wilson operated steamboats to Chester and Philadelphia, but her excursions to New Jersey were the trips that many Wilmingtonians remember best. (Courtesy of the Delaware State Archives.)

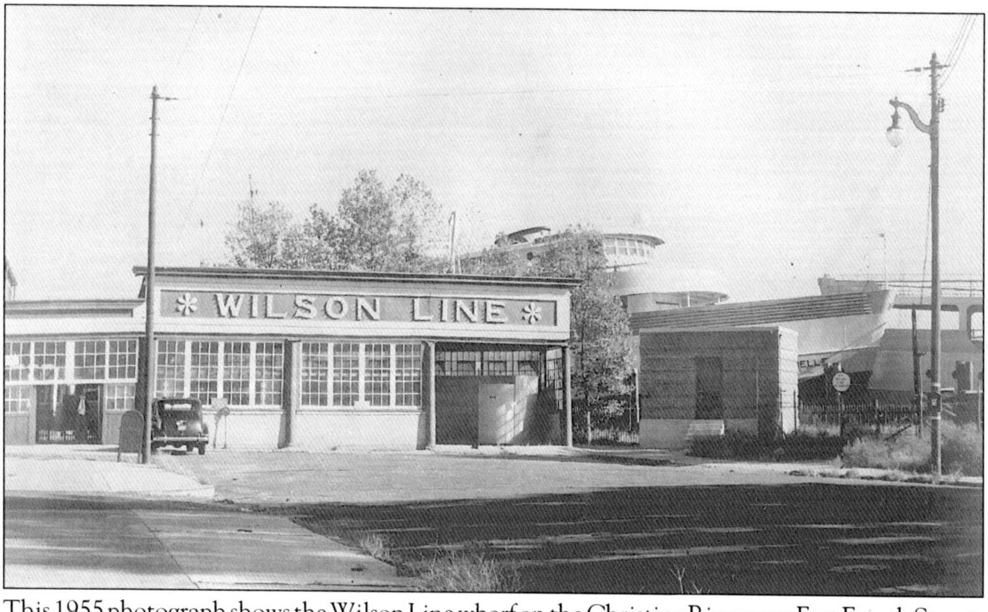

This 1955 photograph shows the Wilson Line wharf on the Christina River near East Fourth Street. Note the steamships in the background. J. Shields Wilson started the line with tugboats in 1876. In the 100 years of its operation, the line ran freight services and excursion boats in a number of places. It even developed the first hydrofoil passenger service in New York harbor. (Courtesy of the Hagley Museum and Library.)

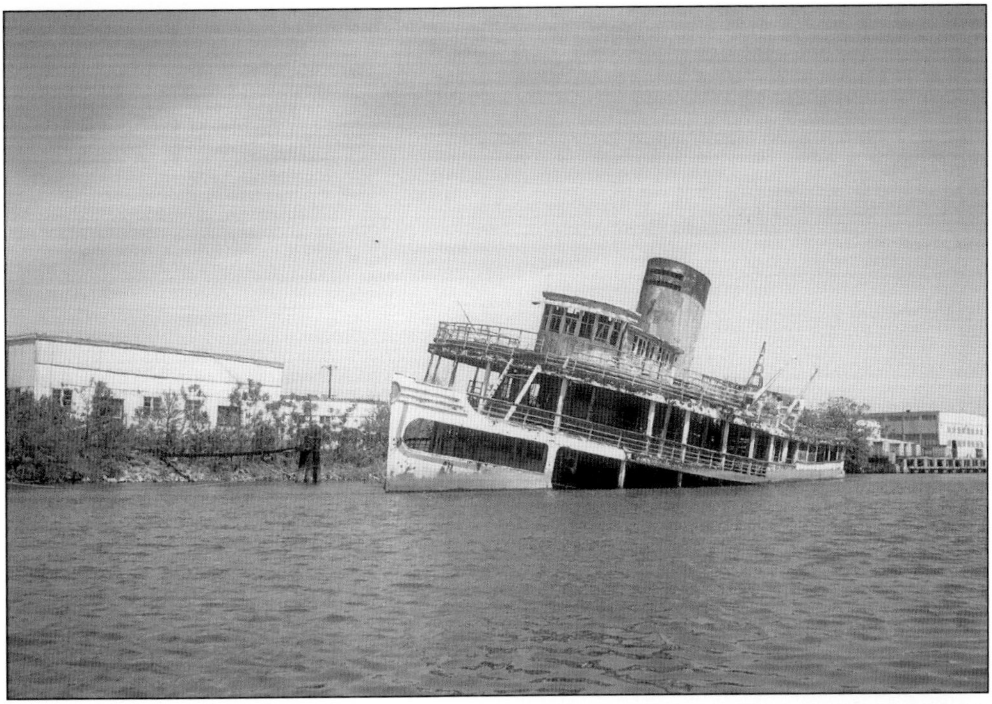

The proud Wilson liner *State of Pennsylvania* met her fate in the Christina River after a long and happy career. Pusey & Jones had launched the ship on the Christina in 1923. Her maiden voyage was a moonlight cruise (fare: 50¢) to Riverview Beach. She was built to have lots of deck space and featured a 3,000-square-foot ballroom where a live orchestra played dance music.

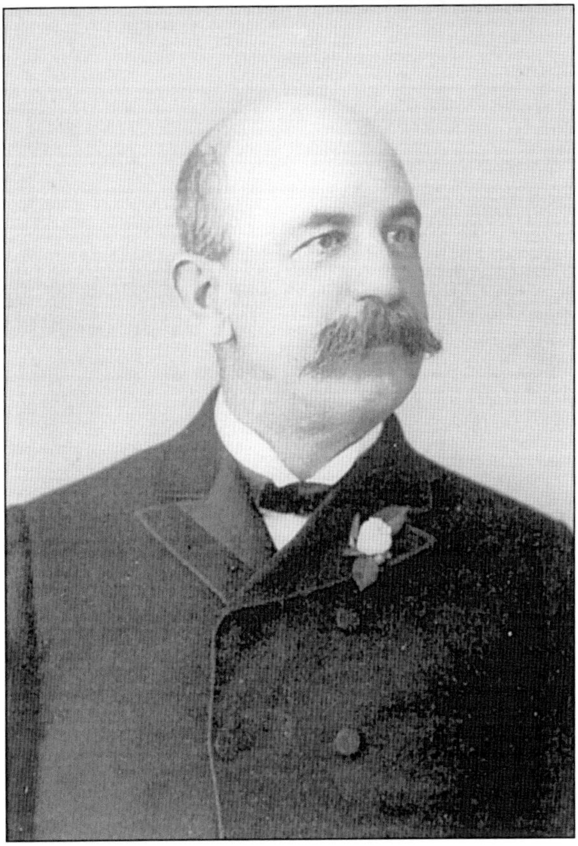

In about 1870, Enoch Moore, a shipbuilder and marine railway operator, occupied part of what later became the Wilson Line area. In 1880, Moore employed 50 men and constructed wooden vessels of up to 350 tons. His specialty was wooden steam freight barges. Another boat builder, Banner and Munn, who made metal lifeboats, steam launches, and sail boats, also worked in this area. (Courtesy of the Historical society of Delaware.)

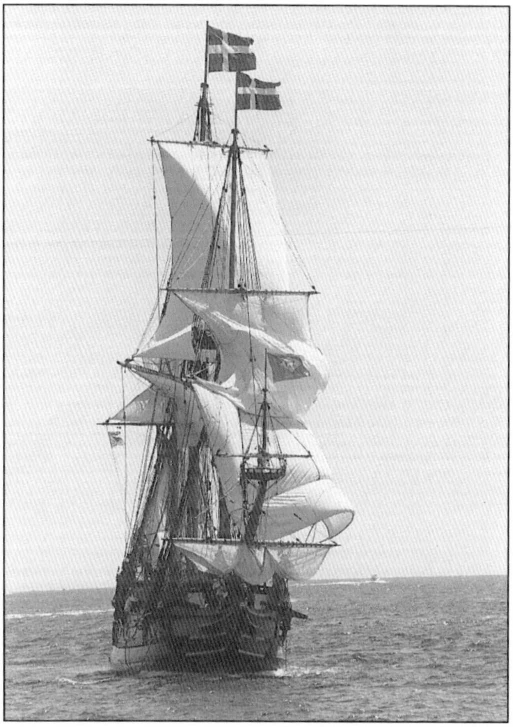

In 1638, Swedish colonists started a small settlement on the peninsula. This replica of the *Kalmar Nyckel*, one of the two ships in which they arrived, calls Wilmington her home port. Built at a cost of $4.3 million, she was launched in September 1997 and commissioned in May 1998. (Courtesy of Chris Queeney.)

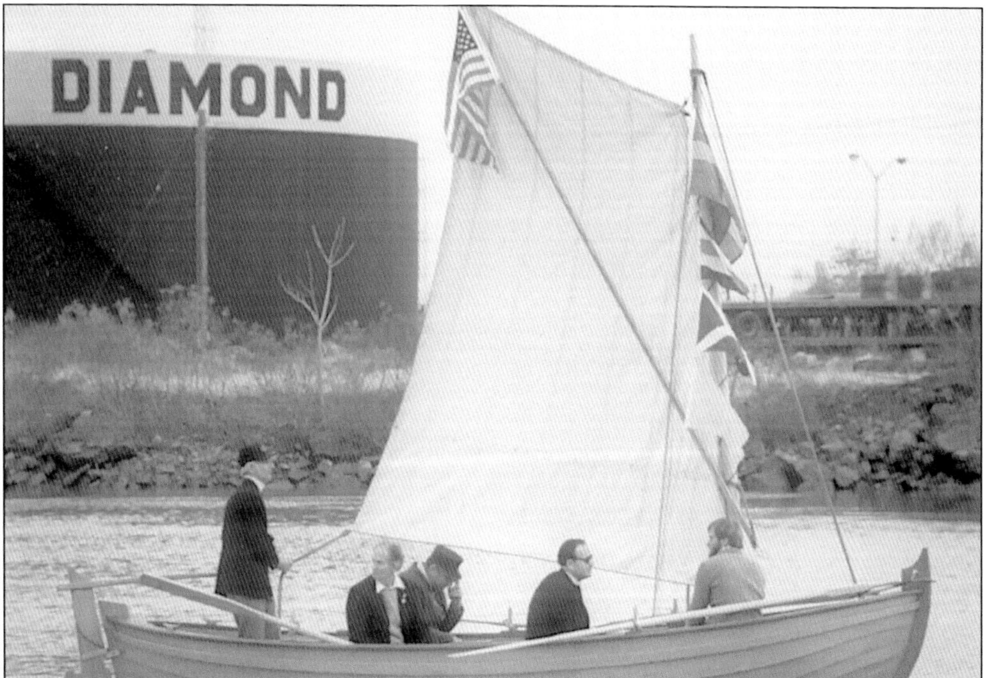

The *Little Key*, built in the earliest phase of the reproduction of the *Kalmar Nyckel*, takes her first sail on the Christina in 1986. On board are, from left to right, Captain Quinlan, Malcolm Mackenzie, Ralph Gilgenost, Nick du Pont, and Phil Shelton. (Courtesy of Malcolm Mackenzie.)

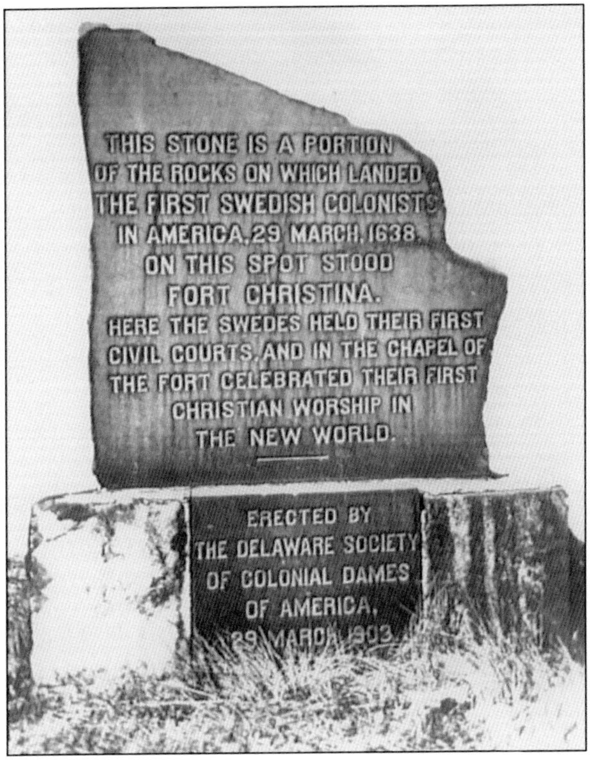

The story of Sweden's only colony in America seems to have lived as a mystical tale for two centuries after its founding. Though the Christina River was named for the young queen at the time of the original settlement, neglect hid the actual place of landing. In 1903, the Colonial Dames placed this marker on the landing site. (Courtesy of the Delaware State Archives.)

When shipbuilding and other industries found the peninsula to be an ideal location, the historical significance of the area was lost amid railroad spurs and heavy machinery. This tiny sign seems a meager tribute to the colony of New Sweden. (Courtesy of the Delaware State Archives.)

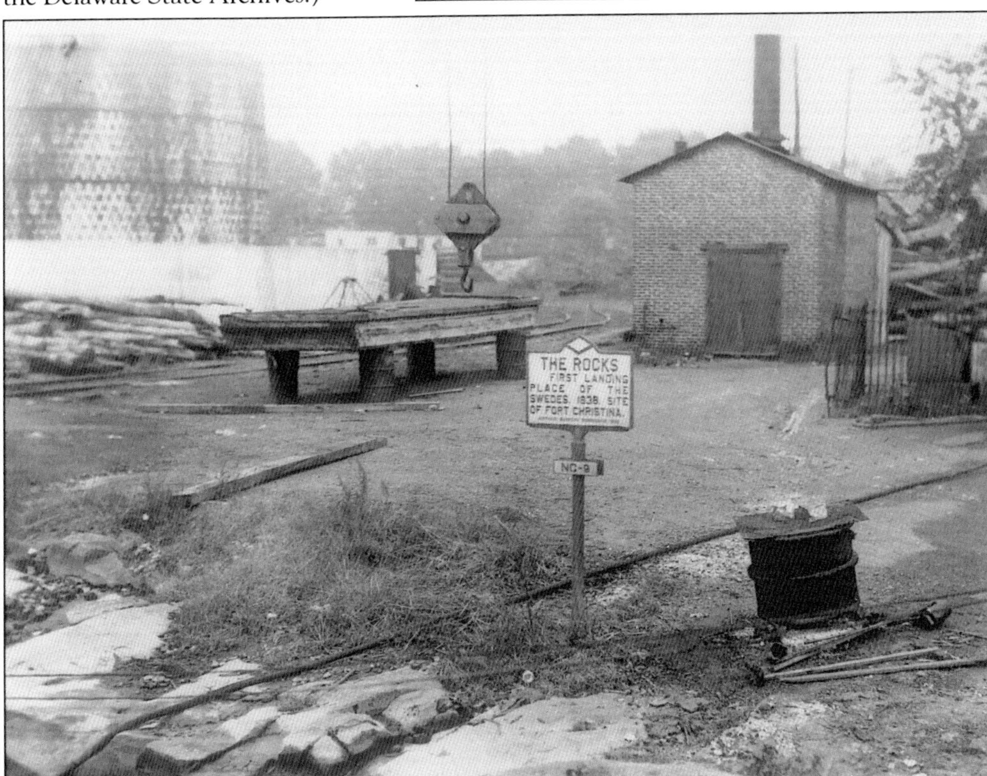

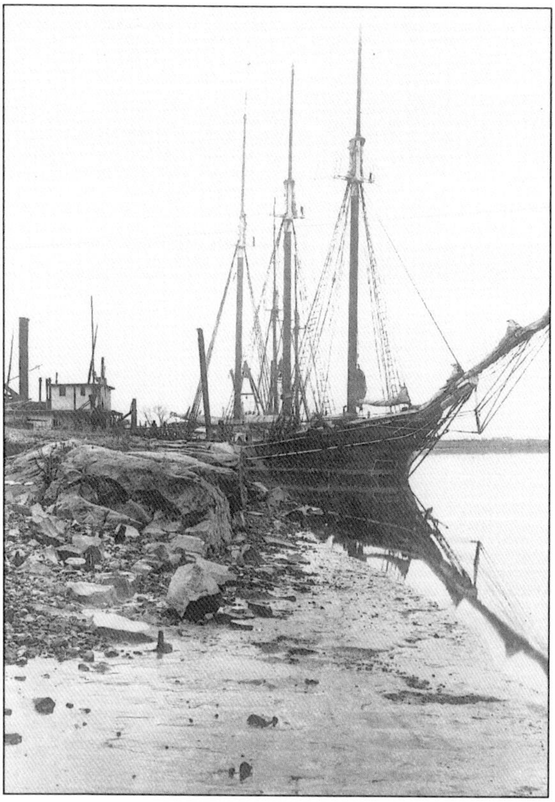

A three-masted schooner tied up alongside the peninsula in 1898 is a much more dramatic image than the rocks in front of it. Yet these are the stones where the Swedes are said to have landed in 1638, when they first arrived at what would later become Wilmington. (Courtesy of the Delaware State Archives.)

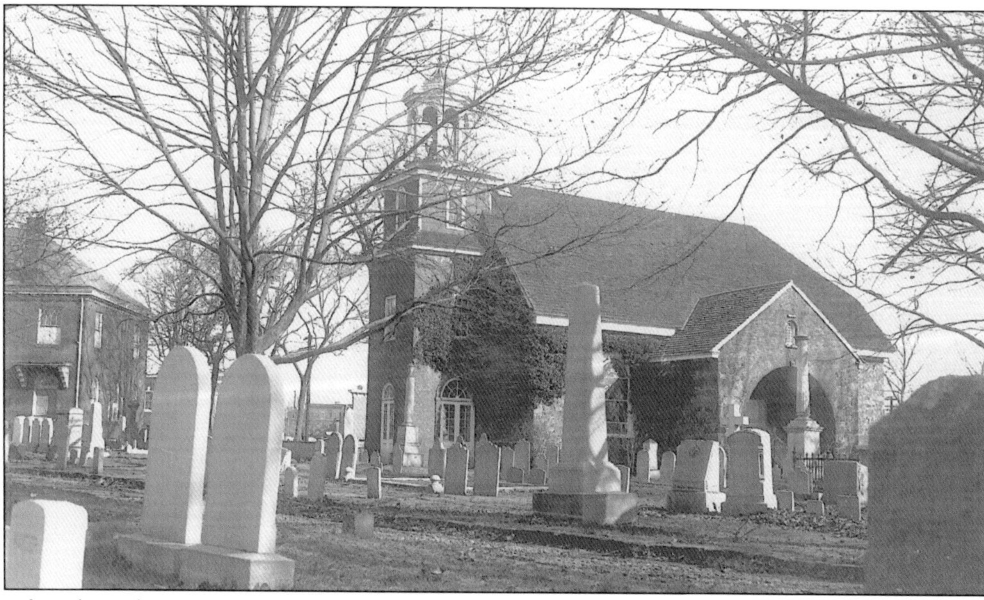

After the colony fell to the Dutch, many descendants of the early Swedish settlers remained in the area. For their benefit, construction began on Old Swedes Church in 1698. It is now a national historic landmark and the oldest continually operating church in the nation. This 1933 photograph shows the church much as it looks today with its tower, an addition of about 1800. (Courtesy of the Delaware State Archives.)

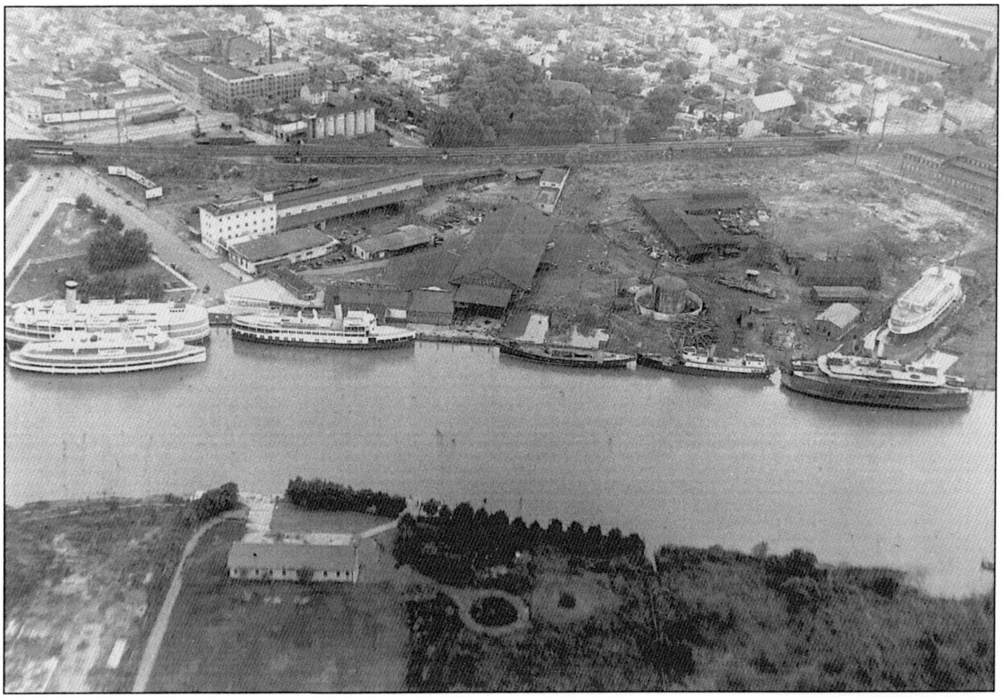

This aerial photograph of about 1930 shows Wilson Line ships, the railroad line, and miscellaneous industrial structures. The area along the far bank of the river to the right is approximately where the Christina Monument would be located within a few years. (Courtesy of the Delaware State Archives.)

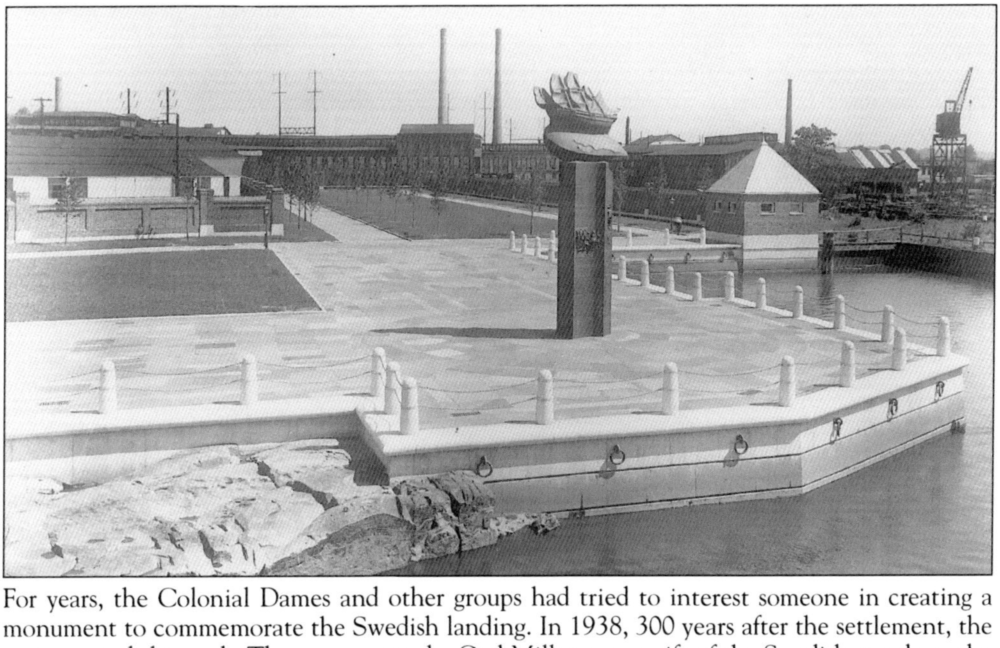

For years, the Colonial Dames and other groups had tried to interest someone in creating a monument to commemorate the Swedish landing. In 1938, 300 years after the settlement, the state created this park. The monument, by Carl Milles, was a gift of the Swedish people to the American people. Note the Jackson & Sharp buildings surrounding the park. (Courtesy of the Delaware State Archives.)

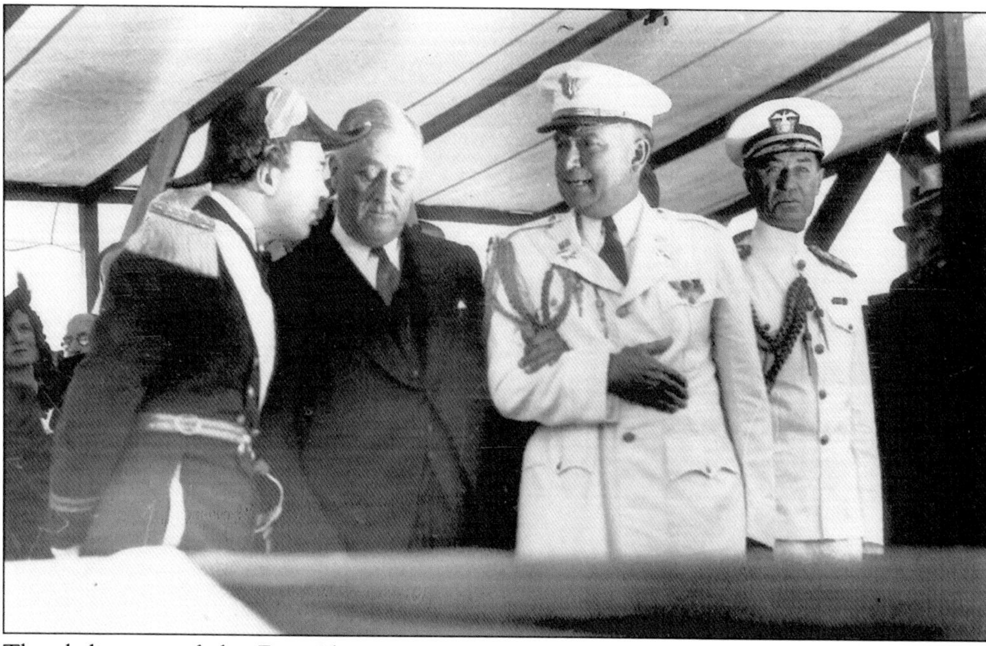

The dedication of the Fort Christina Monument was an important part of Wilmington's tercentenary celebration in 1938. Dignitaries came from Sweden and distant parts of the United States to take part in this event. Here are, from left to right, Prince Bertil of Sweden, President Franklin D. Roosevelt, a U.S. Army aide, and a U.S. Navy aide. (Courtesy of the Delaware State Archives.)

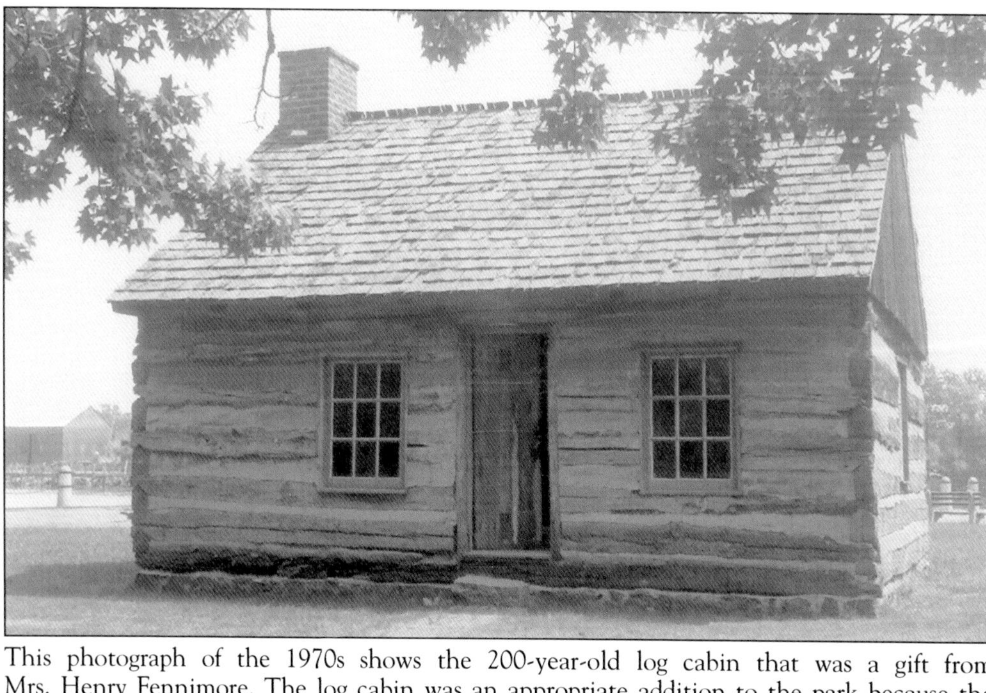

This photograph of the 1970s shows the 200-year-old log cabin that was a gift from Mrs. Henry Fennimore. The log cabin was an appropriate addition to the park because the Swedes were the first to use this type of construction. Unfortunately, the cabin became a target for vandals, and it is now boarded up. (Courtesy of the Delaware State Archives.)

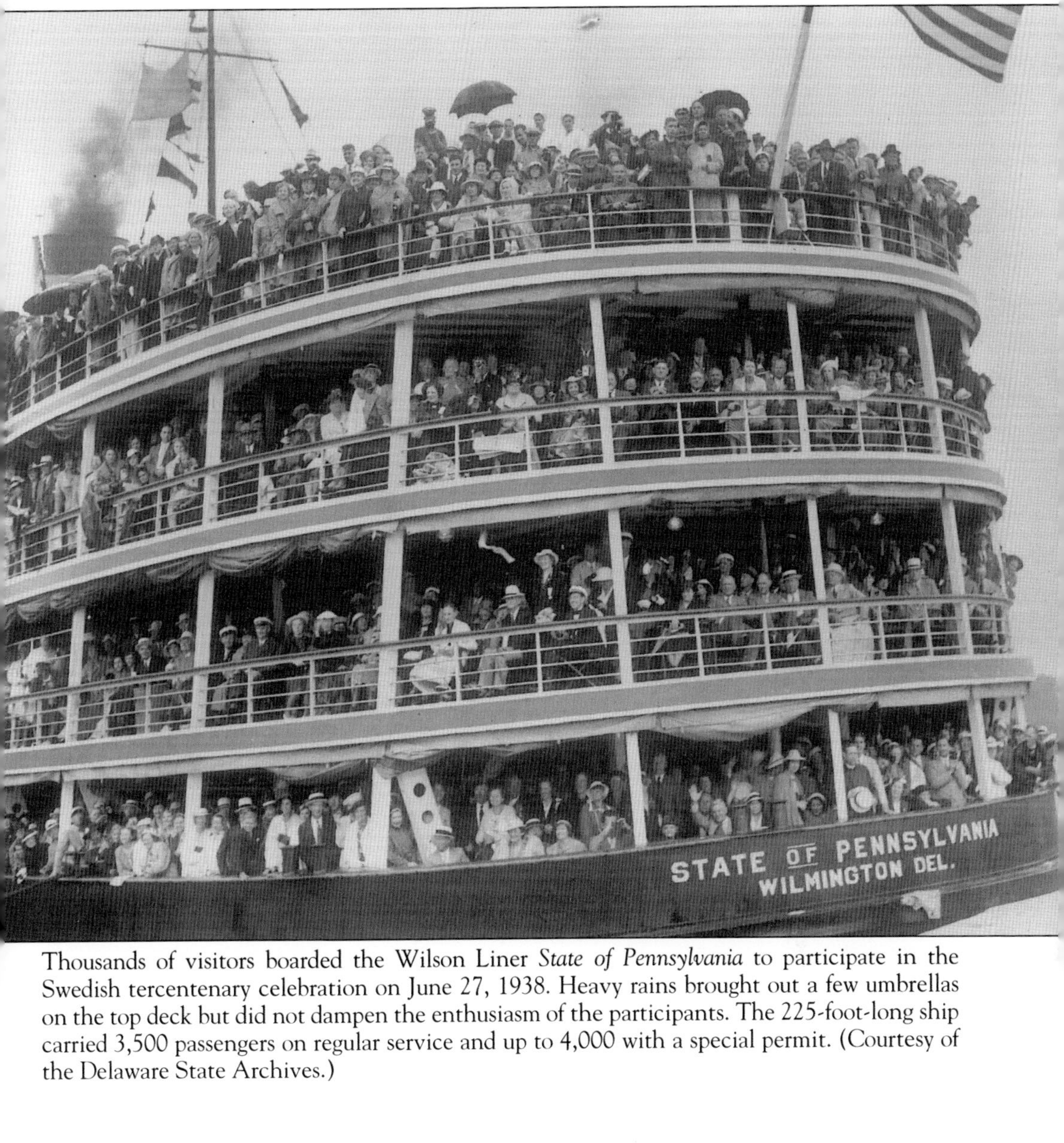

Thousands of visitors boarded the Wilson Liner *State of Pennsylvania* to participate in the Swedish tercentenary celebration on June 27, 1938. Heavy rains brought out a few umbrellas on the top deck but did not dampen the enthusiasm of the participants. The 225-foot-long ship carried 3,500 passengers on regular service and up to 4,000 with a special permit. (Courtesy of the Delaware State Archives.)

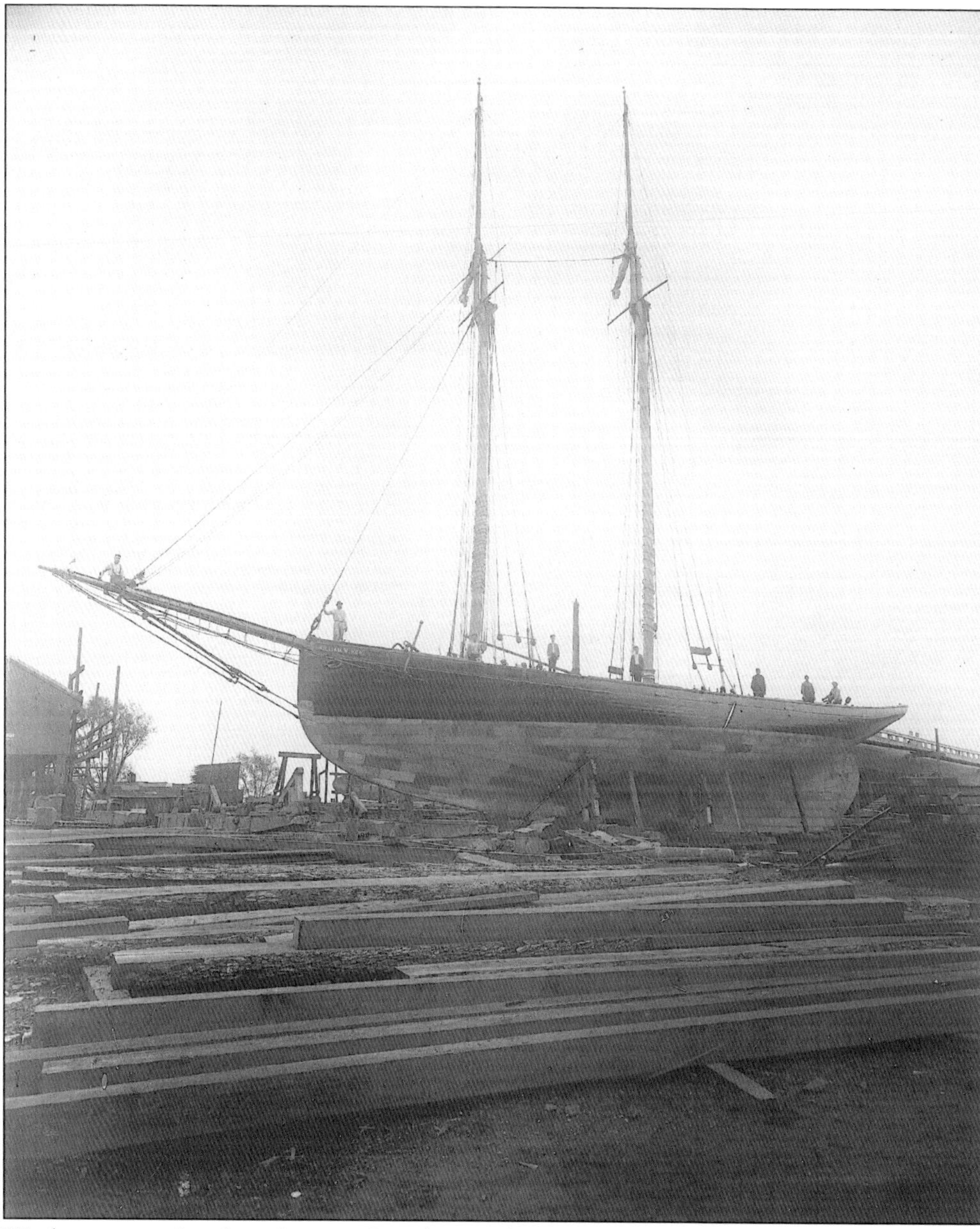

Workers pause for this photographer during the construction of the two-masted wooden schooner *William W. Ker* at the Jackson & Sharp Company in 1894. Job Jackson and Jacob Sharp went into business in 1863, producing railroad cars to carry peaches from Delaware's expanding orchards. By 1890, the company covered 20 acres on the peninsula, had over 1,000 employees, and could have up to 80 railroad cars under construction at one time. Jackson & Sharp also built many wooden sailing vessels for both pleasure and commercial use. The plant employed skilled wood workers, upholsterers, metal workers, painters, and craftsmen of all the types needed to create the details in the finished railroad cars and boats. The sawdust from Jackson & Sharp's extensive wood-working operations did not go to waste; vacuums sucked it up to be used for fuel for the boilers that powered their machinery. (Courtesy of the Delaware State Archives.)

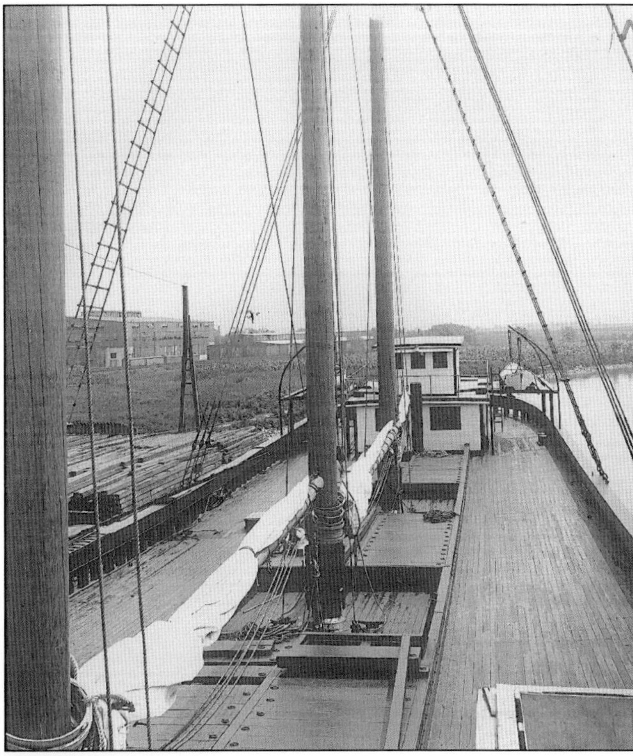

We are looking back over the stern of the three-masted wooden schooner *Altamaha* in 1913. Jackson & Sharp sold out to American Car and Foundry, but the plant continued in operation and enlarged its work force. Commonly called the Delaware Car Works, the company also produced many boats as well as railroad cars. (Courtesy of the Delaware State Archives.)

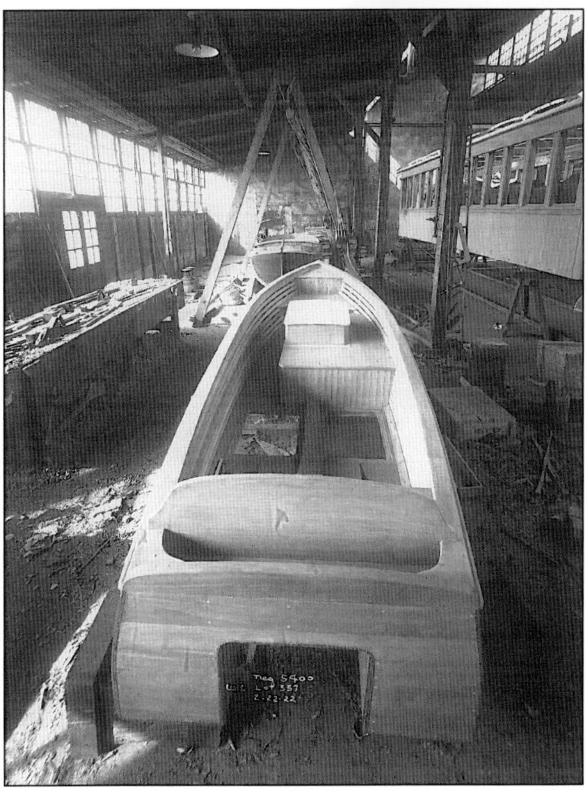

This 1922 photograph shows the construction of a wooden inboard motor boat in one of the Jackson & Sharp buildings. Another partly finished small boat is in the background, and on the right is the body of a wooden railroad car that is not yet attached to wheels. (Courtesy of the Delaware State Archives.)

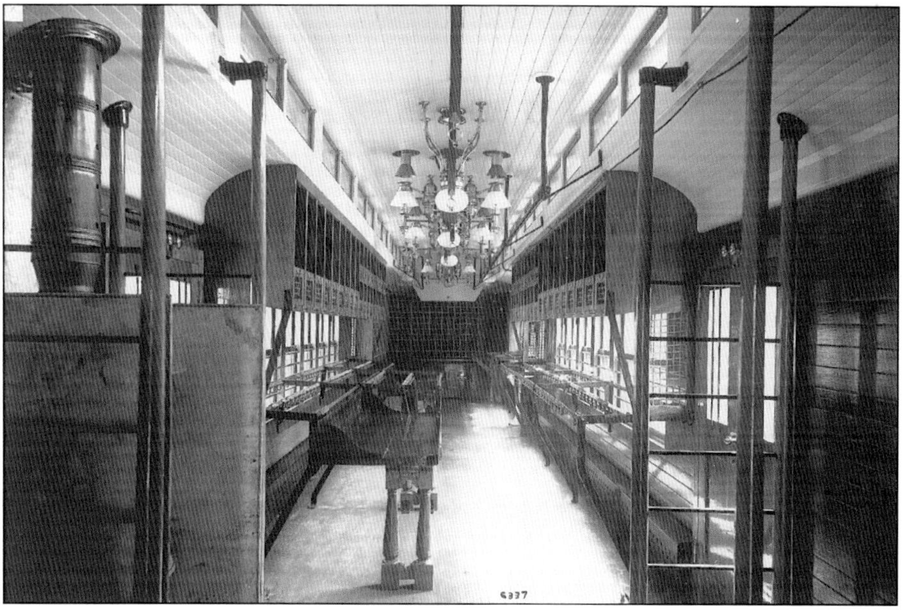

The interior of this mail car, built at the Jackson & Sharp (American Car and Foundry) plant in 1908 for the Atlantic Coast Line, helps to tell the story of how mail was handled in the early 20th century. Workers picked up mail at stations along the line, sorted it into bins and bags, and dropped it at the appropriate stations. (Courtesy of the Delaware State Archives.)

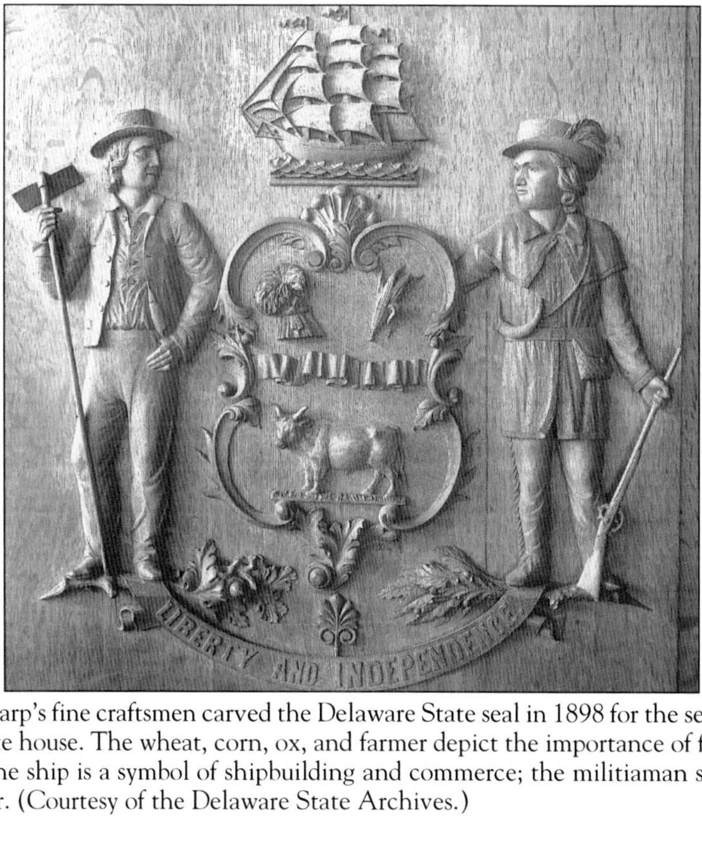

Jackson & Sharp's fine craftsmen carved the Delaware State seal in 1898 for the senate chamber of the old state house. The wheat, corn, ox, and farmer depict the importance of farming to the state, while the ship is a symbol of shipbuilding and commerce; the militiaman symbolizes the citizen-soldier. (Courtesy of the Delaware State Archives.)

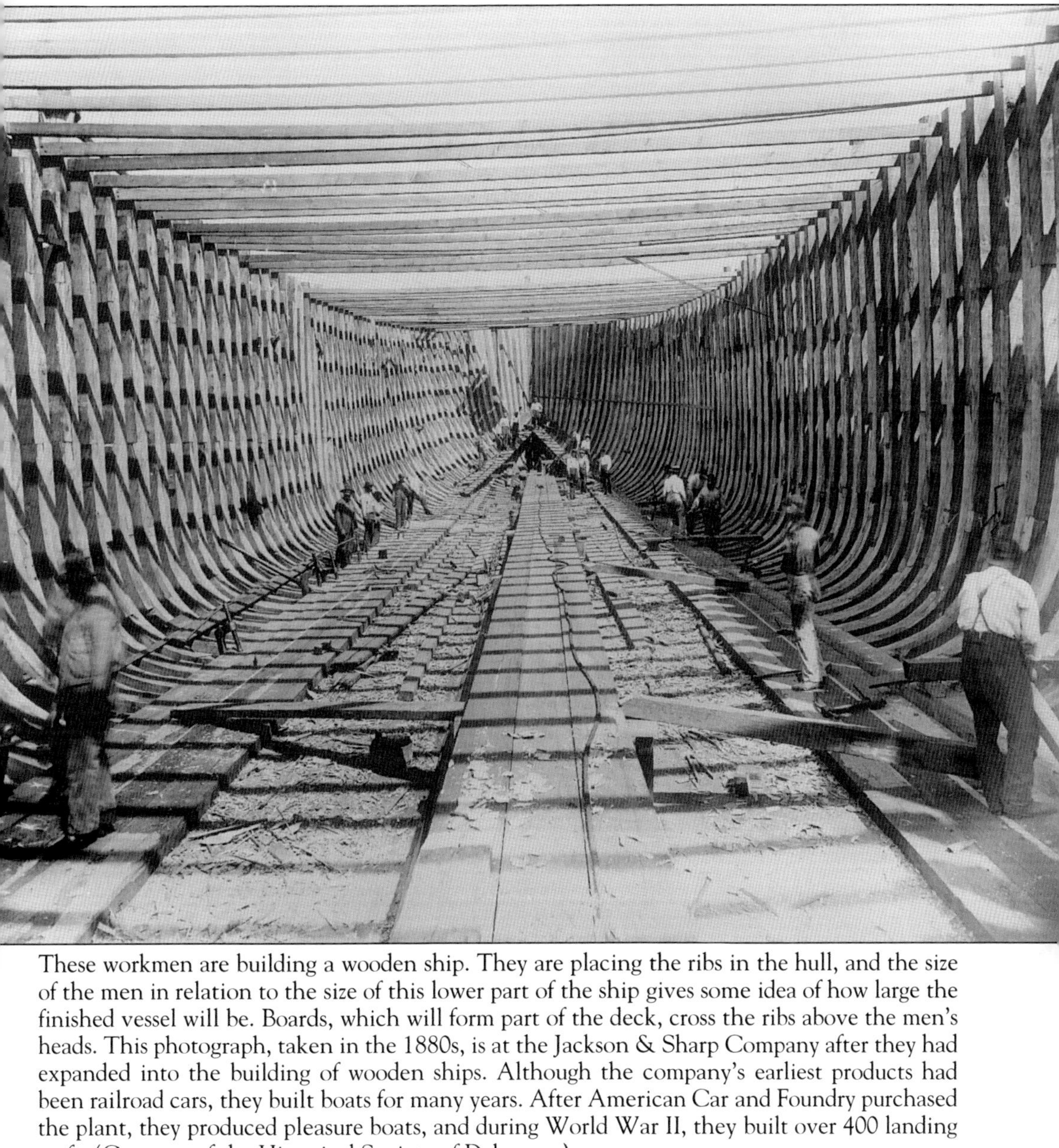

These workmen are building a wooden ship. They are placing the ribs in the hull, and the size of the men in relation to the size of this lower part of the ship gives some idea of how large the finished vessel will be. Boards, which will form part of the deck, cross the ribs above the men's heads. This photograph, taken in the 1880s, is at the Jackson & Sharp Company after they had expanded into the building of wooden ships. Although the company's earliest products had been railroad cars, they built boats for many years. After American Car and Foundry purchased the plant, they produced pleasure boats, and during World War II, they built over 400 landing craft. (Courtesy of the Historical Society of Delaware.)

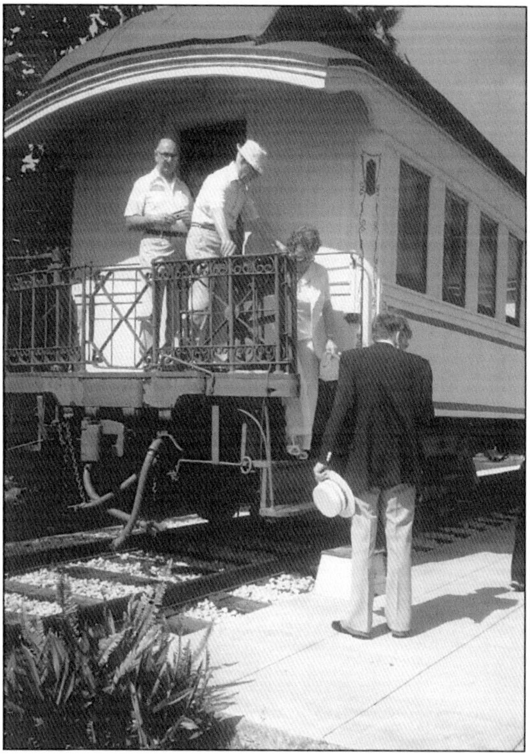

Jackson & Sharp built the private railroad car, *The Rambler,* in 1886, for Henry Morrison Flagler, the prime developer of Florida's east coast as a resort area. After Flagler's death, the car was abandoned, but the restored car is now at the Henry Morrison Flagler Museum in Palm Beach, Florida. Visitors can see the interior of the car that still bears the Jackson & Sharp nameplate.

In 1887, Jackson & Sharp built this railroad car advertising the benefits of Florida. At the time, there was probably no better way to promote the development of a winter playground in a balmy southern climate than to send the message on the rails. This was just one of the many railroad cars Jackson & Sharp built for advertising and other specialized uses. (Courtesy of the Delaware State Archives.)

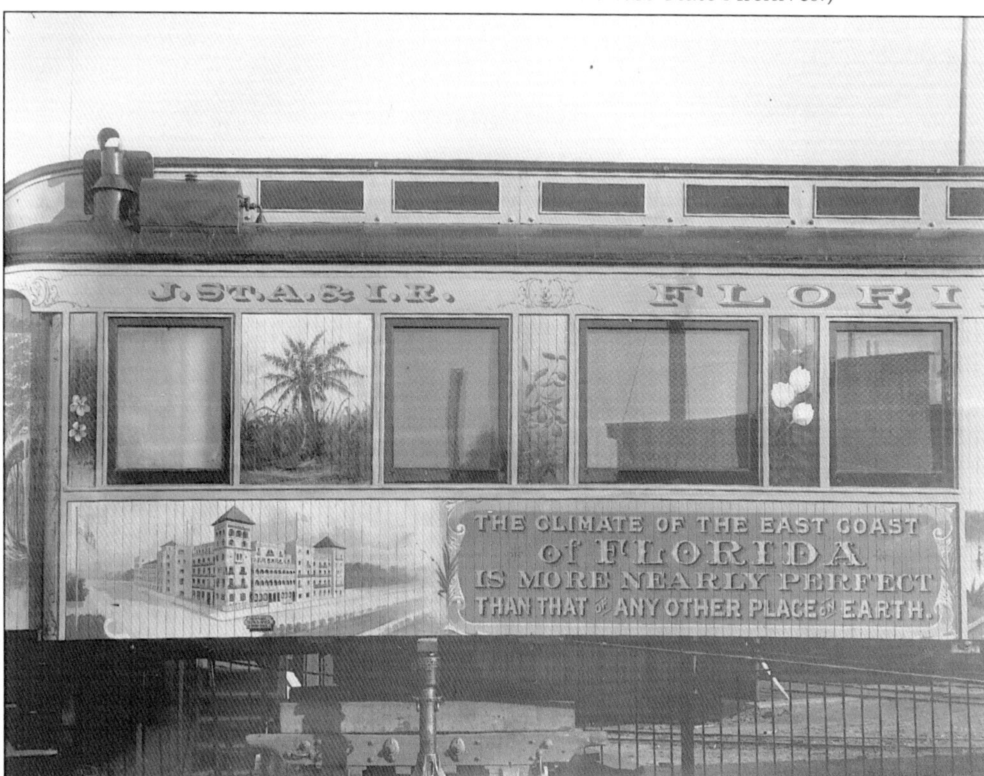

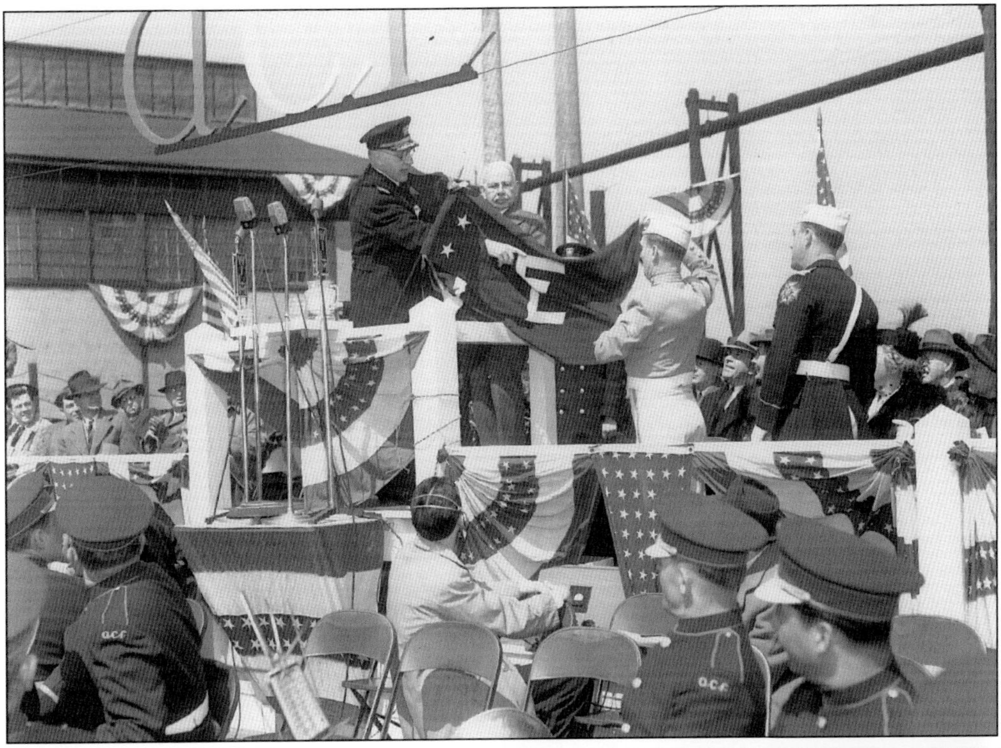

American Car and Foundry, successor to Jackson & Sharp, received the U.S. Navy "E" pennant for excellence in production in World War II. A crowd gathers here to watch as officials of the company ceremoniously accept the official "E" banner. Note the ACF (for American Car and Foundry) on the band uniforms. (Courtesy of the Delaware State Archives.)

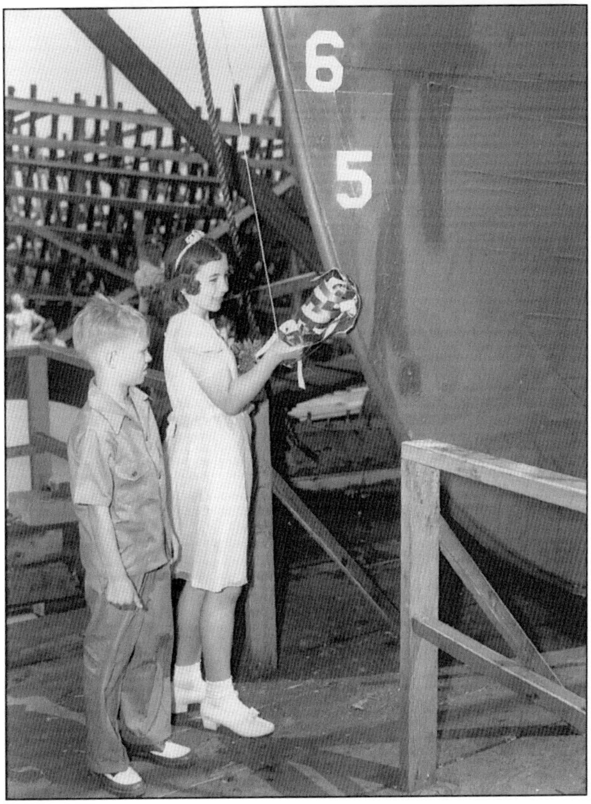

Dolores Ann Speck, a ten-year-old sponsor, aims for the nose of the mine sweeper J-804 that slid down the ways at American Car & Foundry on June 18, 1942. Kenneth A. Hannum, her ten-year-old escort, looks on. (Courtesy of the Delaware State Archives.)

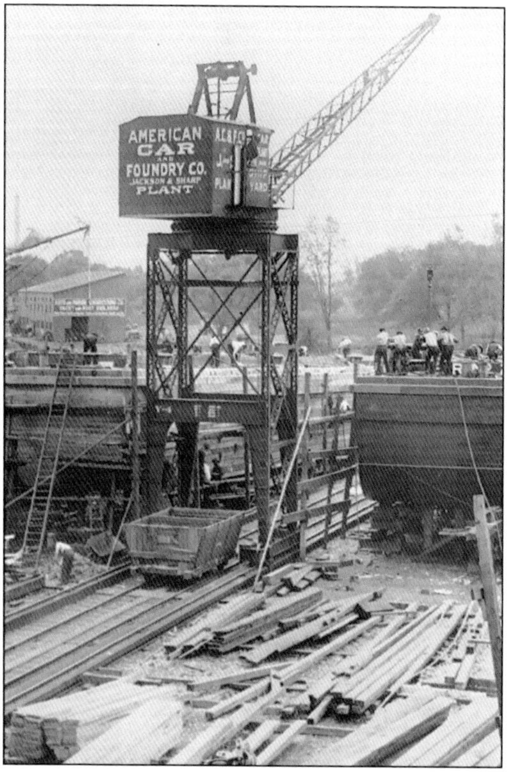

After World War II, American Car and Foundry built wooden barges. Men are at work here near one of the cranes on the peninsula. The sign clearly identifies American Car and Foundry's heritage as the Jackson & Sharp plant. (Courtesy of the Hagley Museum and Library.)

In the 1970s, the community organization Cityside began calling attention to the waterfront by sponsoring Maritime Days, which included a regatta. Here, Mayor William McLaughlin (in profile facing the girl holding the silver cup) presents trophies. Roy Smith, president of Cityside, is on the far left in the white hat, and Kevin Free, later a state representative, is standing on the dock. Others are unidentified. (Courtesy of A. Roy Smith and Mildred Ward.)

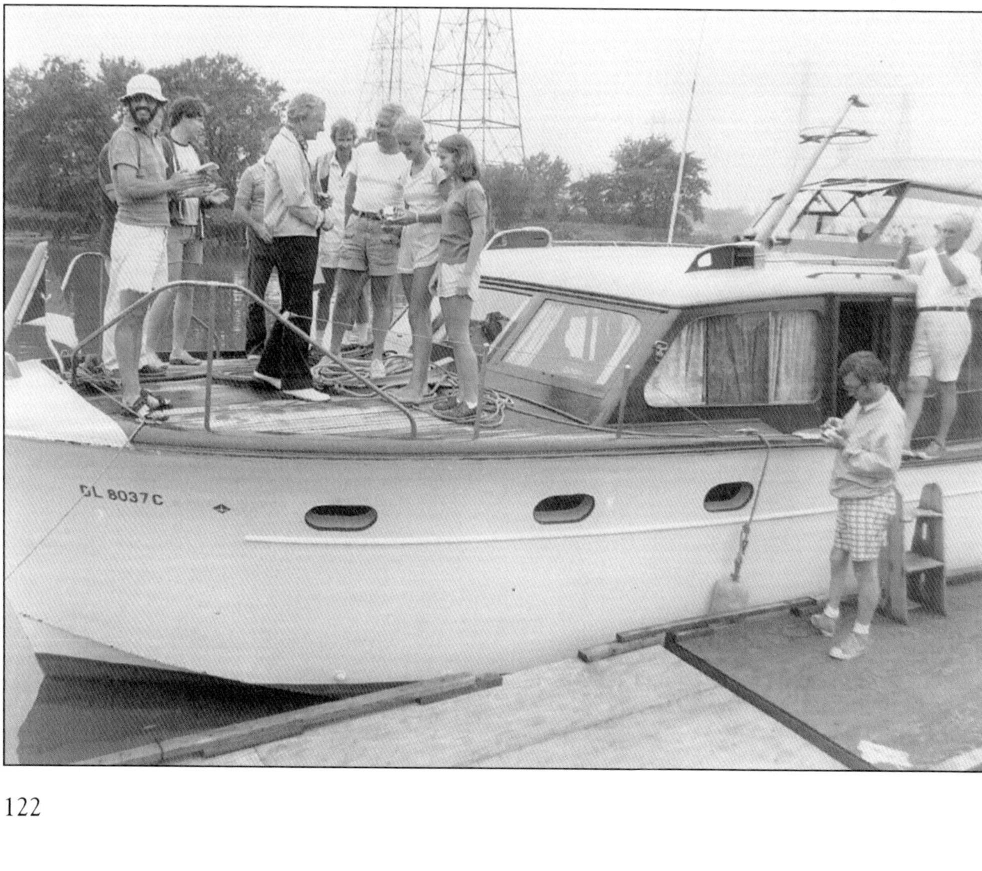

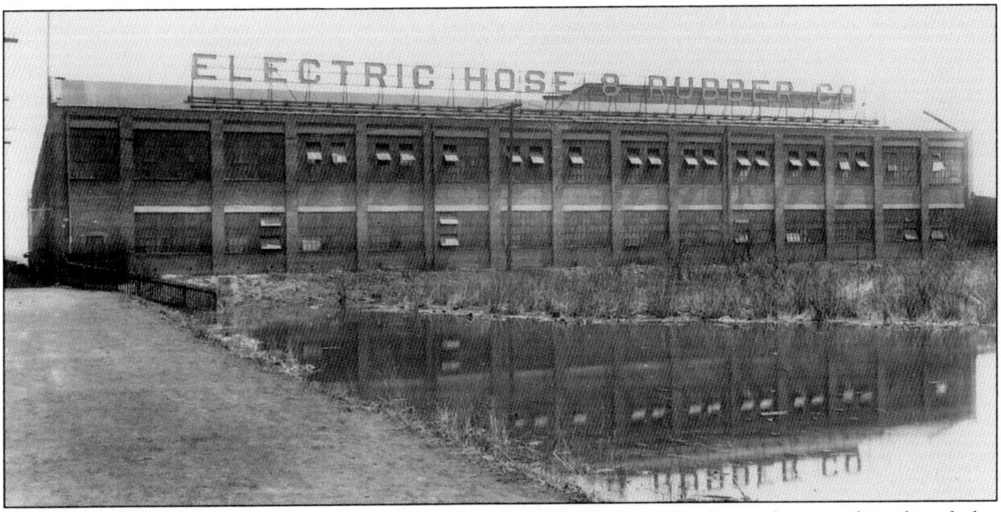

The Electric Hose & Rubber Co. buildings face the peninsula from the north side of the Brandywine as it curves to meet the Christina. The buildings are near the spot where Shellpot Creek once emptied into the Brandywine as shown on the map on page 10. The company started as the Chicago Electric Wire Co., which covered electric wire with an insulating material for use under water. (Courtesy of the Delaware State Archives.)

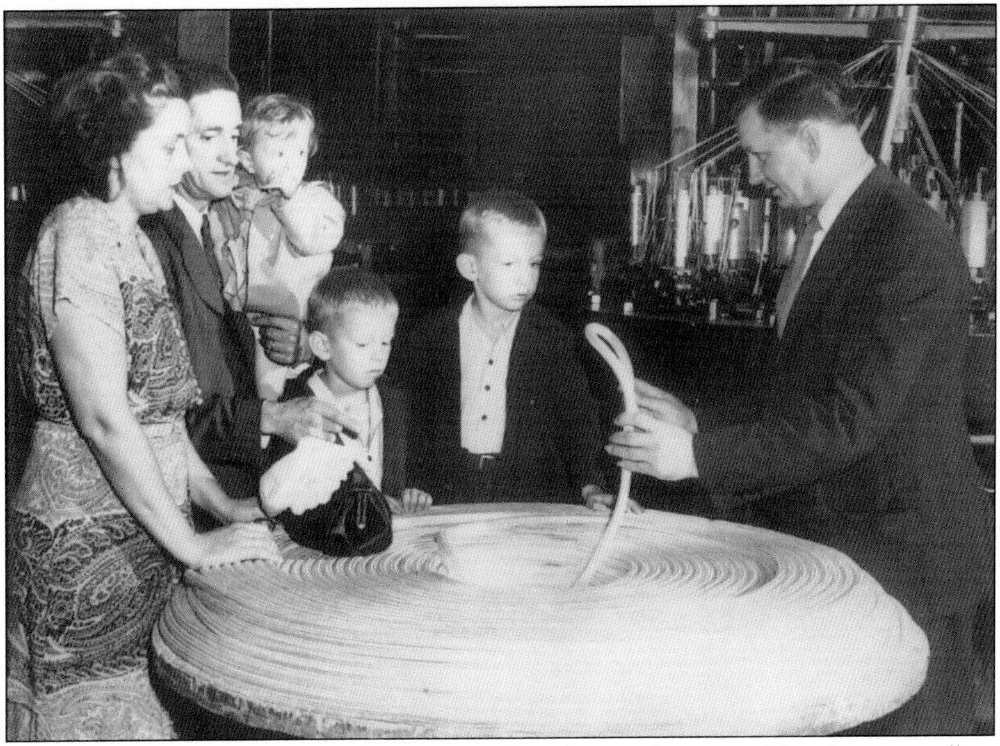

Realizing that their process for the waterproof insulation of wire would make an excellent garden hose, the company began to make "Chicago Electric Hose." This was such a success that they incorporated as Electric Hose & Rubber, even though they stopped making electrical wire. Here, a company representative is explaining their product to a family in what appears to be the 1940s. (Courtesy of the Delaware State Archives.)

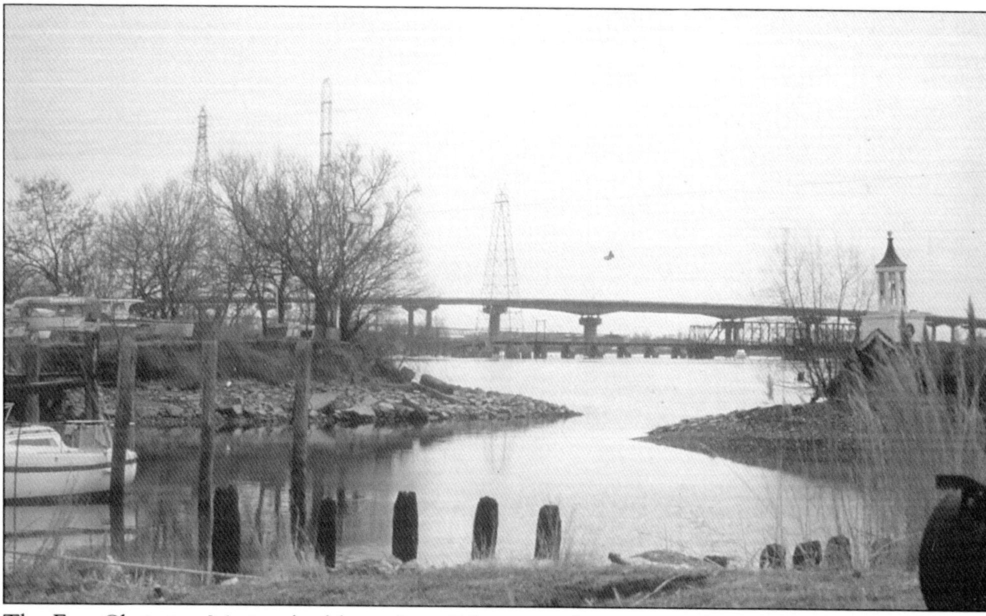

The Fort Christina Marina had lots of small boats in the water and in storage in the 1970s. A rather eclectic mix of buildings and other structures appeared toward the end of the peninsula. Here, we see an old tower from a Howard Johnson's restaurant with the Seventh Street bridge, the I-495 bridge, and electrical towers in the background. (Courtesy of Malcolm Mackenzie.)

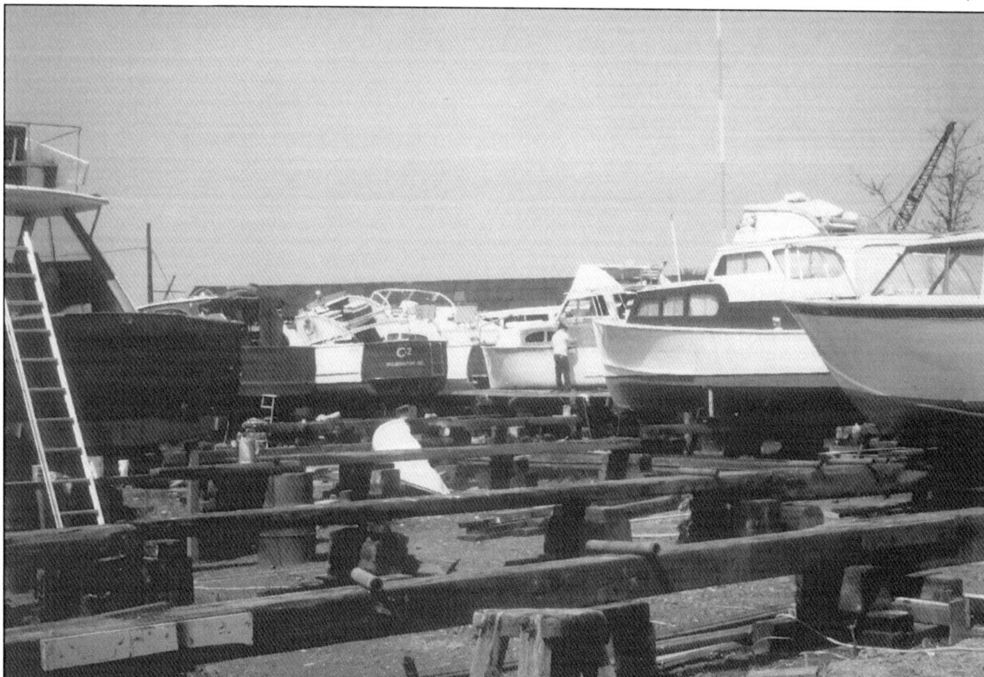

Many people stored their boats at the Seventh Street Boat Yard in the 1970s. Located near the end of the peninsula, this was a convenient place for owners to work on their boats and launch them before going out into the Delaware River. Dick Grant opened the Up The Creek Restaurant near here.

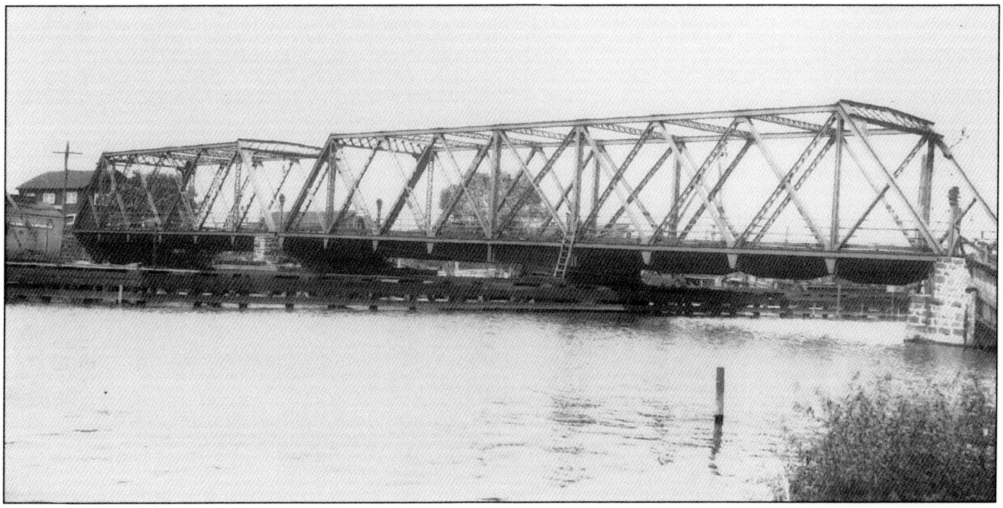

A Frank R. Zebley photo of the 1930s shows the Seventh Street bridge, which connected the end of the peninsula to the Cherry Island marshes. This iron bridge, built in about 1900, replaced an earlier wooden bridge. Since there was no traffic from the peninsula to Cherry Island, the bridge was inoperable for many years and is now gone. (Courtesy of the Delaware State Archives.)

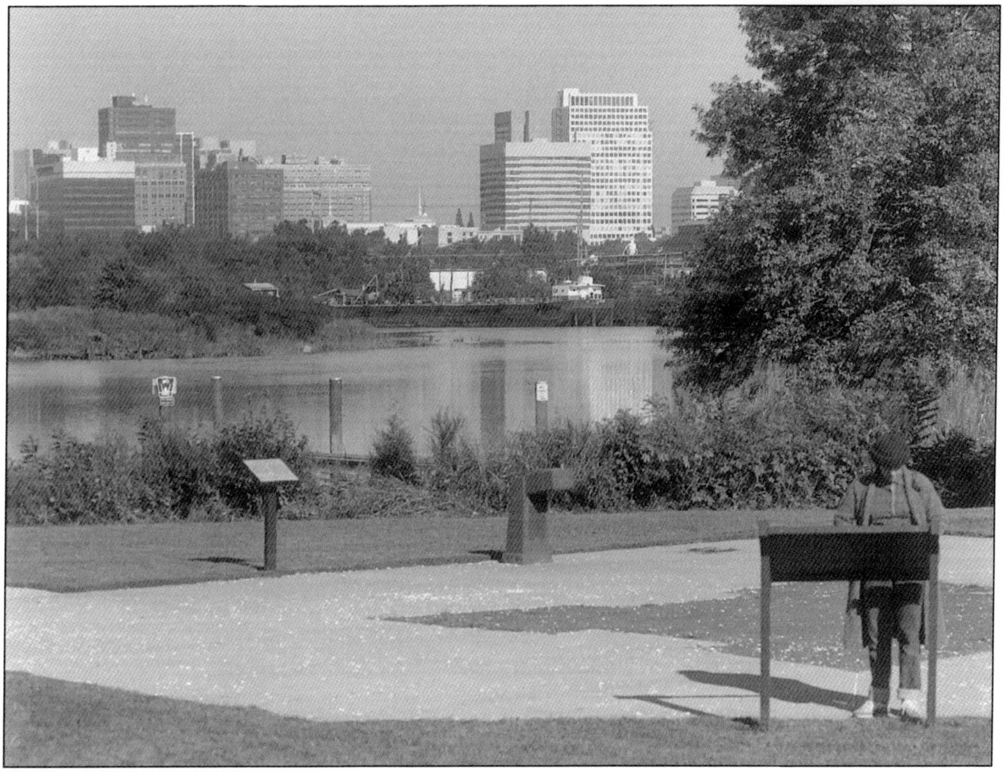

The city of Wilmington created the Seventh Street Park near the end of the peninsula with an outline on the ground showing the shape of the Swedish fort that once protected the settlement. This photograph from the 1970s, by Tim Bayard, shows the park's excellent view of the city to the west. (Courtesy of Tim Bayard.)

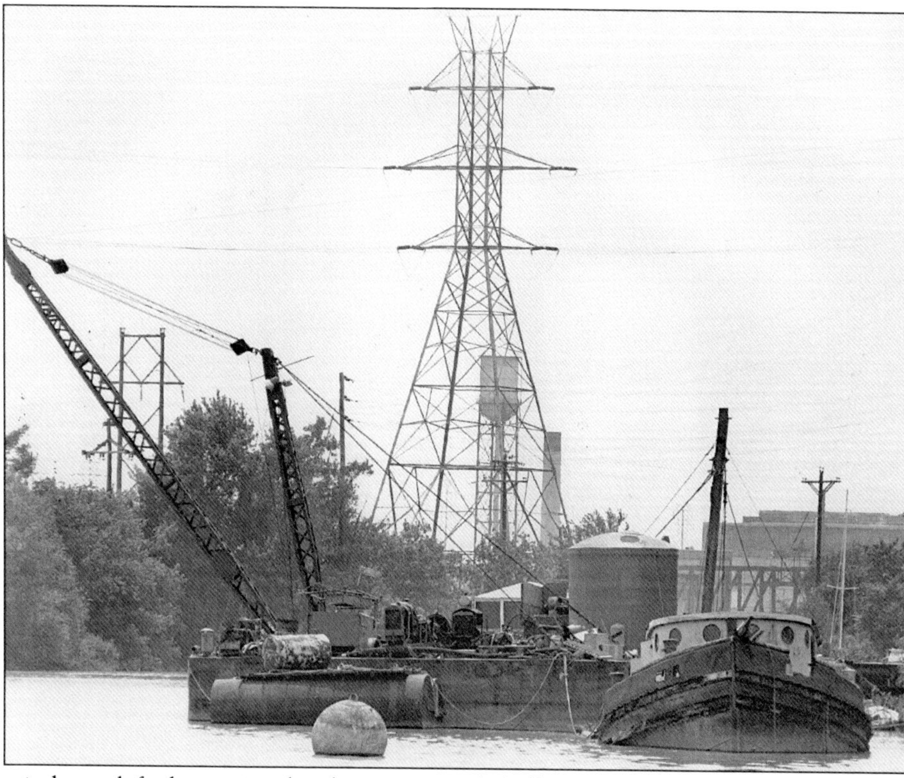

After industry left the peninsula, the curves and shallows of the rivers became a haven for derelict and abandoned boats. A mid-1970s photograph by David W. Van Allen shows an old boat and barge slowly succumbing to the ravages of tide and time. (Courtesy of the Wilmington Department of Parks and Recreation.)

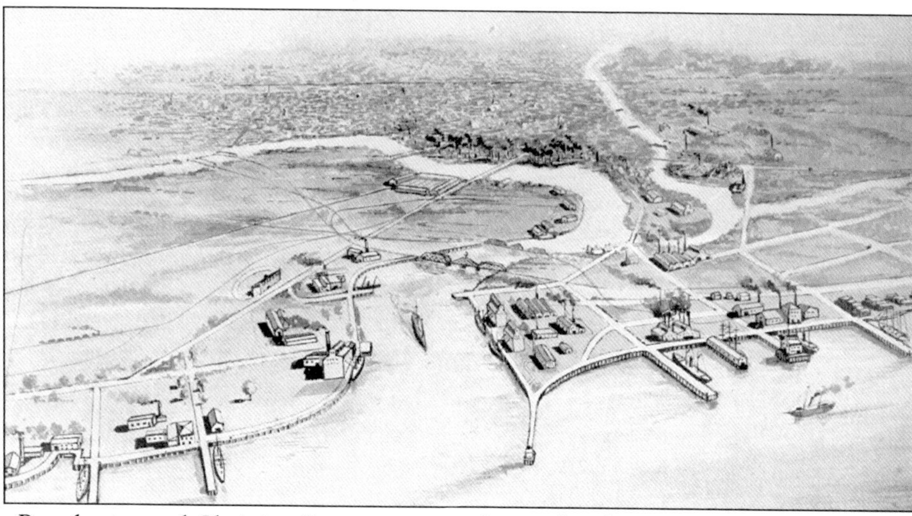

The Brandywine and Christina Rivers meet on the south side of the peninsula and flow into the Delaware, today's location for Wilmington's port. This imaginative bird's-eye view of the riverfront appeared in a 1898 book extolling the prosperity of the city's industries. The image seems to present hopes for the growth of industry along the Delaware. (Courtesy of the Historical Society of Delaware.)

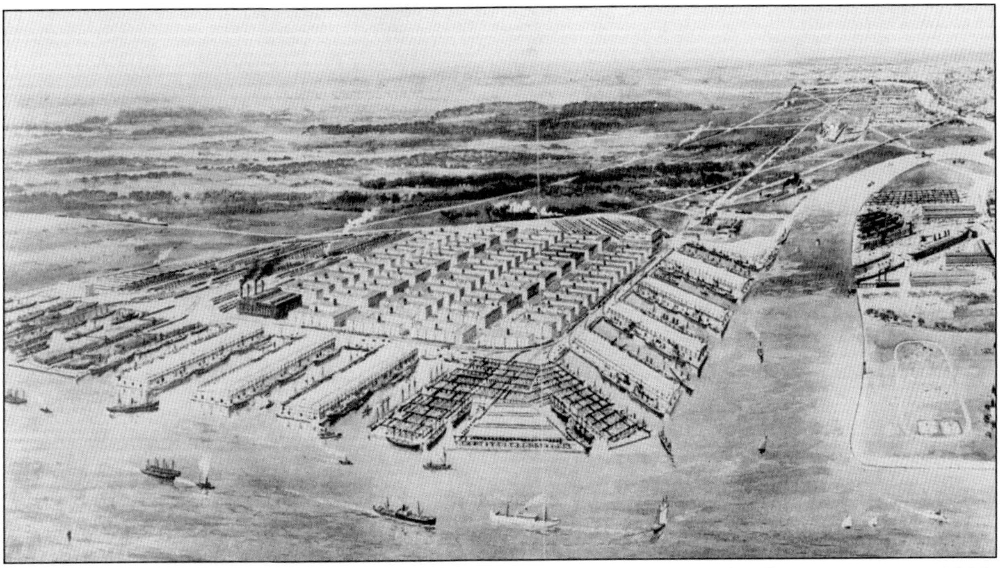

The chamber of commerce prepared this even more optimistic view of today's port area in 1919. The shipping facilities on the upper Christina were no longer adequate, so some proponents of a new port came up with grandiose ideas. However, the concept of a new port was a sound one, and the new marine terminal opened in 1923. (Courtesy of the Historical Society of Delaware.)

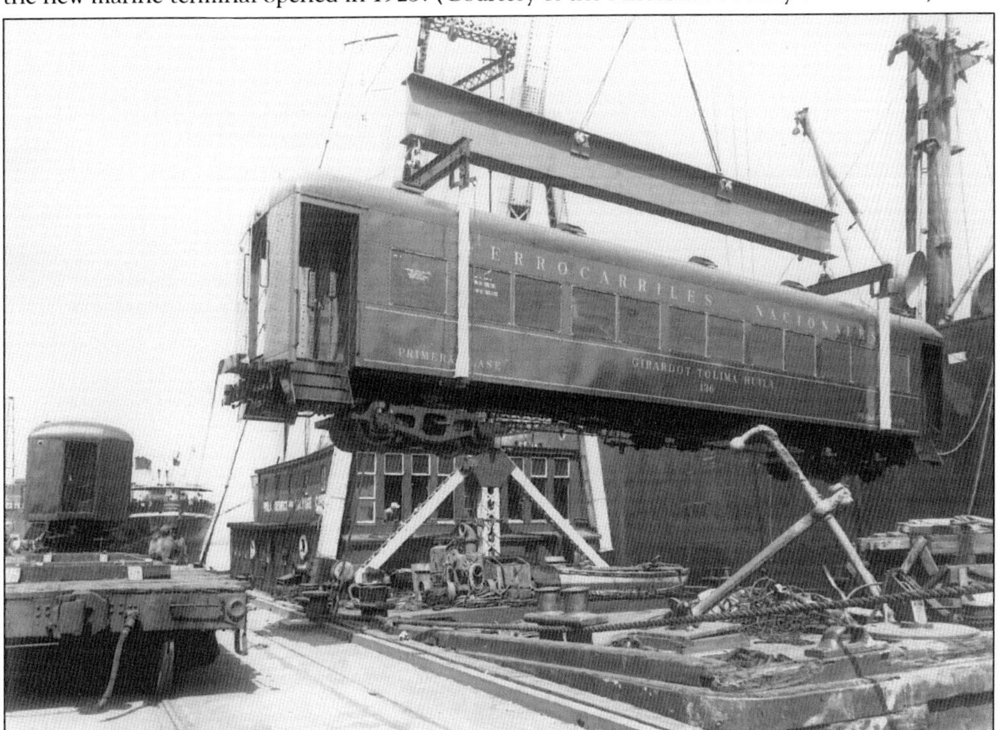

Wilmington's industries produced plenty of products for overseas customers. This railroad car, built by American Car and Foundry, is being loaded onto a ship headed for South America. The car is complete with all interior fittings and exterior signage in Spanish. (Courtesy of the Delaware State Archives.)

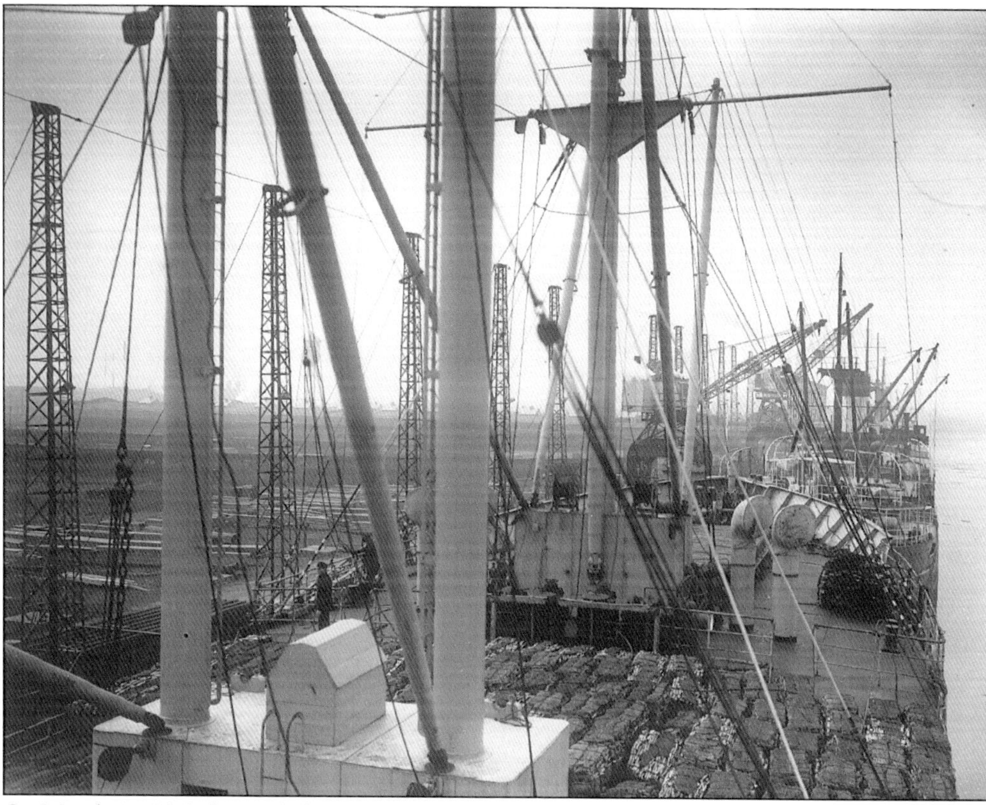

On March 4, 1936, the English steamer *Harbledown* tied up at the Wilmington Marine Terminal. Today, the Port of Wilmington boasts the largest on-dock storage facility in the United States, making it number one in North America for the import of bananas, fruit, produce, and juice concentrate. (Courtesy of the Delaware State Archives.)

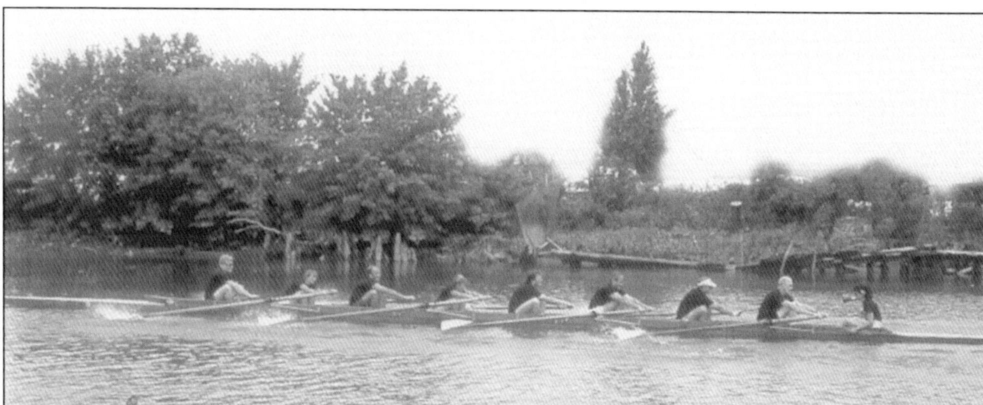

In the past 20 years, the rivers that form the Wilmington waterfront have seen an increase in recreational and business uses that take advantage of the benefits of the rivers. Here, the Wilmington Rowing Center has a mixed eight rowing shell on the Christina. From left to right in this photograph by John Schoonover are Ron McConnell, Helga Ganci, Hans Franke, Shawn Nied, Henry Hauptfuhrer, Mike Upton, Mike Day, Howard Smith, and Gail Hauptfuhrer. The painful demise of the old industries may have made way for a new, but equally viable waterfront. (Courtesy of John Schoonover.)